# ALFRED MARSHALL IN RETROSPECT

# Alfred Marshall in Retrospect

Edited by
Rita McWilliams Tullberg

EDWARD ELGAR

Published by
Edward Elgar Publishing Limited
Gower House
Croft Road
Aldershot
Hants GU11 3HR
England

Edward Elgar Publishing Company
Old Post Road
Brookfield
Vermont 05036
USA

**British Library Cataloguing in Publication Data**

Alfred Marshall in retrospect
  1. Economics. Theories of Marshall, Alfred, 1842–1924
  I. Tullberg, Rita McWilliams *1943–*
330.1

**Library of Congress Cataloging in Publication Data**
Alfred Marshall in retrospect / edited by Rita McWilliams Tullberg
  p.  cm.
  Includes bibliographical references and index.
  1. Marsall, Alfred, 1842–1924. 2. Neoclassical school of economics. I. Tullberg, Rita McWilliams, 1943–
HB103.M3A67 1990
330.15'5–dc20                                  90–43353
                                                        CIP

ISBN 1–85278–344–3

Printed in Great Britain by
Billing & Sons Ltd, Worcester

# Contents

Acknowledgements                                                      vi
List of contributors                                                 vii
Prologue  *Austin Robinson*                                            1

1   Alfred Marshall's family and ancestry  *R. H. Coase*               9

2   Marshall's theories of competitive price  *John K. Whitaker*      29

3   Alfred Marshall and the general equilibrium theory of
    value and distribution: an examination of notes XIV and XXI
    *Robert W. Dimand*                                                49

4   Smooth operator: How Marshall's demand and supply curves
    made neoclassicism safe for public consumption but unfit for
    science  *Philip Mirowski*                                        61

5   Marshall on taxation  *Peter D. Groenewegen*                      91

6   Marshall on free trade  *Phyllis Deane*                          113

7   The spread of Alfred Marshall's economics in Italy, 1885–1925
    *Mauro Gallegati*                                                133

8   Marshall and ethics  *A. W. Coats*                               153

9   Marshall and business  *John Maloney*                            179


Appendix A. A list of the Marshall correspondence in the
Marshall Library, Cambridge  *Frances Willmoth*                      199
Appendix B. General bibliography                                     209
Name index                                                           223
Subject index                                                        227

# Acknowledgements

The present volume was planned as a commemoration of the publication of the first edition of Alfred Marshall's *Principles of Economics* in 1890. However, a retrospect of Marshall's work cannot be confined to an examination of this one book. Long delays occurred before Marshall's ideas, formulated years earlier in notes and lectures, finally appeared in book form. He described the first five editions of the *Principles of Economics* as 'volume one' and for many years planned to complete his life's work with a second volume. The plan was finally abandoned and, after another long delay, the separate works *Industry and Trade* and *Money, Credit and Commerce* were published, the latter only one year before Marshall's death in 1924 at the age of 82. Since then, a great deal of unpublished or inaccessible material has become available, largely through the efforts of A. C. Pigou and more recently of J. K. Whitaker.

Contributors to this volume have therefore taken the opportunity to examine and appraise the whole span of Marshall's work, from his earliest post-graduate years to his publications as an octogenarian. In addition, one chapter focuses on the impact of Marshallian theory and doctrine in Italy whilst he was still living and in the years immediately following his death, and another chapter throws light on the puzzle of Marshall's ancestry. A Prologue sets the scene in Cambridge in the 1920s as the era of Marshallian high influence was drawing to a close.

Two research tools have been added for the benefit of those with a special interest in Alfred Marshall. Appendix A lists all the Marshall correspondence deposited in the Marshall Library, Cambridge. Appendix B brings together the individual bibliographies given at the end of each chapter and includes references to all the editions of the *Principles*.

I should like to express my warmest appreciation to my colleagues for their professional advice and generous assistance in the preparation of this book and to Hasse Tullberg for his never-failing patience and support.

Rita McWilliams Tullberg
Stockholm, July 1990

# Contributors

R. H. Coase, *The Law School, University of Chicago*

A. W. Coats, *Department of Economics, Duke University, North Carolina and Department of History, University of Nottingham*

Phyllis Deane, *Faculty of Economics and Politics, University of Cambridge*

Robert W. Dimand, *Department of Economics, Brock University, Ontario*

Peter D. Groenewegen, *Economics Department, University of Sydney*

Mauro Gallegati, *Instituto di Scienze Economiche, Università di Urbino*

John Maloney, *Department of Economics, University of Exeter*

Philip Mirowski, *Economics, and History and Philosophy of Science, University of Notre Dame, Indiana*

Austin Robinson, *Faculty of Economics and Politics, University of Cambridge*

Frances Willmoth, *Archivist, Marshall Library of Economics, University of Cambridge*

John K. Whitaker, *Department of Economics, University of Virginia*

# Prologue

# Cambridge economics in the post-Marshallian period

*Austin Robinson*

My task is the strictly limited one of trying to convey to you an impression of the Cambridge school of economics as it was at the end of the period of Marshall's dominance. I arrived at Cambridge in the summer of 1919 after two and a half years of war service. I escaped from classics into economics some 15 months later and attended my first lecture in economics in October 1920 after a long vacation during which I had read first Taussig's *Principles*, and then Marshall's *Principles*, as well as other things.

When I got back to Cambridge, I found myself working for my first year of economics under the supervision of Ryle Fay, economic historian, devoted disciple of Alfred Marshall, and full of the Marshall saga, but almost completely innocent of any real understanding of the *Principles*. I taught myself economics as a by-product of defending Marshall against Fay's misunderstandings.

Fay was not, however, responsible for teaching me theory. I went for a short time to Dennis Robertson's elementary course, but my long vacation's reading had carried me beyond that and I changed to Pigou's advanced course. I had two years in which to prepare for Part II of the Economics Tripos and I went both years to Pigou. The others who lectured to me during the two years were Hubert Henderson on 'Money', Frederick Lavington on 'Industry', Gerald Shove on 'Labour' and Barbara Wootton on 'Public Finance'. Apart from these five, I was lucky in being brought into touch with Maynard Keynes by Fay very soon after I had started in Cambridge and was invited to be one of his Monday evening political economy club.

One thing will immediately strike a reader. These six represented the totality of those then teaching 'honours economics' in Cambridge. Of the six, two, Pigou and Keynes, had been taught by Marshall himself; the others had all been taught by Pigou in the creed that 'it is all in Marshall'.

Pigou at that time, before his heart gave him trouble, was a brilliant expositor. He could make difficult ideas comprehensible. He seldom used mathematics. He himself had been a history scholar of King's College; he had then moved over to the Moral Sciences Tripos which in those days included economics. His audience was some 30 undergraduates who had mostly been educated at school as historians or classicists and were happier thinking in plain English; there was yet no Ph.D. at Cambridge and no teaching for it. Those few who had serious hopes of remaining in Cambridge to teach economics chose a research subject and wrote a thesis which they presented to the fellowship-electors of their college. There were no lectures beyond the undergraduate stage.

My memory of Pigou's lectures is not only of their clarity. He gave us Alfred Marshall in what I think was his sincere belief that Alfred Marshall had worked through the problems involved with his powerful critical mind and had reached an unassailable conclusion. He did not think it was necessary or profitable to give us the fallacies that Marshall had demolished. It was his job to train us to tackle the detailed practical problems of economic life. If after a lecture one tried to ask him to clarify some point, the answer one would get, I remember from experience, was 'It is all in Marshall'. For our thinking in the monetary field (*Money, Credit and Commerce* was not yet published), he sent us to Marshall's evidence in 1887 to the Gold and Silver Commission, on which his own exposition was based.

If what we got from Pigou was an orthodoxy, Marshall's own economics was derived from a combination of many oral discussions and wide experience with very extensive reading. He himself attributed the development of this thinking not only to the great English-based economists, Ricardo and Mill, but even more to Roscher, Cournot, von Thünen and other foreign economists. Those of us who learned Marshallian economics never felt that we were being insulated from foreign thinking or were deriving our own thinking from generalisations of purely British experience. Marshall had, for instance, spent a number of months in America seeking to find whether a theory of free trade based on British experience was applicable to a young developing country. And we, of course, read the great Americans—Taussig, Fisher, Clark, Carver and others.

Pigou was not alone in thinking along these lines. Keynes, writing in 1922 the general introduction for the earliest volumes in the series of *Cambridge Economic Handbooks,* could then say:

> Even on matters of principle there is not yet a complete unanimity of opinion amongst professors. Generally speaking, the writers of these volumes believe themselves to be orthodox members of the Cambridge School of Economics. At any rate, most of their ideas about the subject, and even their prejudices, are traceable to the contact they have enjoyed with the writings and lectures of the two economists who have chiefly influenced Cambridge thought for the past fifty years, Dr. Marshall and Professor Pigou (Keynes, 1983, p. 857).

The view that one studied economics not as an intellectual exercise but in order to contribute practically and successfully to human welfare was not, of course, a new accidental product of Marshall's continuing domination of Cambridge. It had been Marshall's own objective. May I quote the last paragraph of his inaugural lecture when appointed to the Cambridge Chair:

> It will be my most cherished ambition, my highest endeavour, to do what with my poor ability and my limited strength I may, to increase the numbers of those whom Cambridge . . . sends out with cool heads but warm hearts, willing to give some at least of their best powers to grappling with the social suffering around them; resolved not to rest content till they have done what in them lies to discover how far it is possible to open up to all the material means of a refined and noble life (Pigou, 1925, p. 174).

That is the thinking on which I was brought up. I still regard the training of active applied economists as the first duty of a university faculty of economics. I still regard those who, with a training in economics, are actively engaged in directly tackling the problems of diminishing poverty, or studying the ways in which that can best be done, as being as truly economists as those who concern themselves with purely academic exercises. A Ricardo, a Marshall, or a Keynes emerges only once or twice in any generation. Nine-tenths of us are destined to become applied economists.

The Marshallian orthodoxy lasted in Cambridge only down to about 1930. I would associate its end with the arrival of Piero Sraffa and the lectures he gave to a younger generation which included Richard Kahn, Joan Robinson and a very able group of young graduate students for the new Ph.D. degree. Sraffa, with painful hesitation, began to question some of Marshall's findings. Once Marshall's infallability had been breeched, others jumped in.

It is impossibly difficult to trace the development of Cambridge thinking during this period. Ideas were being exchanged in conversation or in lectures. But in many cases one person's idea was built on someone else's previous idea which had not yet been published. Marshall's long delays in publishing *Industry and Trade* and *Money, Credit and Commerce* made it difficult for Pigou to publish. Gerald Shove had inhibitions about publishing some of his ideas. Richard Kahn and Joan Robinson were held up by Shove. Thus there was for a time a considerable accumulation of private oral tradition, with the unfortunate result that Cambridge got out of step with colleagues in other universities.

This phase was brought towards an end by Keynes' *General Theory*. But its final demise came with the war, the wartime integration of the Cambridge faculty and the London School of Economics, and the post-war appointment of a number of lecturers who had not been educated in Cambridge.

There was, I think, a second and equally important factor which led to the end of the Marshallian orthodoxy. The essential characteristics of the British economic system were changing dramatically. When Marshall first shaped his model of the British economy in the 1860s and 1870s it was in the age of the relatively small family firm. And Marshall rightly saw that the small family firm had its closest analogies not in the physical sciences but in the biological sciences. The small family firm, particularly in the then dominant cotton and woollen industries, was born, matured, failed to keep abreast of new developments, and finally died. This was the picture that I acquired from Frederick Lavington and confirmed through visits to firms while a student; I had already learned it from experiences of aircraft firms before I came up to Cambridge. Large firms were then rarities. In the cotton industry the speculative market for raw cotton and the big specialist export houses made it possible for the small manufacturer to compete on equal terms at the time when Marshall was collecting his material for *Industry and Trade*. But by the 1930s the textile industries were no longer as dominant as they had been 40 years earlier. Big firms in the metal and chemical industries acquired new managements and survived. The family firm was no longer dominant. The multi-product and multi-national firm of today had, it is true, not yet arrived, but Marshall's model of the 1860s and 1870s was becoming increasingly out-of-date. It was no longer necessary to ask how a firm was born by observation of a representative firm or to ask why the third generation of a family firm was declining from clogs to clogs. Curiously it was because Marshall's model of his own generation was accurate that it ceased to be an accurate model of a different generation.

I do not know how precisely the Marshallian tradition in which I was educated reflected the original thinking of Marshall himself or had become simplified or adulterated during the half century before I absorbed it. Re-reading Marshall, I get the feeling that his primary interest was in economic dynamics—how to increase the rate of growth of the economy, and how to maintain the level of employment. What I think I got from those who taught me was concerned with the best use of the limited resources of any period. I have plenty of memories of discussions of the trade cycle; but it was only with Keynes' *General Theory* that I learned to think about a theory of employment and unemployment and about the means of promoting technical progress. This may very likely have been my own failure to absorb ideas that were in fact presented to us. But I now find in Marshall ideas that I had not fully appreciated in the 1920s.

The demise of Marshallian economics had, I think, also another explanation. The world which he had modelled in 1860–70 had itself changed. Initially high transport costs had implied small, widely distributed manufacture in many industries, mitigated to some extent only by railways and by coastal or canal transport. The improved road system and the internal combustion engine had changed that. Energy for Marshall was primarily derived from coal, heavy to transport and thus determining the location of industry; electricity has completely changed the transport and influence of energy supply. When Marshall wrote, international trade principally took the form of the shipment of raw foodstuffs and raw materials from primary producing backward countries to advanced countries making and exporting manufactures; the invention of powerful fertilisers and artificial textile and other materials has completely changed that. At the same time, capital has become much more mobile, and machinery has taken the place of personal skills. An advanced country is advanced only in innovation, design and development, and not in subsequent manufacture; a backward country with low wages can quickly acquire the capacity to manufacture products and to grow rapidly in income per head. The thinking of an economist needs to be adapted to this fundamentally different world. What is the meaning today of comparative advantage?

Marshall was still alive during my undergraduate time at Cambridge, but I never met him. I remember looking through the hedge of Balliol Croft with another undergraduate economist and seeing him sitting with his black cap on his head in the garden shelter in which he did most of his writing. Fay was to have taken me to tea with him in 1923 when I had lately been made a fellow of Corpus Christi College, but Marshall's heart misbehaved and the visit was called off. I first went to Balliol Croft shortly after Marshall's death when Pigou commissioned me to find accommodation for the Marshall Library and to move Marshall's books to it. Thus I soon got to know Mary Marshall well. She happily became part-time librarian, bicycling to the library and lending to undergraduates the books that she and Alfred had accumulated over the previous half century. Sitting there, she gave us a remarkable sense of continuity with Alfred.

For my generation at Cambridge there was no question of the greatness and the mastery of Marshall. On different occasions many years later I asked two of Marshall's best pupils, Pigou and Layton,[1] whether they still regarded Marshall as the best economist they had ever known. Both regarded that as beyond question—an absurd question to ask.

It was a tragedy that, anxious to protect himself against very sophisticated minor criticisms, Marshall adopted a literary presentation of his *Principles* that often disguised the difficulties and gave an impression of woolly thinking. I myself as an undergraduate got much more from *Industry and Trade*, dealing as it did with the problems which most interested me, than I did from the *Principles*. But if one wished to know Marshall one had hitherto to read the volume of *Memorials of Alfred Marshall* edited by Pigou.[2] There, previously unpublished fragments of his writing and his letters, not only to Edgeworth, Gonner, Bowley and other economists, but also to Bishop Westcott, Llewellyn Davies and Horace Plunkett, reveal a Marshall much more frank and much more human than do the reticent paragraphs of the *Principles*. While I welcome the emphasis on the *Principles* in its centenary year, these are the books that I would persuade anyone to read who wished to feel the greatness of that great man.

If I try to contrast the Cambridge faculty of 1920 with that of 1990, I think the great change is that in 1920 there was an orthodoxy; we spent little time arguing pure theory; one got out into the field to acquire information; there was a widespread shortage of statistical data; Marshall's *Industry and Trade*, for example, was built upon non-quantitative oral discussion. In 1990 there is no similar orthodoxy; there is on the other hand a plenitude of statistics; a researcher has plenty of published evidence, but no equally clear basis on which to analyse it.

### Notes and references

[1] A. C. Pigou succeeded Marshall as Professor of Political Economy at Cambridge in 1908. W. T. Layton (Baron Layton) was appointed lecturer in economics at Cambridge in 1908 together with J. M. Keynes. He later had a distinguished career in political and public service and as editor of the *Economist*.

[2] The work of J. K. Whitaker and others is making many more of Marshall's unpublished manuscripts and letters available than has hitherto been the case.

## Bibliography

Keynes, J. M. (1983) [1922–23], Introduction to *Cambridge Economic Handbooks* for 1922 and 1923, reprinted in D. Moggridge, ed., *The Collected Writings of John Maynard Keynes*, London: Macmillan for the Royal Economic Society, vol. 12.

Pigou, A. C., ed. (1925), *Memorials of Alfred Marshall*, London: Macmillan.

# 1.  Alfred Marshall's family and ancestry *

*R. H. Coase*

I have described the first sentence of Keynes' memoir (Pigou, 1925, pp. 1–65) as a 'masterpiece of concealment'. Alfred Marshall's birthplace is there given as Clapham, 'a leafy London suburb', as Corry explained, whereas he was actually born in Bermondsey in the midst of the tanneries. Alfred's mother gets the bare mention of her name. The reason for this became obvious when I learnt that she was a butcher's daughter. His father at the time is said to have been a cashier at the Bank of England whereas he was a clerk (Coase, 1984, pp. 519–27). In fact, he never held any important position in the Bank. It is true that he was made a 'cashier' in 1867 (some 25 years after Alfred's birth) but the conferring of this title in the Bank of England, we are told, was usually a reward for 'long and faithful service'.[1] At his marriage, Alfred Marshall's father described himself as a 'gentleman'. By doing so, he elevated his social status and concealed his real position. Alfred Marshall's family lived on the edge of gentility and the truth had to be suppressed if this was necessary to maintain respectability. The result has been to enhance Alfred's social position but to diminish his achievement.

The second sentence in the memoir tells us that the 'Marshalls were a clerical family of the West' and we can almost hear the clink of tea-cups on vicarage lawns. As always in the memoir, or nearly always, there is some truth in this. Keynes tells us that Alfred's great-great-grandfather, William Marshall, was the 'half legendary herculean parson of Devonshire' and that his great-grandfather, John Marshall, a

* The information on which the paper is based has been gathered over a long period from a great variety of sources with the aid of many research assistants. The correspondence and notes relating to this research will be deposited in the Regenstein Library of the University of Chicago. I hope they will be of assistance to those who wish to do further research on Alfred Marshall's family and ancestry. Such research is clearly needed. There are gaps in the story I tell and some of my inferences are based on very scanty evidence. The notes of Mary Marshall, to which reference is made in this paper, will be found in the Keynes Memoir file in the Marshall Library, Cambridge. I am indebted to the Liberty Fund for a grant which financed much of the research on which this paper is based.

clergyman who married Mary Hawtrey, was the headmaster of Exeter
Grammar School. This is correct. But Keynes adds, after the reference
to this 'clerical family of the West', 'sprung from William Marshall,
incumbent of Saltash, Cornwall at the end of the seventeenth century'.
As the 'parson of Devonshire' was born in 1676 in Cornwall and his
father does not appear to have been a clergyman, it would seem that
the 'incumbent of Saltash' from whom the Marshalls sprang was
either an invention or, which I regard as more probable, that the
'parson of Devonshire' became divided in the minds of Alfred's
family into two people, which has the effect of making the clerical line
appear longer. The genealogical information used by Keynes in
writing the memoir was compiled by Ainslie, a daughter of Uncle
Henry,[2] and it is not surprising that she only knew what the family
wished her to believe. It is true that John Marshall had other relatives
(Marshalls) who were clergymen, but the fact is that the two
mentioned are the only clergymen in the direct line to Alfred
Marshall. As we all have eight great-grandparents and sixteen great-
great-grandparents, it is hazardous to discuss genetic influences unless
all lines of descent have been studied and hazardous even then until
their DNA has been inspected. Nonetheless, it is not to be expected
that the author who writes with such enthusiasm on 'The Great
Villiers Connection' would neglect the influence of heredity.
However, as we shall see, if one indulges in such conjectures, there
are stronger candidates than the Marshalls or the Hawtreys (all that are
mentioned by Keynes) as the source of the genes which helped to
produce the author of the *Principles of Economics*.

Let us turn to Alfred's immediate family. After the reference to
John Marshall, Alfred's great-grandfather, the next paragraph of the
memoir starts: 'His father . . .'. This is puzzling since it is apparent
that Keynes has skipped a generation. In fact there is no reference at
all to Alfred's grandparents in the memoir. In the case of Alfred's
grandparents on his mother's side, this is understandable since any
reference to them would have taken us into the labouring classes. But
why was William Marshall, Alfred's grandfather on his father's side,
not mentioned? His history, I think, explains why. All that Mary
Marshall says in the notes that she gave to Keynes is that he was a
paymaster in the navy and it is certainly true that on his gravestone in
Leith in Scotland (where he died) he is described as 'formerly
paymaster R. N.'.[3] It must be unusual for a graveyard inscription to

contain an untruth but the fact is that Alfred's grandfather never was a paymaster in the navy.

I will recount his history so far as I have been able to discover it. His father, John Marshall, the headmaster of Exeter Grammar School, had three sons, two of whom became clergymen. Alfred's grandfather was the odd man out. Why he was considered (or considered himself) unsuitable for a clerical position, I do not know. My hypothesis is that he lacked the brain power needed for this particular occupation. He was born in 1780, but I have found no mention of him until the announcement (in the *Gentleman's Magazine*) of his marriage in 1810, when he was just under 30 years old. He is there described as 'assistant paymaster-general at the Cape of Good Hope'.

This position, to which he had obviously just been appointed, was that of assistant paymaster-general to the Cape garrison in South Africa, the permanent occupation of the Cape by the British having started in 1806. William Marshall and his bride set sail on 24 June 1810 and reached Cape Town on 1 October 1810. He held this position for several years, during which time four children were born, two of whom died as infants. One that survived was William, the father of Alfred Marshall. Judging from the house in which he lived and other indications, it would seem that Alfred's grandfather was in the upper stratum of British society at the Cape.[4] However, sometime after March 1816, he gave up this position and went to Mauritius. Mauritius had been a French colony (called 'Ile de France') but was captured by the British in 1810. At the end of the war in 1814, it became a British possession by the Treaty of Paris.

In Mauritius he first took a position in the commissary of police.[5] He then made an ill-fated move by purchasing, at a public auction in December 1817, the farm of the *batelage* or exclusive privilege of shipping and landing goods in the harbour of Saint Louis, for two years. Within a few months, William Marshall discovered that he had made a serious blunder. In a memorial addressed to the Acting Governor, dated April 1818, he explained that he could not pay the second installment of the sum he had bid and he asked for relief. His explanation for this *débâcle* was that he had paid too high a price for the farm, approximately twice the sum for which it had been sold in previous years. He gave two reasons why he had done this. First, he had been 'led to suppose by public report . . . that the Port would be kept open until the 1st March, 1820', whereas it was shut on 1 April 1818. Second, the bidding at the auction advanced in small sums which he had thought 'the result of a fair competition' from which he had concluded 'that if any other person could afford to give so much, [he] could do likewise'. Economists will recognise this as a variant of the efficient market hypothesis. However, he claimed that the bids above 17 500 dollars (he paid 23 000 dollars) were not made by others who wanted to purchase the farm but by the government auctioneer and the price paid was not therefore 'the result of a fair competition'. In addition, some of his boats and implements were destroyed by a hurricane in March 1818. As a result, his expenses during the first year amounted to 60 000 dollars, while his receipts were 40 000 dollars.[6] The Mauritius dollar (a money of account) was worth about 4 shillings. His initial payment, plus first-year losses, therefore amounted to about £6 000 (a large sum of money in those days)[7] and this together with his living expenses apparently largely exhausted his capital. It seems that the Acting Governor refused to forward his memorial to the Secretary of State for the Colonial Department unless he based his claim for relief solely on the losses from the hurricane. The next Acting Governor did, however, forward William Marshall's memorial with the comment that it was 'reasonable . . . to afford Mr. Marshall some relief . . . there appearing no chance whatever, of Mr. Marshall being able to fulfill his Engagement'. He added that 'Mr. Marshall is represented to me as a diligent, respectable man, who was anxious to obtain Employment, but who, unfortunately, was not sufficiently informed at the time, of the exact extent of the concern into which he was entering'.[8] One has the impression that Alfred's grandfather was not very smart.

How this matter was resolved I do not know. But in 1823 Alfred's grandmother died and his grandfather left Mauritius with his six young children. He settled in Leith in Scotland where he became a merchant. As was perhaps to be expected, this business venture does not appear to have been a success since by 1827 his occupation is given as a clerk.[9] He died in 1828, characteristically without having made a will, was buried with a false inscription on his gravestone and was forgotten. It is not difficult to understand why Alfred Marshall's family did not keep his memory alive.

Custody of the children was given to John Bentall, a brother of their mother, and they went to Totnes in Devon where, according to Mary Marshall, another brother took charge of them. What happened to these orphans who were to constitute Alfred Marshall's immediate family? The eldest was his father, the others consisted of an aunt and four uncles. I need add nothing to what I have already said elsewhere about that extremely disagreeable man, his father. But what of the others? Of Aunt Louisa, Mary Marshall tells us that Alfred Marshall was 'devotedly fond . . . She made the care of her brothers and their families her first duty in life'. Alfred Marshall owed a special debt to her (and so do we) since it was his belief that the summer holidays he spent with her saved his life after being overworked by his father in the rest of the year (Pigou, 1925, p. 2).

Let us now consider his uncles, starting with Uncle Edward. He enlisted in the Royal Navy in January 1829, aged 12, as volunteer first class. A year after his enlistment, he was made midshipman. In 1833, he was promoted to mate and in 1843 to lieutenant. He was made commander in 1853 and captain in 1857. He served on many stations, at the Cape of Good Hope, in the Mediterranean and on the east coast of Africa among others and in ships with such colourful names as *Thunderer*, *Thunderbolt*, *Snake* and *Devastation*, and even one with the somewhat dubious name of *Sappho*. For three years, Commander Marshall was in charge of the *Virago* on the Pacific station. It will have been noticed that his career is similar to that of Horatio Hornblower in the C. S. Forester novels and I believe the only reason that there never was an Admiral Edward Marshall was because he died, Captain Marshall, in 1862, aged 45.[10]

Next consider Uncle Henry. I know nothing of his early life but at the time of his marriage in 1854, when he was 33, he was a merchant in Calcutta, India. He was still a merchant in India in 1858 but had returned to England by 1859, perhaps as a result of the Indian Mutiny. He died in 1880 and was described in his will as a timber merchant. Uncle Henry was a businessman.

Next there is Uncle Thornton. In his teens he was apprenticed to a pharmacist and studied medicine at Guys Hospital, London. At the end of 1843, aged 21, he applied for employment in the medical department of the army and was appointed an assistant surgeon. He served in New Zealand and Australia and was promoted to surgeon in 1855. There is not much to tell about him since he suffered from ill health and died in 1861, aged 38.[11]

We now come to the last member of this 'clerical' family, Uncle Charles, the only one that Keynes mentions in the memoir and the most interesting of Alfred Marshall's uncles. He was, said Mary Marshall, 'Alfred's favourite uncle'. Certainly Alfred Marshall had good reason for gratitude. By providing him with a loan, Uncle

Charles played an important, perhaps decisive, part in making it possible for Alfred Marshall to go to Cambridge to study mathematics, a step that would ultimately lead to his becoming an economist. It was also a legacy from Uncle Charles, according to the memoir, which enabled Alfred to make his visit to America in 1875. When I found that there were no legacies in Uncle Charles' will, I had doubts about whether Keynes was correct. However, I discovered that there was a letter in the Oxley Library in Brisbane written by Uncle Charles' widow to her solicitor complaining that Uncle Henry (the executor of the will) was paying the legacies out of income. Apparently there were legacies not mentioned in the will, perhaps contained in a letter.

Given the important part which Uncle Charles' financial assistance played in Alfred's life, Keynes adds that

> the story of the sources of this uncle's wealth, which Alfred often told, deserves a record . . . . Having sought his fortunes in Australia and being established there at the date of the gold discoveries, a little family eccentricity disposed him to seek his benefit indirectly. So he remained a pastoralist, but, to the mirth of his neighbours, refused to employ anyone about his place who did not suffer from some physical defect, staffing himself entirely with the halt, the blind and the maimed. When the gold boom reached its height, his reward came. All the able-bodied labourers emigrated to the gold-fields and Charles Marshall was the only man in the place able to carry on (Pigou, 1925, p. 4).

Edgeworth thought this passage should have been omitted because behaviour based on an eccentricity had no general significance.[12] I think it should have been omitted because there is not a word of truth in it.

Let us try to reconstruct the real story of Uncle Charles' life and of how he acquired his wealth. Mary Marshall in her notes for Keynes says that Uncle Charles 'who disliked his brother William's control at Totnes . . . ran away and became a cabin boy'. In the memoir, Keynes adopts the phrase and applies it metaphorically to Alfred who, he said, ran away 'to be a cabin-boy at Cambridge and climb the rigging of geometry and spy out the heavens'. But it seems likely that Mary Marshall's tale was true and that Uncle Charles really did run away and became a cabin-boy. I say this because, when he was 20, we find his occupation given as 'mariner' in the census of 1841.[13]

After 1841 I have found no reliable information about his activities until 1849, when he is recorded as owner (with Robert Campbell) of the sheep station Ellangowan on the Darling Downs in Australia.[14] According to one account, he arrived in Australia in 1847.[15] How he

obtained the capital to buy his interest in this sheep station I do not
know, perhaps in some business venture outside Australia or as the
result of an inheritance. There is a description of a meeting with him,
almost certainly in 1849, in reminiscences by John Watts, who was
manager of a neighbouring property:

> We had a dispute with Ellangowan, then belonging to Mr. Charles Marshall,
> who had purchased it from the Forbes . . . . When we got to Ellangowan,
> Marshall was just preparing for shearing, and had to manage the washpool
> himself. Here we found him, and he said: 'Oh, come up to the house and have a
> glass of grog and we will talk it over as soon as I have finished here'. So in due
> course we found ourselves at the house, and it was arranged that the matter
> should stand over until after shearing but before this could be done Mr. Marshall
> had sold the station to J. Gammie . . .'.[16]

From 1849 on it is possible to give a very complete account of his
activities on the Darling Downs. In 1850 he became a joint owner of
Glengallan with Robert Campbell.[17] In the same year he was
appointed a justice of the peace, an indication of his standing among
the pastoralists on the Darling Downs.[18] In 1852 he became sole
owner of Glengallan.[19] Glengallan was a large sheep station of about
60 000 acres with a grazing capacity for about 1 800 cattle and 20 000
sheep.[20] The Reverend H. Berkeley Jones, who published a book
about his travels in Australia, says this of his visit to Glengallan in
1852: 'Mr. M. possesses a very valuable station, and in the course of a
few years, with small capital and untiring perseverance, has
accumulated nearly a lac of rupees' (Berkeley Jones, 1853, p. 164). In
1854 Uncle Charles brought in John Deuchar as a partner. Deuchar
was a stock breeder with considerable experience; before joining
Uncle Charles, he had been manager of a station owned by the
Aberdeen Company. With Deuchar's assistance, Glengallan prospered
and its stock became famous. Deuchar was, however, a flamboyant
character and he (but not Uncle Charles) went bankrupt. The
partnership was dissolved in 1869.[21] In 1873, Uncle Charles brought
in W. B. Slade as partner. Slade also proved to be an excellent stock
breeder but Uncle Charles died in 1874 and his interest in Glengallen
passed to his widow. Marshall and Slade became Knighton and Slade
when she remarried. There is no reason to doubt that Uncle Charles
made a fortune. He married Charlotte Augusta Dring Drake in 1857, a
daughter of General William H. Drake who, in 1871 became Sir
William. At the time of his marriage, Uncle Charles was 36; Charlotte
was 20.

How did this man who had run away to become a cabin-boy come to acquire his wealth? Alfred Marshall gives the answer. He had a sheep station on which he employed the halt, the blind and the maimed (a 'little family eccentricity' according to the memoir, although there is no evidence that any other of Alfred's relatives possessed it). At any rate, when gold was discovered in Australia, the workers on other stations left for the goldfields and Uncle Charles was the only man who was able to continue sheep farming, at least on the Darling Downs. It is an inherently improbable tale. Those working on a sheep station as shepherds or in other capacities were, in general, engaged in tasks which the halt, the blind and the maimed could not perform. It is difficult to imagine what useful work a blind man riding his seeing-eye horse could do on a 100-square-mile sheep station. But it is not necessary to insist on this. There are many reasons for thinking that this tale is a fabrication.

We should note first of all that by 1850, Uncle Charles was already a man of some substance while the first payable gold discovery in Australia was not made until 1851. Second, the historical accounts of the sheep stations on the Darling Downs indicate that they all continued operating after gold was discovered. The number of sheep in New South Wales, Victoria and Tasmania actually increased during the period of the gold boom and there is every reason to suppose that this was true on the Darling Downs (which was at this time in New South Wales). Waterson says that in this period 'the area exuded prosperity—1856 to 1866 was the golden age . . .' (Barnard, 1958, p. 217; Waterson, 1968, p. 13). No doubt numbers of workers did go to the goldfields although, curiously enough, in the case of Glengallan, the only mention I have found of such a movement involves Uncle Charles himself. Nemeniah Bartley visited the Turon goldfields in 1851 and there met 'Marshall, a son of the chief cashier of the Bank of England and his West Indian friend, Davson'. 'Son' is obviously a mistake for brother and the description of Alfred Marshall's father as 'chief cashier of the Bank of England' is another example of that 'little family eccentricity' of exaggerating their social position. Bartley adds: 'Fearfully and wonderfully was the "damper" compounded by Marshall and Davson; wedges of putty were digestible in comparison therewith' (Bartley, 1892, p. 52); from which we can infer that Uncle Charles was no weakling.

More important perhaps in undermining Alfred Marshall's tale is that it is inconsistent with all we know about the employment practices of this tough ex-seaman. He was a no-nonsense employer. In 1849, while he was still at Ellangowan, he accused George Munday at the Court of Petty Sessions of absconding from his service. Munday denied that he was Uncle Charles' servant and the case was dismissed. At the same time Samuel Bishop was brought before the court to answer Uncle Charles' complaint of 'neglect of duty and insolence'. It was held that the charge was not proven.[22] We get a more complete view of Uncle Charles' attitude from the correspondence with his new partner, W. B. Slade, written in 1873 and 1874 while on a trip to England, and now in the Oxley Library in Brisbane.

Uncle Charles emerges as a fair-minded man but one who, in his employment practices, was above all concerned with what he would gain from following one course of action or another. Just before he died he remarked that the number of hands employed seemed large for the quantity of stock kept and he hoped that there would be a considerable reduction.[23] In dealing with individuals he was sympathetic but businesslike. Here is an example:

> I often wonder whether you will be able to find work for old Pugh after he has finished the wool shed. I like the old fellow very much and shall be sorry that he has left our employ. He is mostly thoroughly trustworthy and can be depended upon in an emergency . . . Though of course if you have no work for him you cannot help him.[24]

Most of the comments on employees in the letters relate to the South Sea islanders he had taken on and whose term of employment was nearing its end. He wanted them properly treated:

> While in Brisbane I saw the Immigration Agent Mr. Gray, and it was arranged that on your sending down the South Sea Islanders on expiration of their respective terms, you should remit their 3 years' wages and he would see that they were properly cared for and not cheated by shopkeepers.[25]

In another letter he says that he had 'promised the boys that if they behaved well I would send them each a Medal'.[26] He had eight medals struck with their names engraved on them. He takes pains to see that this is well done, thinks about getting them reproduced in a newspaper 'to show that the boys are not treated quite as slaves'[27] but apparently decided not to do so because it would look like 'ostentation'.[28] He comments: 'They will be delighted to get their medals for good conduct, and I feel they deserve them'.[29] As the South Sea islanders had been so useful, he hoped that some would return but if they did not, that replacements would be obtained. If Slade intended to do this,

Uncle Charles gave some words of advice, '. . . go down directly . . . the ship arrives and select them yourself. If you trust an agent to pick them you will get a very inferior lot'.[30] This suggestion seemed designed to avoid employing 'the halt, the blind and the maimed'.

It is easy to see from this correspondence why Uncle Charles was able to build up a fortune. In his letters he is concerned with every detail of the business, shows great shrewdness and his aim is always to increase the profits of the firm. Thus he notes that 'documents of importance, and especially Bills at sight' should be sent 'by the shorter route via Brindisi. The week's interest on £1 000 is 30/8 at 8 per cent and of course bears no proportion to the difference in rate of postage'.[31] One quotation gives an excellent illustration of his thinking:

> I hope you will not be obliged to let the number of sheep go down too low from sales. The clip forms so important a source of our profits that we must not let it fall off if possible. I begin to think it is a mistake culling sheep only on account of coarse wool. During the last two years I have observed that coarse sheep have paid much better than fine ones. The C wool fetches very nearly, and often quite as much as that marked A (principally on account of its greater length of staple) and the difference in weight of the fleeces . . . is fully in favour of C quality. The carcase is also of course larger and so more valuable. Of course it would not do to dispense with the stud flocks on account of the sale of rams, but I feel quite sure that for the general flocks the coarser long wool quality of sheep will pay best . . . and of course our great object in sheep farming is to keep the stock that *pays best* [emphasis in original].[32]

Uncle Charles was a good businessman but he would have made a good economist. In May 1874, he reports that the Hogarth Meat Preserving Company, in which he has an interest, had been losing money and that instructions had been sent to Australia to stop working: 'At present prices of stock, and tin [*sic*] meat in England, it is impossible to carry on meat preserving without loss'. He believes that other meat preserving establishments in Australia will also stop working. He concludes: 'The effect of this will not be to make meat rise in England, for South America will supply the market but stock must fall [in Australia]'. He adds that he is telling Slade this 'in order that you may act cautiously in buying'.[33]

Alfred Marshall, discussing joint supply, has this to say in the *Principles*:

> . . . the price of mutton in the wool-producing districts of Australia was at one time very low. The wool was exported; the meat had to be consumed at home; and as there was no great demand for it, the price of the wool had to defray

almost the whole of the joint expenses of production of the wool and the meat. Afterwards the low price of meat gave a stimulus to the industries of preserving meat for exportation and now its price in Australia is higher (Marshall, 1961, vol. 1, p. 389).

My feeling is that Uncle Charles would have done as well and perhaps better.

It seems clear that Uncle Charles built up his fortune over a long period as a result of hard work, intelligence, perseverance and attention to detail. Apart from his pastoral activities (which must have given him the bulk of his income), he had other business interests in Australia of which the meat preserving company already mentioned is one example. He dealt in land, had rental property in the neighbouring town of Warwick and had investments in Australian mining companies. These companies do not seem to have been a profitable investment for him and he comments: 'My tin [speculation] has proved the truth of what I have held as a golden maxim namely "never to invest in anything that you do not understand and have no part in its control"'.[34]

Claude Guillebaud has remarked on Alfred Marshall's uncanny ability to detect error in any statement about economic facts. Why then did he accept and repeat a story so improbable on its face and, as we now know, at variance with Uncle Charles' actual behaviour? I think I may know the answer. Even before the discovery of gold there had been a severe shortage of labour on the Darling Downs and the owners of sheep stations there petitioned for the resumption of transportation which had been stopped in 1840.[35] Transportation was in fact resumed in 1849, and in 1850 it became possible for those running sheep stations on the Darling Downs to secure convict labour. Uncle Charles did not hesitate. In 1850 he is listed for seven 'exiles', in 1851 for another and 1852 for three more, including one taken on by Robert Campbell in 1850. In addition, four passports for the employment of 'ticket-of-leave' men were issued to him in 1851 and two more in 1852. He was probably also able to use the 'ticket-of-leave' men assigned earlier to Robert Campbell.[36] A 'ticket-of-leave' was a document issued to a convict allowing him to work for wages in the private sector, thus preparing himself for economic self-sufficiency after the expiration of his sentence. It was a status that a convict would normally not wish to imperil by, for example, leaving his district without a police pass. So in the years immediately following the gold discovery of 1851, when the drain on local labour would have been most intense, a substantial portion of the labour force employed by Uncle Charles at Glengallan consisted of convict labour. This, I believe, is what the tale of 'the halt, the blind and the maimed' was intended to conceal. In reality, Uncle Charles did not employ the halt but the haltered. It becomes easy to understand why Uncle Charles' workers did not go to the goldfields. Did Alfred Marshall know that what he was saying was a falsification? It is not possible to be certain but I would regard it as very likely. The family would not wish it to be known that Uncle Charles made the fortune from which Alfred (and other family members) benefited in part through the employment of convict labour.

What I find curious about this concealment through falsehood in the case of Alfred Marshall's family is that, to me, the truth is not discreditable. Two of his uncles were successful businessmen, one very successful, and another had a distinguished career in the navy. The fourth died at too early an age to assess his achievement but we have no reason to suppose that it would not have been highly creditable. The story of these orphans who were Alfred Marshall's uncles is one in which he could take pride, even though there was not a clergyman among them. I should add something about Alfred Marshall's brothers and sister. His elder brother, Charles William Marshall, became manager of the Bengal Silk Company in India. His younger brother Walter died while a student at Cambridge. His sister Mabel fell in love with a young army officer but her tyrant father would not allow her to marry him. She ultimately married the Reverend E. D. Guillebaud. Our feelings of indignation at the high-handed action of Alfred Marshall's father may be somewhat assuaged by the thought that this gave us Claude Guillebaud and the variorum edition of the *Principles*.

One aspect of this story should be noted. As all of Alfred Marshall's uncles spent most of their time abroad, he would have had little contact with them, certainly while he was young. Apart from his summer holidays with Aunt Louisa, he would have had no relief from the oppressive control of his father. That he managed to survive his father's harsh regime with the fire of his genius still alight must have been due to some inner strength, to something within him. I now turn to a possible source of that something.

Keynes' discussion of Alfred Marshall's ancestry is slight and is largely confined to the clerical connections of his great-grandfather, John Marshall, and the family of Mary Hawtrey. The neglect of the ancestry of Alfred Marshall's mother is easy to explain. But the failure to mention his grandfather, William Marshall, had the unfortunate result that no attention was paid to his wife, Alfred Marshall's grandmother. Her name was Louisa Bentall.

That Alfred Marshall's family benefited in a material way from the Bentall connection is clear. John Bentall, a stockbroker, the brother of Louisa, was made guardian of her children after the death of their father in Leith, and they went to live in Totnes with another brother, presumably Thornton Bentall, a banker. Alfred Marshall's father worked as a clerk for John Bentall before joining the Bank of England. The Bentalls no doubt aided Alfred's father and uncles in ways unknown to us. But Alfred Marshall may have benefited from the Bentall connection in a much more important way. It seems possible that he inherited through Louisa Bentall those traits of character and intellect which enabled him to withstand his father and to play a major role in building modern economics.

The Bentalls were distinguished over the centuries by the possession of considerable business ability. Robert Burnel, Lord Chancellor of Edward I, in the 13th century, was a member of the family. He was 'a self-made man who . . . built up a widespread complex of landed property by purchase, exchange, the conversion of loans, and other ways in the course of a prosperous career' (Wagner, 1960, pp. 223–24). It reminds one of Uncle Charles. One of his purchases was an estate in Benthall, Shropshire, and the family (or some of them), seems to have taken the name of Benthall which, in the course of time, became Bentall. Louisa Bentall's father (Alfred's great-grandfather) was a banker. In modern times the department store Bentall's of Kingston near London and Bentall and Co., the agricultural machinery company, were founded by members of the family (Herbert, 1936; Kemp, 1955). A more recent example is Sir Paul Benthall who had a successful business career in India and was later chairman of the Amalgamated Metal Corporation and a director of Chartered Bank, the Royal Insurance Company and other financial concerns in England. A member of the family bought the old family home, Benthall Hall, in Shropshire, in 1934, and in 1958 it was given to the National Trust (National Trust, 1976). But Louisa Bentall had more to contribute. Her grandfather was John Bentall, wine cooper and merchant of Colchester in Essex and his wife was Elizabeth Thornton.

Elizabeth Thornton's family was even more distinguished in business and public affairs than the Bentalls. They were merchants, bankers, members of parliament, and some of them were among the most prominent members of the Clapham Sect. Economists will immediately recognise that this means that Alfred Marshall was related to Henry Thornton, author of *The Paper Credit of Great Britain* of whom Hayek has said that 'in the field of money the main achievement of the classical period' was due to him (Thornton, 1939, p. 36). Both Alfred Marshall and Henry Thornton were descendants of Robert Thornton, Rector of Birkin, Yorkshire, in the 17th century. Robert Thornton was Alfred Marshall's great-great-great-grandfather and Henry Thornton's great-great-grandfather. Ralph Hawtrey had a similar distant relationship with Alfred Marshall. Keynes in the memoir, as originally published, said of this relationship with Ralph Hawtrey, '. . . there is not much in the true theory of money which does not flow from that single stem'. How much stronger a statement could have been made had Keynes known that Alfred Marshall was also related to Henry Thornton. I should add that this comment was omitted when the memoir was reprinted in 1933 in *Essays in Biography*, perhaps because Keynes had found that neither Alfred Marshall nor Ralph Hawtrey were related to the author of *The Treatise on Money* (published in 1930). That Alfred Marshall and Henry Thornton were related has another consequence. E. M. Forster was the great-grandson of Henry Thornton and so Alfred Marshall was also distantly related to him—and thus to a member of those 'trustees of civilization', the Bloomsbury Group.[37] Had Keynes known about this relationship, I feel sure that he would have added a page or perhaps two to the memoir, although what he would have made of it I cannot imagine. That Keynes would have found the true facts of Marshall's ancestry intensely interesting is not open to doubt. He may have been fascinated by 'The Great Villiers Connection' but, as he tells us in the preface to *Essays in Biography*, what he really took pride in was 'the solidarity and historical continuity of the High Intelligentsia of England' (Keynes, 1972, p. xix).

The exclusion of the Bentalls and the Thorntons from their family history in Alfred Marshall's generation is extremely hard to explain. His father, his aunt and his uncles owed a great debt to the Bentalls for looking after them as children and in helping them to get started, while they should have been aware of the Thornton connection since one of Alfred's uncles was named 'Thornton'. Unlike their close relationship with the Bentalls, Alfred Marshall's immediate family did not seem to have had a great deal to do with the Hawtreys and the clerical

Marshalls apart from Aunt Louisa in Devon, who was in touch with them.[38] The only explanation I can give for this neglect of the Bentalls and Thorntons is that it was the result of the erasure of Alfred Marshall's grandfather from the family memory. I know nothing about his early life but my guess is that he started his career with capital derived from his father and his wife and that this was dissipated in ill-considered business ventures with the result that he ended up as a clerk in Leith. Failures would not be talked about in the Marshall family and as a consequence all knowledge of his wife, her family and illustrious relations would be lost.

The effect of all these errors and omissions in Keynes' references to Alfred Marshall's family has been to give a very misleading picture of the circumstances in which Alfred Marshall was brought up. For example, Skidelsky said recently in his biography of Keynes that 'Marshall was yet another product of the well-connected clerical families which colonised English intellectual life' (Skidelsky, 1986, p. 40). Alfred Marshall was not a member of a cultivated, comfortable and well-connected clerical family, with his father's occupation an exception, as Skidelsky seems to suppose. Alfred's home life was such as would have left most people unfit for serious scientific work. Keynes reports in the memoir that E. C. Dermer, a schoolfellow of Alfred's, said that Alfred Marshall as a schoolboy was 'small and pale, badly dressed, looked overworked . . . cared little for games, was fond of propounding chess problems, and did not readily make friends'. I do not doubt the accuracy of this description. Alfred Marshall, in a letter, refers to his father's 'extremely severe discipline' (Coase, 1984, pp. 523–24) and what this implied in Victorian England I shudder to imagine. No doubt his father's 'extremely severe discipline' left permanent scars. Nonetheless, while still a boy, Alfred Marshall rejected the fake scholarship and unscientific attitude of his father, stood his ground and made up his mind to go to Cambridge to study mathematics. When he reached Cambridge, 'the great mother of strong men', it must have seemed like heaven. The memoir tells us nothing about Alfred's undergraduate years except that, when completed, he proposed to study molecular physics. My feeling is that the ideas to which he was exposed when he arrived in Cambridge must have played a very important part in forming his views on the proper conduct of scientific work. If this is so, a detailed study of his life as an undergraduate would help us to understand better many of his basic positions. Be that is it may, what is striking to me about the story I have told is the ability of Alfred Marshall to overcome very unfavourable family circumstances and to emerge, not unscathed, for some aspects of his character are not admirable, but with the power of his intellect intact and with that devotion to scholarship which can serve as a model to us all and which, in his case, was to produce the *Principles of Economics*.

## Notes and references

[1] The statement about William Marshall's position at the Bank of England and the meaning of the title 'cashier' is based on a letter (uncovered in the Marshall Library by Rita McWilliams Tullberg) which was written to J. M. Keynes by Mr Nairne of the Bank of England.

[2] As I learnt from a letter from Mary Marshall to 'Cousin Ainslie', now in the possession of Professor George J. Stigler of the University of Chicago.

[3] I have to thank Mr Donald Rutherford of the University of Edinburgh for providing me with information on William Marshall's activities in Leith.

[4] See Philip, 1981, p. 267. Information was also provided by Professor Peter Wickins of the University of Cape Town.

[5] Information provided by M. Ly-Tio-Fane of the Sugar Industry Research Institute, Mauritius.

[6] William Marshall, 'The Memorial of William Marshall of Port Louis', 6 April 1818, Colonial Correspondence—Mauritius CO 167/145, Public Records Office (PRO), London; *idem*, 'The Memorial of William Marshall of Port Louis, Island of Mauritius', 31 December 1818, Colonial Correspondence—Mauritius CO 167/45, PRO, London.

[7] Alfred Marshall tells us that the average income per head in the United Kingdom was about £15 in 1820 (Marshall, 1890, pp. 45–46fn and 1961, vol. 2, p. 733).

[8] Major General Darling to Earl Bathurst, 18 March 1819, Colonial Correspondence—Mauritius CO 167/45, PRO, London.

[9] In the Edinburgh and Leith Directory, he is described as 'merchant' in 1823–24 and 1824–25, as 'merchant and clerk' in 1825–26 and as 'clerk' in the issues for 1826–27 and 1827–28.

[10] O'Byrne, 1861, p. 728; *Gentleman's Magazine*, 13 N.S. (1862), p. 794; for service records see ADM 9/431/2588, PRO, London.

[11] Peterkin and Johnston, 1968, vol. 1, p. 329; *A List of the Officers of the Army and the Corps of Royal Marines, on Full, Retired, and Half-Pay, 1859–60* and *1862–63*; *Gentleman's Magazine*, 10 N.S. (1861), p. 588; WO 17/577, 17/586, 17/595, 17/604, 17/613, 17/630, 17/631, 17/640, 17/649, 17/658, 17/679, 17/689, 17/699, 17/709, 25/3931, PRO, London.

[12] See the letter from F. Y. Edgeworth dated 30 August 1924 in the Keynes Memoir file, Marshall Library, Cambridge.

[13] He is so described in the entry for the house of Thornton Bentall, Borough and Parish of Totnes, census of 1841.

14 Commissioner for Crown Lands, *Darling Downs Record Book, 1845–52*, New South Wales State Archives (NSWSA), Sydney; CLO/13 Queensland. Chief Commissioner for Crown Lands, *Darling Downs Record Book*, Register of demands made for leases to pastoral runs, 1848–65, Queensland State Archives (QSA), Brisbane.

15 See 'Gooragooby' Dalveen, 'Echos of the past: a black criminal', *Warwick Daily News* (Queensland), 26 March 1935.

16 John Watts, 'Personal Reminiscenses by John Watts', John Oxley Memorial Library, Brisbane, 24.

17 Commissioner for Crown Lands, *Darling Downs Record Book, 1845–52*, NSWSA, Sydney.

18 Hall, no date, p. 60; *Votes and Proceedings*, New South Wales Legislative Council, 1856–710, 1:916–26, JOML, Brisbane; AO/3256, AO/3257, NSWSA, Sydney.

19 Hall, no date, p. 45; Steele, 1978, pp. 60–65; Rev. B. Glennie, 'The Australian Diary of the Rev. B. Glennie, Jan. 16th 1848—Sept. 30th 1860', JOL, Brisbane, 15. In Steele (1978) will be found a number of reproductions of pencil sketches made by Martens of Glengallen in 1853. Some paintings of Glengallen by Martens were commissioned by Uncle Charles and Uncle Henry.

20 *Votes and Proceedings*, N.S.W. Legislative Council, 1854, vol. 2 and 1859–60, vol. 3; Commissioner for Crown Lands, *Darling Downs Record Book, 1848–49*; Darlings Downs Pastoral District, *N.S.W. Government Gazette*, 1848, pp. 945–46.

21 Hall, no date, pp. 36–38, 45–47; Waterson, 1968, p. 283; Glennie (note 19 above), p. 17; CLO/8, CLO/13, QSA, Brisbane.

22 *Moreton Bay Courier*, 29 December 1849.

23 C. H. Marshall to W. B. Slade, 26 June 1874, Glengallan Estate, *Private Papers*, JOML, Brisbane.

24 Ibid., 4 September 1873.

25 Ibid., 18 April 1873.

26 Ibid., 28 August 1873.

27 Ibid., 3 October 1873.

28 Ibid., 27 October 1873.

29 Ibid., 29 October 1873.

30 Ibid., 11 July 1873.

31 Ibid., 24 September 1873.

32 Ibid., 15 April 1874.

33 Ibid., 13 May 1874.

34 Ibid., 15 April 1874.

35 *Moreton Bay Courier*, 25 January 1851; *Sydney Morning Herald*, 3 February 1851.

36 Commissioner for Crown Lands, *Darling Downs Record Book, 1845–52*, Register of Exiles and Register of Ticket-of-Leave Holders, NSWSA, Sydney.

37 According to Harrod (1951, p. 194), this was how Keynes thought of the Bloomsbury Group.

38 Hawtrey, 1903, vol. 1, p. 107. The only other connection of Alfred's immediate family with the Hawtreys I have found is that when Thornton Marshall

applied for admission to Guy's Hospital he was recommended by the Reverend Dr. Hawtrey of Eton.

## Bibliography

Barnard, A. (1958), *The Australian Wool Market, 1840–1900*, Melbourne: Melbourne University Press.

Bartley, N. (1892), *Opals and Agates: or Scenes under the Southern Cross and the Magelhans*, Brisbane: Gardina Gotch.

Berkeley Jones, Rev. H. (1853), *Adventures in Australia in 1852 and 1853*, London: Richard Bentley.

Coase, R. H. (1984), 'Alfred Marshall's mother and father', *History of Political Economy*, vol. 16, no. 4.

Corry, B. (1968), 'Marshall, Alfred', in D. L. Sills, ed., *International Encyclopedia of the Social Sciences*, vol. 10, p. 25.

Hall, T. (no date), *The Early History of Warwick District and Pioneers of the Darling Downs*, Warwick.

Harrod, R. F. (1951), *The Life of John Maynard Keynes*, New York: Harcourt and Brace, and London: Macmillan.

Hawtrey, F. M. (1903), *The History of the Hawtrey Family*, London: G. Allen, two volumes.

Herbert, C. (1936), *A Merchant Adventurer: Being a Biography of Leonard Hugh Bentall, Kingston on-Thames*, London: Waterflow.

Kemp, P. K. (1955), *The Bentall Story, Commemorating 150 Years Service to Agriculture, 1805–1955*, Maldon.

Keynes, J. M. (1972) [1933], *Essays in Biography*, reprinted in D. Moggridge, ed., *Collected Writings of John Maynard Keynes*, London, Macmillan for the Royal Economic Society, vol. 10.

Marshall, A. (1890), *Principles of Economics* , London/New York: Macmillan.

Marshall, A. (1961), *Principles of Economics*, C. W. Guillebaud, ed., London: Macmillan for the Royal Economic Society, ninth (variorum) edition, in two volumes, vol. 1–text; vol. 2–notes.

National Trust (1976), *Benthall Hall, Shropshire*, Plaistow: Curwen Press for the National Trust, 1976.

O'Byrne, W. R. (1861), *A Naval Biographical Dictionary*, London: O'Byrne Bros.

Peterkin, A. and Johnston, W. (1968), *Commissioned Officers in the Medical Services of the British Army, 1660–1960*, London: Welcome Historical Medical Library, two volumes.

Philip, P. (1981), *British Residents at the Cape, 1795–1819*, Cape Town: David Philip Ltd.

Pigou, A. C., ed. (1925), *Memorials of Alfred Marshall*, London: Macmillan.

Skidelsky, R. (1986), *John Maynard Keynes: Hopes Betrayed, 1883–1920*, New York: Viking Penguin, and London: Macmillan, 1983.

Steele, J. G. (1978), *Conrad Martens on Queensland: The Frontier Travels of a Colonial Artist*, Brisbane: University of Queensland Press.

Thornton, H. (1939) [1802], *An Enquiry into the Nature and Effects of the Paper Credit of Great Britain*, F. A. Hayek, ed., London: G. Allen and Unwin.

Wagner, A. R. (1960), *English Genealogy*, Oxford: Clarendon Press.

Waterson, D. B. (1968), *Squatter, Selector, and Storekeeper: A History of the Darling Downs, 1859–1893*, Sydney: Sydney University Press.

Watts, J. (undated), *Personal Reminiscenses by John Watts*, Brisbane: Oxley Memorial Library, 24.

# 2. Marshall's theories of competitive price

*John K. Whitaker*

Marshall's puzzling treatment of the long-period determination of price and output in competitive markets is well known and much commented upon. What I attempt here is to provide the most plausible detailed interpretation of his views on such matters. Since the path followed has been well blazed by previous commentators, I can claim at most only an element of synthetic originality and perhaps some refinement of detail. The main innovation is to distinguish three distinct versions of Marshall's price theory that are at least latent in his discussion; hence the title. Recognition of these three versions helps to articulate the exposition and also helps to explain why Marshall's ideas have received such differing interpretations and have led in so many different directions.

Space limitation forbids a detailed exegesis of Marshall's text. Indeed I dispense almost entirely with the usual embroidery of carefully selected quotations, feeling that these can be misleading if not placed in their full context.[1] I have also not found it possible to provide a detailed comparison with and commentary on previous interpretations.[2] For these reasons, my title might better have been 'Some variations on Marshallian themes'.

I

Marshall's three versions of competitive price theory reflect differences in respect to product homogeneity and internal economies. More precisely, the different versions arise from the differing responses that may be given to the following questions.

1. Is the industry's output homogeneous, with one producer's output a perfect substitute for another's, or is the output heterogeneous so that there is product differentiation between individual producers?

2. Are internal economies of scale absent (or exhausted at a firm size that is negligible compared to industry output) or do internal

economies continue to be reaped as a firm expands to produce a substantial fraction of industry output?

With two possible answers to each of two apparently independent questions there seem to be *four* alternatives:

Case A: Sustained internal economies absent, output homogeneous
Case B: Sustained internal economies absent, output heterogeneous
Case C: Sustained internal economies present, output heterogeneous
Case D: Sustained internal economies present, output homogeneous

But one of these alternatives, Case D, is seen by Marshall as incompatible with the persistence of competition in the long run. An industry with such characteristics would soon turn into an oligopoly or 'conditional monopoly'—conditional because the market remains contestable—with one or more firms expanding to exploit ever-increasing scale economies and driving out the others by underselling them in the open market. This fourth case was to have been dealt with in the never-written second volume of the *Principles* the first volume of which deals with the theory of normal value.[3] Normal value is restricted to either *unconditional* monopoly or to the persisting competition of many producers.

Leaving the case of unconditional monopoly aside—the treatment in Book V, Chapter 14 of the *Principles* is unproblematically lucid—there remain three cases of persisting competition falling within the ambit of the theory of normal value. These correspond to Cases A–C above, although it has been a long-standing source of puzzlement and controversy to account for Marshall's belief in the persistence of competition in Case C where internal economies persist.[4] I now consider each of these cases in turn and then take up the problem of external economies.

## II

Case A, with homogeneous products and no sustained internal economies, is most obviously exemplified by agriculture which receives much attention in the *Principles*. With homogeneous products the 'law of one price' applies, after allowing for transport costs. A firm has no need to devote effort and resources to building up a clientele or drumming up sales since output can be sold readily in an organised market open to all. In the absence of sustained internal economies, firms remain small and easily manageable. There is little call for the creative adaptation of internal organisation and production methods to a changing scale of operations and thus no need for management of unusual ability. (It needs to be emphasised that to Marshall existing technology is not a known book of blueprints freely available to all firms. Each firm must work out for itself just how to apply existing background technology to the firm's own operations, often arriving at an idiosyncratic solution as it expands its scale or adapts to changed factor prices.) The modest demands made on management in Case A are perhaps reinforced by a tendency, in agriculture at least, for background technology to advance less rapidly than in large-scale manufacturing.

The consequence of all this is that there is no great difficulty in keeping a firm in existence indefinitely at a viable level of efficiency. A finite life for each firm and systematic turnover of firms are not features characterising a competitive industry in Case A. This is not to say that entry or exit of firms is precluded. There is likely to be entry as the entire industry's output expands, or exit as it declines. But any long-period equilibrium will tend to be characterised by a fixed group of firms, each of unchanging size and each displaying repetitive behaviour.[5] This is, of course, the paradigm of the modern textbook.

Marshall never gave a clear account of the way in which, in this kind of setting, long-run average and marginal costs vary with a firm's output, but two things are evident. First, all firms determine output in the long period by equating long-run marginal cost to price.[6] Second, a firm's costs depend upon the output of the industry as a whole as well as upon the firm's own output. The dependence on industry output might reflect the bidding up of input prices as the industry expands its demands. But more important to Marshall were external economies reaped by industry expansion.

Although all firms have the same long-run marginal cost in a long-period equilibrium, they need not have the same long-run average cost. This is broadly because of the existence of 'differential advantages' among firms. These reflect either differences in the efficiency of management between firms or differential access to superior units of some heterogeneous input, well-advantaged land being the obvious and leading example. The implication is, of course, that there is a limited supply of managers or land of the highest quality. In calculating average costs, the cost of management and land should be entered as the opportunity cost to the *industry* excluding any effects of capitalising differential advantages arising only within the industry: these comprise the producer surplus or rents (explicit or implicit) generated in the industry. The hidden presumption is that management and land are homogeneous, or at least less hetero-geneous, in alternative uses outside the industry than they are within the industry. In the case of managers this is justified by Marshall's assumption that, as for all skilled labour, special aptitude in a particular line of business is revealed only after commitment to it. Hence, the attractive force is the earnings of average ability: all managers in an industry will have similar opportunity costs since they do not know whether they will prove better or worse than average if they move elsewhere. An extreme justification for all land having the same opportunity cost to the industry would arise if it had no alternative use, the opportunity cost then being always zero.

The clearest insight Marshall provides into the relation between costs and output is through the 'particular expenses' curve.[7] This represents an array, in increasing order, of the cost, excluding producer surplus, of each unit of output produced in a long-period equilibrium. By construction, the graph of the array slopes positively, the ordinate indicating unit cost and the abscissa the number of units of output produced with that or smaller cost. (See Fig. 1 where $PE$ is the particular expenses curve, $DD$ and $SS$ are the industry's long-period demand and supply curves, and $Q_o$ and $P_o$ are the quantity and price corresponding to long-period equilibrium.) The shaded area in Fig. 1 measures total producer surplus generated within the industry, and the supply curve slopes positively because of limitation on the availability of managers and land of the highest quality.[8] External economies account for the fact that $SS$ lies above $PE$ to the left of $Q_o$. $SS$ is drawn on the assumption that at any output, such as $Q_1$, external economies are those that would accrue if industry output were also $Q_1$. While $PE$ is drawn on the assumption that at any output, say $Q_1$, that is less than $Q_o$ the external economies are the greater ones accruing when industry output is $Q_o$. If external economies are absent, Marshall indicates that $PE$ and $SS$ coincide to the left of $Q_o$. This reveals that the unit costs arrayed in $PE$ must be viewed as *marginal*, not average, costs, since $SS$ is a lateral summation of the supply curves of individual firms based on long-run marginal costs. The effects of external economies are revealed by a downward shift in $PE$ as long-period equilibrium output rises due, say, to a rightward shift in $DD$.

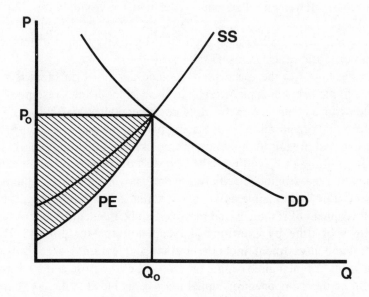

Figure 1

III

Case B, that of an industry with heterogeneous output but no sustained internal economies, retains only a vestigial presence in the *Principles*, partly because one of its chief manifestations—the retail trade—was to have been dealt with more fully in Marshall's unwritten Volume II. But some manufactures, such as textiles, where internal economies are exhausted at a modest output, might also fall under this head (Marshall, 1961, vol. 1, p. 281). In its simpler forms, where exceptional management skills are not required to keep a firm jogging along reasonably efficiently for ever, as will now be supposed, Case B can be thought of as Case A with product differentiation added. Otherwise Case B merges into Case C and does not need to be discussed separately.

Marshall evidently believed that most manufactured or processed goods were differentiated products and that their sellers faced negatively sloped demand curves, at least for price reductions. Yet he also wished to use the concepts of *the* price and output levels for an industry comprising a large set of competing sellers of such differentiated products, products generically similar and clearly demarcated from those offered by sellers outside the industry. Not only this, but in a celebrated footnote (ibid., p. 458) he speaks of the demand curves facing individual sellers as sufficiently negatively sloped to require significant price cuts to expand sales.

In the long run the 'particular' demand curve a firm faces is not given to the firm but engineered by it. Each seller devotes resources to building up a clientele or network of customers: what Marshall termed an 'external organisation'. Advertising plays some part in establishing this external organisation, but more important is the drumming up of business through travelling salesmen and other personal contacts, something that cannot be achieved overnight. Like the firm's internal organisation and tangible assets, the external organisation is built up by investment of resources and may have to be maintained against the ravages of time by exertions and expenditures for upkeep. The cumulated investment in both internal and external organisation represents the intangible capital or goodwill of the firm, and a normal return on this component of capital must be included in the cost base. (However, as in the case of tangible investments, past investments in goodwill that were mistaken or have been rendered obsolete must be eliminated from the base. Otherwise, given enough time, a new entrant could replicate the firm at lower cost.) Of course, a firm's demand curve is shifted not only by its own actions but also by the actions of other sellers or changes in the general circumstances affecting the industry or related industries, such as technology, factor prices or consumer incomes.

Marshall provides little indication of how the glaring gaps in his exposition are to be filled. What determines the precise shape and location of a seller's demand curve at any time? Does a seller interact strongly in his selling efforts with a few close rivals or are interactions with other sellers widely spread over the industry and thus so attenuated as to be ignorable? (There are some hints that the former alternative sometimes applies.) Is entry of a new firm likely to affect all existing firms by a little or a few existing firms by a lot? That is, is entry-deterring behaviour likely to occur? Is there a symmetry of demand response to increasing and decreasing price, or is demand perfectly elastic for price increases and only less than perfectly elastic for price decreases, as Negishi (1985, ch. 2) suggests in a reinterpretation of Adam Smith's treatment of markets?[9] Some credence is given to this last possibility by the consideration that Marshall invariably uses the particular demand curve in the context of price reductions and ignores the possible incentive for a seller to raise prices when his particular demand curve remains negatively sloped as price is raised above the level set by other sellers. That is, Marshall does not recognise clearly the monopolistic element in monopolistic competition.

Despite the vague, even inchoate, nature of Marshall's views, it does seem most plausible to regard him as groping towards something like Chamberlin's large-group case with selling costs (Chamberlin, 1938, pp. 80–100 and 149–69; see also Stykolt, 1956), but it would be anachronistic to suppose that he saw it in detail. Still, indulging for the moment in such anachronism, let us picture a typical Case B firm in large-group equilibrium, supposing for simplicity that there are constant costs in production. (See Fig. 2 where $AR$ represents the firm's particular demand curve, $MR$ the corresponding marginal revenue curve, and $LAC$ the long-run average and marginal cost of production assuming tangible inputs are always adjusted in a cost-minimising way.) The firm finds it most profitable to produce $q_0$ and sell at price $p_0$, as shown in Fig. 2 where the shaded area represents the return to intangible capital plus any excess profits or return to differential advantage. Assuming the last away, the second category— excess profits (deficient profits if negative)—must be excluded by the conditions of large-group equilibrium. This follows because entry into the industry, or exit from it, are both unrestricted. Suppose, however, that the shaded area is larger than required to give a normal return on the firm's intangible or goodwill capital. Then the firm will have an incentive to invest in improving its external organisation. In itself this tends to shift $AR$ to the right and will tend to induce further investment in internal organisation and tangible capital. But similarly situated firms will have a similar incentive, and their actions will tend to shift the original firm's $AR$ to the left. Starting in long-period large-group equilibrium and imagining that a rise in consumer incomes shifts the $AR$ curves of all firms in the large group to the right, there is set in train a process of investment by existing firms and entry of new firms. The adjustment process will be complex and there is no simple way of ascertaining what the new large-group equilibrium will look like if and when it is finally established. Possibly the structure of relative prices set by different firms will remain stable even though absolute prices change. This would make it easier to think in terms of 'the' price level for the industry. It would also make more justifiable the

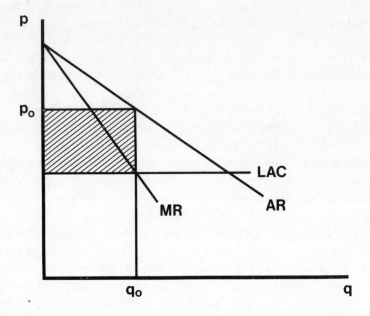

Figure 2

construction of quality weights to be used in aggregating the heterogeneous outputs of different sellers to get a measure of 'the' quantity supplied by the industry as a whole. But all such matters remain entirely in the realm of conjecture since Marshall is silent.

IV

The third case, Case C with differentiated products and persistent internal economies, has loomed largest in the eyes of interpreters of the *Principles*, though it actually plays only a small role in the first edition of 1890. It is in this context that the finite life cycle of the firm and the related concept of the representative firm come into prominence. Like the trees in a virgin forest, each firm has a typical life cycle, starting small and weak, slowly building up internal and external organisation and a special clientele until it is fully mature, and then gradually subsiding into inefficiency and eventual extinction as the energy and grasp of the founder wanes and less able successors replace him.

The basic presumptions are:

1. Successful management of Case-C firms requires exceptional managerial and entrepreneurial skills and energies.

2. Such exceptional skills and energies are unlikely to be maintained as a firm's founder passes control to molly-coddled heirs or hired managers or goes public.

3. The building up of internal, and especially of external, organisation is inevitably a slow process and a firm does not have enough time during its vigorous phase to establish a sales connection sufficiently large to dominate the industry.

Product differentiation, perhaps aided by constraints on external financing, plays a vital role in justifying the last presumption. Sales can be expanded rapidly only by accepting a reduction in price so great as to more than counterbalance the benefits of any new internal economies reaped in production. A profitable expansion of output requires a prior extension of external organisation. Having nothing further to say about Marshall's views on product differentiation it will, however, be expositionally simpler to take the third presumption axiomatically and reason 'as if' all firms in the industry are price takers, selling a homogeneous product at a common price but with output constrained by limits set by the external organisation.

The exacting managerial demands characteristic of Case C seem to arise partly because firms grow to be quite large, although not dominatingly so, partly because the increasing-returns technology is typically complex, and partly because the potential benefits of expansion make the struggle for markets ruthless and even the maintenance of existing clientele especially difficult.

One has to say that the general line of argument underlying Marshall's treatment of Case C seems unpersuasive, although it was perhaps less so when the Victorian family firm was the dominant form of industrial organisation. Even Marshall seems to have had growing doubts as joint-stock companies rose increasingly to prominence. *Industry and Trade* of 1919 still adverts to the life-cycle possibility, but half-heartedly and peripherally, although the eighth edition of the *Principles* in 1920 emphasises it still.

It is clear that, when it came to the long period, Marshall was extremely reluctant to apply equilibrium methods to Case C industries, and did so only with extravagant warning and reservations. His treatment might seem something of a *jeu d'esprit*, could such a notion be applied to someone as unfrivolous as Marshall, but it is evident that it had appeared to him upon discovery as an important conceptual clarification, resolving a major empirical puzzle. For it helped reconcile his firm conviction that internal economies and competition coexisted widely.

In the long-period equilibrium of Case C, firms are virtually on a par with machines or skilled workers. Indeed, Marshall uses the term 'appliances of production' to comprise all three.[10] Each firm, machine or skilled worker (including managerial personnel among the latter) has a finite span of economic life. For all three categories, maintaining a steady stock of balanced age distribution in the industry requires a steady flow of new replacements. Commitment of the new replacements to this particular industry is largely irreversible. Thus, the commitment, whether of a new firm, a new machine, or a new entrant to a skilled occupation, must be based on the lifetime stream of earnings expected. When long-period equilibrium rules, and has been long sustained, the relevant earnings stream may be assumed correctly foreseen. To sustain the long-period equilibrium at a given level of industry output, the prices of the industry's output and variable inputs (materials and unskilled labour) must be such as to just sustain the requisite replacement flow of firms, machines, skilled workers, and so on, neither more nor less. Comparing the equilibria corresponding to different levels of industry output, and hence to different positions of the demand curve facing the industry, enables the industry supply curve to be determined. It is the locus of alternative equilibrium combinations of quantity and price for the industry's output. In these hypothetical comparisons, background technology and supply conditions for variable inputs must be held constant.

Assume for simplicity that in long-period equilibrium all firms are equivalent and have identical life cycles: the only differential advantages left are those of age. A firm of specified age will have the same output and average cost irrespective of its date of inception. On the other hand, at any date, firms of different ages will have different levels of output and average cost. Here, and in the subsequent argument, cost—whether average or marginal—is to be interpreted as including only the cost of tangible inputs such as labour, plant and materials. The cost of the intangible or goodwill capital invested in the firm's internal and external organisations is to be excluded. Tangible inputs are assumed to be fully adjusted in a cost-minimising way *given the firm's current internal organisation* which determines the applicable production function. Output is constrained by the firm's current external organisation, and it is not the case that output can be expanded until marginal cost equals 'the' market price. Rather, marginal cost will normally be below market price, equalling marginal revenue if the firm indulges in price cutting to force sales. But young firms, striving to establish themselves, may produce with marginal and average cost above market price, pushing their product at a loss in order to establish a clientele or 'connection' with 'goodwill' value. Older, senescent firms will have higher average cost than well-established vigorous firms, increasingly so as vitality declines, and will reach their demise as average cost rises to the level of market price, there being no prospective future profits to recoup present losses. Their internal organisation might be said to have atrophied through X-inefficiency.

In long-period equilibrium there will always be a balanced age distribution of firms and the observable distributions of firms by output and average cost will remain invariant over time. But any firm will age inexorably, like the individual tree in the virgin forest. A snap-shot of the industry at any time is revealed by a version of the particular expenses (*PE*) curve.

The *PE* curve now arrays either the total outputs of the various firms by current average cost or the output units of all firms by the incremental cost of producing them. (Either way a smooth *PE* curve approximates an underlying step function.) Arraying by incremental or marginal cost seems of limited relevance given that the Case A competitive supply curve no longer applies and that each firm's production function shifts as the firm's internal organisation changes. An array by average cost is more easily implemented empirically and will now be assumed.[11] A typical *PE* curve is shown in Fig. 3 (where *SS* is the long-period supply curve, *DD* is the industry's demand curve, and $Q_o$ and $P_o$ are the long-period equilibrium quantity and price for the industry). The position of the *PE* curve will not change over time so long as the industry remains in the same long-period equilibrium. But each firm will pass through an identical life cycle that takes average cost along the *PE* curve from *a* to *b* and back to *c*, although not necessarily at a uniform speed. The discounted sum of the successive positive or negative surpluses of total revenue over total cost that a firm generates along this trajectory (already incorporating a normal return to investments in tangible capital) should be just enough to remunerate the firm's stream of investment in intangible capital. It is this condition that determines exactly where $P_o$ must lie in relation to the *PE* curve in order to sustain long-period equilibrium for the industry.

The positive slope of the *PE* curve does not reflect any differential advantages accruing to certain firms as it did in Case A, for such differences are now assumed away. Instead, it manifests the variation of average cost over a life cycle common to all firms. As shown in Fig. 3, the *PE* curve may terminate to the right vertically above the point $(Q_o, P_o)$ and not at this point as in Case A (see Fig. 1). This is because young firms may rationally plan to make initial losses.

The long-period supply curve *SS* is shown in Fig. 3 as negatively sloped. Marshall believed this would typically be the case given sustained internal economies. External economies might reinforce the effect, while a bidding up of the prices of inputs as the industry expands might militate against it. But internal economies are the crucial force at work. Marshall's basic presumption was that when alternative long-period equilibria are compared, higher industry output is not matched by a proportionate increase in the number of firms, so that firms will be larger on average over their life cycles, and will thus reap greater internal economies. To put this in another way, when industry output is larger, a given firm finds itself in an environment more conducive to expansion and so reaches a greater absolute size at maturity. Such a crucial proposition calls for detailed justification. Unfortunately Marshall gave none, although the key must lie in a presumption that the largely unspecified difficulties of building up an external organisation and connection depend on *relative* market share rather than absolute size.

Marshall introduced the concept of the representative firm in order to simplify the treatment of long-period equilibrium in Case C. At one level, the representative firm is an empirical approximation. An astute observer can identify a real firm whose average cost will give a good approximation to industry supply price when industry output is in some specified narrow range.[12] At a more conceptual and elusive level, the representative firm may be viewed as an analytical construct that converts real heterogeneity to hypothetical homogeneity. The industry equilibrium might be conceived as involving only representative firms, all unchanging, rather than the actual ever-ageing ever-changing body of firms all differentiated by age at least.

Given the second interpretation, it is tempting to compare two different long-period equilibria by supposing that exactly the same set

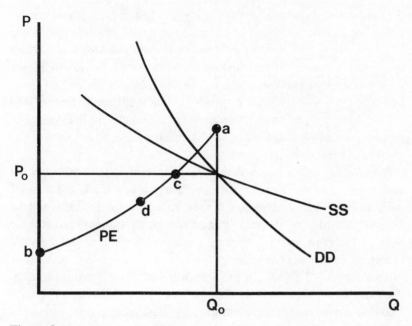

Figure 3

of identical, immortal and unchanging representative firms is present in both situations, so that the relevant points on the long-period industry supply curve might be obtained from the long-period supply curve of any representative firm. But there is no way of independently determining the latter. It will not do to revert to the alternative empirical identification of a particular firm as representative. For this actual firm is taken as representative only for a pre-specified level of industry output. And since this firm is inevitably ageing and changing over time, any imputation of a true long-period supply curve to it must itself be purely hypothetical. The second usage of the representative firm concept offers apparent analytical simplification only at the cost of baffling conceptual complexity. It is clearer, if more cumbersome, to work with the entire distribution of firms.[13]

Marshall's stress on the irreversibility of the long-period industry supply curve in Case C does not raise severe conceptual difficulties. Essentially he assumes that the long-period supply price of any level of the industry's output will be lower the more that level falls below the industry's past-peak equilibrium output. The explanation is straightforward. Irreversible and practically immortal investments in either tangible capital or knowledge (the latter to be thought of as the detailed know-how required to apply the given background technology to production) have been justified by the high past-peak level of output. They still contribute to production at the lower current level of output, and thus yield positive quasi-rents, but these quasi-rents are now less than would justify making the investments anew. They may be treated just like land. Such arguments can legitimately be confined within the bounds of equilibrium analysis, and could apply in principle to Cases A and B as well, although Marshall presents them only in the context of powerful scale economies.

Marshall's well known tax-subsidy argument is essentially an argument for subsidising a Case C industry so that it can expand and benefit from scale economies. These scale economies need not be external but may be internal to the firms in the industry since these become larger on average over their life cycles when industry output is larger. Taxation of the Case A industry is merely one of various possible ways of financing the subsidy, but a way permitting easy demonstration that overall welfare gain is *possible*. Accusations that Marshall erred in this demonstration by neglecting producer surplus are unfounded.[14] Loss of producer surplus in the taxed Case A industry was properly accounted for; possible gain of producer surplus in the subsidised Case C industry was ignored, but only on the basis that including it would make the demonstration hold *a fortiori*. That external economies were not the crux is suggested by Marshall's presumption that they would occur in both Case A and Case C industries. Thus, external economies gained through the subsidy would tend to be offset by external economies lost through the tax.

## V

Marshall can be said to have originated the concept of external economies, yet what appeared to him the most important of them seem more internal than external. These are the economies resulting from the increased specialisation and subdivision of function made possible by output growth. Probably influenced by Herbert Spencer's view on the increased complexity accompanying biological evolution, Marshall's stress on this class of economies harks back to Adam Smith's familiar dictum that the division of labour is limited by the extent of the market. To be counted as external, the economies resulting from an increased subdivision of function must obviously involve vertical disintegration and the creation of new firms and sub-industries or 'trades' as the original industry's output rises, an outcome that will be encouraged by the prevalence of diseconomies of scope. Yet this still leaves a dilemma. If the new trades are no longer counted as part of the original industry, the latter's supply curve refers to a gradually narrower set of functions as output expands, which seems unsatisfactory. Yet if they are included, it appears that internal economies are merely shifted from the original industry to the new trades. Actually, this is not necessarily so. The problem is not so much persistent scale economies in the new trades as their inherently monopolistic character at inception. This was made clear by Stigler (1951), and much earlier by Carl Menger (1871, pp. 216–18). For example, as an isolated village grows, a *single* full-time shoemaker becomes viable. With further growth, a *single* two-person shoemaking organisation, each member a specialist, replaces the do-it-all one-man shoemaker form of organisation, and so on. Some basic indivisibility (for example, a specialist must be full time) sets a minimum scale to each form of organisation, but it does not follow that a given form of organisation would become more efficient on an even larger scale (for example, if there were ten do-it-all one-man shoemakers rather than one). However, if there are always economies of further subdivision present, there is always a new and more efficient form of organisation just over the horizon. Increase in industry output will make it viable, but only at its minimum scale, implying a single unit of the new form rather than many competing units.[15] The 'monopoly' involved in this is, however, a 'conditional' one. Anyone can revert to some less subdivided mode of production (for example, individuals can make their own shoes). More importantly, if entry is free, the new unit's market is contestable. The unit may thereby be forced to price as if it was in perfect competition with other similar units, as Samuelson (1947, pp. 78–79) pointed out long ago.

It is, I think, some such contestability argument, rather then market imperfection inhibiting exploitation of internal economies, that must sustain Marshall's view that economies of vertical disintegration can be treated as external and compatible with competition: views subsequently echoed by Pigou (for example 1932, pp. 219–20) and Young (1928). But market imperfections and the life cycle of firms can assist in maintaining competition if internal economies come to prevail in the trades and sub-industries created by an increased differentiation of function.

## VI

Marshall's treatment of the matters dealt with here is sufficiently baffling and fraught with apparent inconsistencies that no-one can claim to have deciphered an entirely coherent vision that must have been at the back of his mind. Nor can it be hoped that any one interpretation will command universal assent. I do not entirely convince even myself as I go back to grapple once more with a puzzling passage of Marshall's. At best one can hope that continuing interpretive efforts will manifest that increasing complexity and better adaptation to its end that Marshall discerned in the development of the industrial organisation.

### Notes and references

[1] The interested reader will need to consult and ponder upon at least the following pages from the variorum edition of Marshall's *Principles* (Guillebaud, 1961), volume one of which is a reprint of the eighth edition of the *Principles* from 1920.

*Volume one*: pp. vi–ix, xiii–xvi, 138–39, 148–49, 153–56, 240–42, 265–66, 271–73, 277*, 280–82, 284–89*, 299–304, 311–13, 314–18*, 341–43*, 355–59, 361–62, 367*, 370–71, 373–74, 376–80*, 390, 391–92n*, 396–98*, 404, 406, 408–409, 411, 441, 445, 451–52, 456–61*, 467–70, 472–74*, 485–86, 497*, 500–503*, 516–22, 538, 540, 596–97, 599–606, 614–15, 616–17n, 618–19, 625–26, 630–31, 635, 649–53, 656–57, 662–63, 667, 805–12*, 832, 847–52*.

*Volume two*: pp. 69–72, 334–35, 344–46, 382–83, 392–93, 441, 447, 452, 458, 471, 521, 524–29*, 539, 548–49, 577, 579, 587, 653, 660–61, 802–803, 805–806*, 812.

The pages marked by an asterisk contain the most important passages. Portions of Marshall's *Pure Theory of Domestic Values* (Whitaker, 1975, volume 2, pp. 186–236, especially 219–36) and *Industry and Trade* (Marshall, 1919, especially pp. 182–87, 314–16) should also be consulted.

[2] The most important references (key items asterisked) are Andrews (1951); Blaug (1985, pp. 376–96 and 411–14); Ellis and Fellner (1943); Frisch (1950)*; Hague (1958)*; Hollander (1961); Jenner (1964–65); Levine (1980); Loasby (1978); Maxwell (1958); Negishi (1985, ch. 5); Newman (1960)*; Robertson (1924 and 1930)*; Robbins (1928); Samuelson (1967); Shove (1930)*; Viner (1931)*; Williams (1978); Wolfe (1954)*.

[3] Case D is prominent in *Industry and Trade* (Marshall, 1919), on which see Liebhafsky (1955) and Gonce (1982), for example.

[4] In Whitaker (1987 and 1989), I distinguished only Cases A and C, which correspond to the most significant dichotomy. Distinctions between the three cases stand out much more clearly in the first edition of the *Principles* (Marshall, 1890) than they do in the eighth edition. But even in the eighth edition the discussion of firms' demand for inputs, including much of Book VI, seems to proceed on Case A terms. All short-period equilibrium issues are left aside in what follows. In the short period, with the number and capital of all firms held fixed, the relevant

dichotomy simply turns on whether products are differentiated or not. That is, it is between Case A and Cases B + C.

[5] 'In agriculture and other trades in which a man gains no very great new economies by increasing the scale of his production it often happens that a business remains of about the same size for many years, if not for many generations' (Marshall, 1961, vol. 1, p. 283).

[6] The use of the qualifiers 'long-run' and 'short-run' seems to be due to Viner (1931). Marshall himself sticks to 'long-period' and 'short-period'. His emphasis on the cost of entire processes of production rather than particular units of output corresponds to a distinction between long-run and short-run costs. Below it will be necessary to introduce complications due to intangible or goodwill capital.

[7] The treatment of this is extremely terse. See Marshall (1961, vol. 1, pp. 473–74 fn. and 810–12fn. and especially vol. 2, pp. 805–806). See also Whitaker (1975, vol. 2, pp. 226–27).

[8] This assumes that the industry is not bidding up prices of variable inputs such as labour and raw materials as it expands. The identification of the shaded area in Fig. 1 with producer surplus applies equally whether the *PE* curve arrays output by its marginal or average unit cost.

[9] The asymmetry arises because buyers are assumed to know the market price level and the price asked by the seller to whom they are attached, but not the specific prices of other sellers. Thus, if a firm increases its price above the market level, its own clientele actively seeks out other sellers. But if it lowers its price clienteles of other firms do not switch to the price-cutting firm.

[10] See, for example, Marshall (1961, vol. 1, pp. 374, 376 and 377; and vol. 2, pp. 548–49).

[11] Marshall seems to have first developed the idea of the *PE* curve in the context of agriculture to demonstrate a graphical relationship between land rent and the supply curve. The doctrine achieved its final form, and the *PE* curve its name, in the 1891 second edition of the *Principles*. (See footnote 7 for references.) Marshall then made an uneasy attempt to encompass both agriculture and industry (both Case A and Case C) in a single discussion, introducing some confusion as to whether output units are ranked by the cost incurred in producing the unit specifically or by the overall average cost of the firm producing them. The *PE* curve is shown incorrectly as extending to the right of the industry output level, while the possibility that it may rise above the industry price level, as in Fig. 3, is not noted. For pertinent discussions see Viner (1931) and Blaug (1985, pp. 384–88, 412–13). Both agree that the *PE* ranks by average cost and that *PE* may rise above market price.

[12] In Fig. 3 this would be a firm whose average costs of *tangible* inputs are at some point such as *d* sufficiently below market price to yield a surplus that, if continued for the entire life of a firm, would just cover the cost of the necessary investment in *intangible* capital. It is only in this sense that price might be said to be determined by the costs of the representative firm. Although the idea of long-run *marginal* cost is occasionally hinted at, its relevance to Case C is emphatically disclaimed in Appendix H of the *Principles* (Marshall, 1961, vol. 1, pp. 805–12 and especially p. 805). Current average costs seem to be the only solid basis for proceeding, but the cost of intangible capital must be included too.

[13] As cogently argued by Wolfe (1954) and Newman (1960). A generalisation of the above hypothetical argument would imagine that the number of representative firms increases as industry output is enlarged, but less than proportionately.

[14] See, for example, Samuelson (1967, pp. 112–13). Marshall's arguments are presented more fully and satisfactorily in this early *Pure Theory of Domestic Values* (Whitaker, 1975, vol. 2, pp. 219–36) than in the *Principles* (Marshall, 1961, vol. 1, pp. 467–73). The relevant producer surpluses would be those due to 'differential advantages', especially land rents, other than those of mere age.

[15] Suppose, for example, that more shoes per head are produced by $n+1$ individuals, each with a different specialty, than by $n$ individuals, each somewhat less specialised. Whether the $n+1$ individuals form a single firm or work as independent craftsmen, there will be only one of each when that mode of organisation first becomes viable.

## Bibliography

American Economic Association (1953), *Readings in Price Theory*, Homewood, Ill: Irwin.

Andrews, P. W. S. (1951), 'Industrial analysis in economics', in T. Wilson and P. W. S. Andrews, eds, *Oxford Studies in the Price Mechanism*, Oxford: Oxford University Press.

Blaug, M. (1985), *Economic Theory in Retrospect*, Cambridge: Cambridge University Press, fourth edition.

Chamberlin, E. (1938) [1933], *The Theory of Monopolistic Competition*, Cambridge, Mass: Harvard University Press.

Ellis, H. S. and Fellner, W. J. (1943), 'External economies and diseconomies', *American Economic Review*, vol. 33, September, pp. 493–511. Reprinted in American Economic Association, 1953.

Frisch, R. (1950), 'Alfred Marshall's theory of value', *Quarterly Journal of Economics*, vol. 64, November, pp. 495–524. Reprinted in Wood, 1982, vol. 3, no. 61.

Gonce, R. A. (1982), 'Alfred Marshall on industrial organisation: from *Principles of Economics* to *Industry and Trade*', in Wood, 1982, vol. 4, no. 123.

Hague, D. C. (1958), 'Alfred Marshall and the competitive firm', *Economic Journal*, vol. 68, December, pp. 673–90. Reprinted in Wood, 1982, vol. 3, no. 71.

Hollander, S. (1961), 'The representative firm and imperfect competition', *Canadian Journal of Economics and Political Science*, vol. 27, May, pp. 236-41.

Jenner, R. A. (1964–65), 'The dynamic factor in Marshall's economic system', *Western Economic Journal*, vol. 3, no.1, pp. 21–38. Reprinted in Wood, 1982, vol. 1, no. 18.

Levine, A. L. (1980), 'Increasing returns, the competitive model, and the enigma that was Alfred Marshall', *Scottish Journal of Political Economy*, vol. 27, November, pp. 260–75.

Liebhafsky, H. H. (1955), 'A curious case of neglect: Marshall's *Industry and Trade*', *Canadian Journal of Economics and Political Science*, vol. 21, August, pp. 339–53. Reprinted in Wood, 1982, vol. 4, no. 101.

Loasby, B. J. (1978) 'Whatever happened to Marshall's theory of value?', *Scottish Journal of Political Economy*, vol. 25, February, pp. 1–12. Reprinted in Wood, 1982, vol. 3, no. 93.

Marshall, A. (1890), *Principles of Economics*, vol. 1, London: Macmillan, first edition.

Marshall, A. (1923) [1919], *Industry and Trade*, London: Macmillan, fifth edition.

Marshall, A. (1961), *Principles of Economics*, C. W. Guillebaud, ed., London: Macmillan for the Royal Economic Society, ninth (variorum) edition, in two volumes, vol. 1–text; vol. 2–notes.

Maxwell, J. A. (1958), 'Some Marshallian concepts, especially the representative firm', *Economic Journal*, vol. 68, December, pp. 691–98. Reprinted in Wood, 1982, vol. 3, no. 72.

Menger, C. (1871), *Principles of Economics*, English translation by J. Dingwell and B. F. Hoselitz, Glencoe, Ill.: Free Press, 1950. Page references are to the 1981 edition, New York: New York University Press.

Negishi, T. (1985), *Economic Theories in a Non-Walrasian Tradition*, Cambridge: Cambridge University Press.

Newman, P. K. (1960), 'The erosion of Marshall's theory of value', *Quarterly Journal of Economics*, vol. 74, November, pp. 587–600. Reprinted in Wood, 1982, vol. 3, no. 75.

Pigou, A. C. (1932) [1920], *The Economics of Welfare*, London: Macmillan, fourth edition.

Robbins, L. C. (1928), 'The representative firm', *Economic Journal*, vol. 38, September, pp. 387–404. Reprinted in Wood, 1982, vol. 3, no. 48.

Robertson, D. H. (1924), 'Those empty boxes', *Economic Journal*, vol. 34, March, pp. 16–21. Reprinted in American Economic Association, 1953.

Robertson, D. H. (1930), 'Increasing returns and the representative firm', *Economic Journal*, vol. 40, March, pp. 80–89. Reprinted in Wood, 1982, vol. 3, no. 50.

Samuelson P. A. (1947), *Foundations of Economic Analysis*, Cambridge, Mass: Harvard University Press.

Samuelson P. A. (1967), 'The monopolistic competition revolution', in R. E. Kuenne (ed.), *Monopolistic Competition Theory: Studies in Impact*, New York: Wiley.

Shove, G. F. (1930), 'Increasing returns and the representative firm', *Economic Journal*, vol. 40, March, pp. 94–116. Reprinted in Wood, 1982, vol. 3, no. 50.

Stigler, G. J. (1951), 'The division of labor is limited by the extent of the market', *Journal of Political Economy*, vol. 59, June, pp. 185–93.

Stykolt, S. (1956), 'A curious case of neglect: Marshall on the "tangency solution"', *Canadian Journal of Economics and Political Science*, vol. 22, May, p. 251. Reprinted in Wood, 1982, vol. 4, no. 104.

Viner, J. (1931), 'Cost curves and supply curves', *Zeitschrift für National-ökonomie*, vol. 3, September, pp. 23–46. Reprinted in American Economic Association, 1953.

Whitaker, J. K. (ed.) (1975), *The Early Economic Writings of Alfred Marshall 1867–1890*, London: Macmillan for the Royal Economic Society, two volumes.

Whitaker, J. K. (1987), 'Alfred Marshall 1842–1924', in J. Eatwell, M. Milgate and P. Newman, eds, *The New Palgrave: A Dictionary of Economics*, London: Macmillan, vol. 3, pp. 350–63.

Whitaker, J. K. (1989), 'The Cambridge background to imperfect competition', in G. Feiwel, ed., *The Economics of Imperfect Competition and Employment*, London: Macmillan, 1989.

Williams, P. L. (1978), *The Emergence of the Theory of the Firm*, London: Macmillan.

Wolfe, J. N. (1954), 'The representative firm', *Economic Journal*, vol. 64, June, pp. 337–49. Reprinted in Wood, 1982, vol. 3, no. 65.

Wood, J. C. (ed.) (1982), *Alfred Marshall: Critical Assessments*, London: Croom Helm, four volumes.

Young, A. A. (1928), 'Increasing returns and economic progress', *Economic Journal*, vol. 38, December, pp. 527–42.

# 3. Alfred Marshall and the general equilibrium theory of value and distribution: an examination of notes XIV and XXI

*Robert W. Dimand*

The name of Alfred Marshall is so closely associated with partial equilibrium analysis that leading textbooks of the history of economic thought, such as Negishi (1989) and Ekelund and Hebert (1990), present contrasting chapters on Marshall and partial equilibrium and on Leon Walras and general equilibrium. Walsh and Gram (1980) and Weintraub (1985), the standard authorities on the history of general equilibrium theory, make no mention of Marshall as a general equilibrium theorist. Against this consensus, Joseph Schumpeter (1954, p. 952) stands almost alone in protesting that 'note XXI in the Appendix to Marshall's *Principles* is conclusive proof of the fundamental sameness of his and Walras' models'. As Schumpeter noticed, Marshall did present a theory of general equilibrium in Notes XIV and XXI of his Mathematical Appendix.

At the end of Book VI, Chapter II, § 10 of his *Principles of Economics*, Marshall (1920, p. 545) observed that

> the efficiencies (total and marginal) of the several factors of production, their contributions direct and indirect to the aggregate net product, or national dividend; and the shares of that dividend which accrue to them severally are correlated by a number of mutual interactions so complicated, that it is impossible to comprehend the whole in a single statement. But yet by aid of the terse, compact, precise language of Mathematics it is possible to lead up to a fairly unified general view.

In a footnote, he added that:

> Such a survey is focussed in Notes XIV–XXI of the Mathematical Appendix: the last of them is easy of comprehension, and shows the complexity of the problems. Most of the rest are developments of details arising out of Note XIV, the substance of part of which is translated into English in [Book] V, [Chapter] IV.

These notes were of great importance to Marshall. He wrote to John Bates Clark in 1908:

> Substantially my theory of capital as it exists to-day is completely outlined in Notes V and XIII–XIV; and my general theory of distribution (except in so far as relates to the element of time) is in like manner contained in Note XXI; to which the preceding notes and especially XIX–XX lead up. . . . My whole life has been and will be given to presenting in realistic form as much as I can of my Note XXI (Pigou, 1925, pp. 416–17).

These notes present the general theory of capital and distribution in the presence of mutual interdependence that could not be properly treated in the text of the *Principles* because the theory required 'the terse, compact, precise language of Mathematics' from which many readers of the book were excluded, despite Marshall's encouraging remark that Note XXI was 'easy of comprehension'.

The notes in Marshall's Mathematical Appendix have another importance, apart from contributing to a fuller understanding of Marshallian economics. Marshall's 1908 letter to Clark contains a claim of independent discovery and priority:

> By this time [1874] I had practically completed the whole of the substance of my Mathematical Appendix, the only important exception being the mathematical treatment of elasticity (Note III) and Edgeworth's contract curve Note XII bis (ibid., p. 416).

That is, Marshall claimed that his notes on general equilibrium were complete before the 1874 publication of the first part of Walras' *Elements d'économie politique pure*. Marshall did not, however, mention Walras in this letter, in which he stated that:

> Between 1870 and 1874 I developed the details of my theoretical position; and I am not conscious of any perceptible change since the time when Böhm Bawerk and Wieser were still lads at school or College . . . (ibid., p. 417; the letter is also given in Marshall, 1961, vol. 2, pp. 9–11).

Note XIV, using notation developed in Notes V and XIII, considers someone building a house, where H is the present discounted value of the pleasures to be derived from the house, weighted by the probability of experiencing those pleasures, and V is the present value of the aggregate of effort to be expended in construction. Alphas with appropriate subscripts represent 'the several amounts of different kinds of labour, as, for instance, wood-cutting, stone-carrying, earth-digging, etc.' while betas with superscripts stand for the quantities of different kinds of accommodation to be provided; 'sitting-rooms, bed-rooms, offices, etc. . . . '. Marshall then gave the equations that would balance effort and benefit by maximising $H - V$:

$$\frac{dV}{d\alpha_1} = \frac{dH}{d\beta}\frac{d\beta}{d\alpha_1} = \frac{dH}{d\beta'}\frac{d\beta'}{d\alpha_1} = \frac{dH}{d\beta''}\frac{d\beta''}{d\alpha_1} = \ldots$$

$$\frac{dV}{d\alpha_2} = \frac{dH}{d\beta}\frac{d\beta}{d\alpha_2} = \frac{dH}{d\beta'}\frac{d\beta'}{d\alpha_2} = \frac{dH}{d\beta''}\frac{d\beta''}{d\alpha_2} = \ldots$$

Note XIV ended at that point in the first two editions, but Marshall added further elaboration and explanation in the third edition (1895). He glossed the equations, stating that,

> the (marginal) demand price for carpenters' labour is the (marginal) efficiency of carpenters' labour in increasing the supply of any product, multiplied by the (marginal) demand price for that product. . . . This proposition is very important and contains within itself the kernel of the demand side of the theory of distribution (Marshall, 1920, p. 847).

Marshall then turned from an individual building a house with his own labour for his own occupation to a master builder, for whom V would be total outlay and H total receipts. Marshall classified the master builder's expenses as wages for different classes of labour, assorted raw materials, 'interest on the capital value of the organisation of the business (its goodwill, etc.) regarded as the going concern, and remuneration of the builder's own work, enterprise and anxiety' with allowance for risk included in the last two categories of costs. He then presented the first order conditions for maximising $H - V$, and examined the case where the master builder monopolised the supply of villas.

Marshall (ibid., p. 850–51) noted that: 'It would be possible to extend the scope of such systems of equations as we have been considering, and to increase their detail, until they embraced within themselves the whole of the demand side of the problem of distribution'. He warned of a risk associated with such analysis

> those elements being most emphasized which lend themselves most easily to analytical methods. No doubt this danger is inherent in every application not only of mathematical analysis, but of analysis of any kind, to the problems of real life. It is a danger which more than any other the economist must have in mind at every turn. But to avoid it altogether, would be to abandon the chief means of scientific progress: and in discussions written specially for mathematical readers it is no doubt right to be very bold in the search for wide generalizations.

In Note XIV, Marshall gave a paragraph to

> the case of any producer who has a limited trade connection which he cannot quickly enlarge. If his customers have already as much of his wares as they care

for, so that the elasticity of their demand is temporarily less than unity, he might lose by putting on an additional man to work for him, even though that man would work for nothing (ibid., p. 849).

He noted that this 'fear of temporarily spoiling a man's special market' is important for short-period problems, especially in periods of commercial depression, and announced his intention of pursuing this insight in a second volume of his *Principles of Economics*.

In Note XXI, Marshall (ibid., p. 855) offered 'a bird's-eye view of the problems of joint demand, composite demand, joint supply and composite supply when they all arise together, with the object of making sure that our abstract theory has just as many equations as it has unknowns, neither more nor less'. This was in accordance with his remark in the preface to the first edition (ibid., p. x) that:

> The chief use of pure mathematics in economic questions seems to be in helping a person to write down quickly, shortly and exactly, some of his thoughts for his own use: and to make sure that he has enough, and only enough, premisses for conclusions (i.e., that his equations are neither more nor less in number than his unknowns).

Note XXI examines a case of joint demand, in which $n$ commodities are produced with $m$ factors of production. The problem has $2n + 2m$ unknowns, the prices and quantities of the commodities and factors, and $2n + 2m$ equations,

> viz.—(i) $n$ demand equations, each of which connects the price and amount of a commodity; (ii) $n$ equations, each of which equates the supply price for any amount of a commodity to the sum of the prices of corresponding amounts of its factors; (iii) $m$ supply equations, each of which connects the price of a factor with its amount; and lastly, (iv) $m$ equations, each of which states the amount of a factor which is used in the production of a given amount of the commodity.

Marshall went on to show that the number of unknowns would still equal the number of equations in cases of (i) composite demand, where the same factor is used in the production of several commodities; (ii) joint supply, where several things used in producing commodities are joint products of a single process; and (iii) composite supply, in which one of the productive inputs is supplied by several rival sources. 'Thus, however complex the problem may become, we can see that it is theoretically determinate, because the number of unknowns is always exactly equal to the number of equations which we obtain' (ibid., pp. 855–56).

Note XXI shows that Marshall, like Cassel (1932), thought that equality of numbers of unknowns and equations ensured the existence of an equilibrium. Walras also stressed this condition, although in Lesson 7 (Walras, 1954, p. 108) he noted a case where equilibrium would not exist because the demand and supply curves fail to intersect. As was shown by Hans Neisser in 1932 and independently by Heinrich von Stackelberg, and by Karl Schlesinger in 1933, however, such equality is not sufficient to ensure existence of a solution in which all the prices and quantities are positive (see Weintraub, 1985, pp. 59–70). Marshall solved for $n + m$ prices and $n + m$ quantities of commodities and factors, whereas Walras chose one good as a numeraire with a price of unity and solved for $n + m - 1$ relative prices and $n + m$ quantities, eliminating the redundant equation by Walras' Law, the adding-up constraint that the value of excess demand sums to zero across all markets (from summation of the budget constraint that what each agent supplies must be equal in value to what the agent demands). Since prices must be stated in units of something, one good must have a price of one unit of itself, so that Marshall's list of unknowns becomes the same as that of Walras.

Nothing in Marshall's Notes XIV and XXI would be out of place in the writings of Walras. A difference in appearance is that Walras wrote quantity as a function of price, and drew diagrams with quantity on the vertical axis and price on the horizontal, while Marshall wrote price as a function of quantity, and placed price on the vertical axis. (Textbooks now use Walras' equations and Marshall's diagrams.) Demand and supply equations which make prices functions of quantities can be transformed into equations in which quantities are functions of prices, provided that the Jacobian matrix of partial derivations is invertible (nonsingular).

This difference in writing demand and supply functions has contributed to the widespread perception that Marshall's equilibrium equations in the Mathematical Appendix and his stability analysis (for example, Marshall, 1920, pp. 806–807 fn. 1) differ from those of Walras. As Newman (1965, pp. 105–108) showed, however, the adjustment processes of Marshall and Walras are the same—excess demand in the case of pure exchange, and entrepreneurial shifting of resources equalising profit rates in the case of production. Newman noted that Marshall drew diagrams to illustrate his analysis of production, but not his analysis of exchange, while Walras provided diagrams for exchange, but not for production. The differing diagrams proved more memorable to many readers than the fact that Marshall and Walras did not present different diagrams for the same case.

Alfred Marshall himself claimed congruence for his theory of the existence and stability of equilibrium with that of Walras, and asserted his independence and priority in discovery, stating in the first edition (but not later editions) of his *Principles* (1890, p. 425fn.) that: 'This theory of unstable equilibrium was published independently by M. Walras and the present writer'. He advanced his claim in a letter to Walras on 1 November 1883:

> It happens, however, that in order to explain the use of a machine that a pupil of mine had made for me to construct a series of rectangular hyperbolas, I read on October 20, 1873 before the Cambridge Philosophical Society a short paper anticipating incidentally your doctrine of stable equilibrium. A brief note of it is contained in Part XV of the "Proceedings" [Vol. 2, Oct. 1873, pp. 318–19] (not the "Transactions") of that Society (quoted by Jaffé in his notes to Walras, 1954, p. 502, fn. 5).

Walras' priority stands, since a memoir summarising the first part of his *Elements* was presented to the Académie des Sciences Morales et Politiques in Paris in August 1873. Marshall's 1873 note gives only a brief statement about single and multiple intersections of supply and demand curves, which he did not treat diagrammatically in print until 1879. His equations of general equilibrium were first published in his Mathematical Appendix in 1890, so Walras also has priority in publication. What is noteworthy is that Marshall recognised the congruence of his general equilibrium analysis with that of Walras, and that he reached his analysis independently, given Marshall's statement that Marshall (1879) and the relevant notes of his Mathematical Appendix were written before Walras' 1874 publication. Against this claim of priority, it must be noted that while Note XXI (numbered XX in the first edition) did not change significantly between editions, Note XIV grew from a single paragraph in the first edition in 1890 to six pages in the third and later editions (Marshall, 1961, vol. 2, p. 835).

Whitaker (1987, p. 360) criticised Marshall because: 'Even when formulating market interdependence in the mathematical appendix to the *Principles* . . . he simply treated the demand or supply of each commodity as a function of nothing but the price of the commodity itself'. This is the same criticism that Auspitz and Lieben made of Walras, and that Walras made of Auspitz and Lieben, 'treating demands which are functions of several variables as functions of a single variable' (Walras, 1954, Appendix 2, pp. 484, 486). Marshall was concerned with the effect on demand for a good of changes in the prices of its substitutes and complements. His recognition of how an individual's demands for commodities are linked through the budget constraint shows that he appreciated the mutual interdependence of all prices and quantities, even if his functional notation appeared to relate the quantity demanded of a good to the price of that good alone. If disequilibrium positions can be considered, imagining an alteration of one price while holding other prices constant is a legitimate thought experiment, and does not imply any belief that supply and demand functions depend only on the own-price rather than on the entire list of prices.

Marshall eschewed mathematics and general equilibrium analysis in the text of his *Principles*, and relegated even diagrams to footnotes. In the text, he made the simplifying assumption that the marginal utility of money—meaning the marginal utility of 'the amount of money or general purchasing power at a person's disposal at any time' (Marshall, 1920, p. 838, Note II)—remains constant when relative prices change, permitting a partial equilibrium analysis. This method of presentation was not adopted because the former Second Wrangler was uneasy in the use of mathematics, nor, in light of Notes XIV and XXI, because Marshall lacked understanding of general equilibrium. Marshall organised his work so that, using the assumption of constant marginal utility of money, he could concentrate the reader's attention on the analysis of particular problems, the decision-making of individual agents and the determination of equilibrium in single markets. He also wished to make economic principles accessible to an audience which would be repulsed or baffled by Walras' exposition, which, as Jaffé observed, 'is expressed in primitive mathematics, and then paraphrased in crabbed prose' (Walras, 1954, p. 5). At the same time, Marshall provided a concise and elegant mathematical treatment in his Appendix for those readers who could be tempted to tackle 'a fairly unified general view' of mutual interdependence (Marshall, 1920, p. 545).

Coase (1975) and Brems (1975) have represented Marshall as an opponent of the use of mathematics in economics, in articles that do not even hint at the existence of Marshall's Mathematical Appendix. Coase and Brems cite Marshall's letter to A. L. Bowley on 27 February 1906, in which Marshall warned that:

> Mathematics used in a Fellowship thesis by a man who is not a mathematician by nature—and I have come across a good deal of that—seems to me an unmixed evil. And I think you should do all you can to prevent people from

using Mathematics in cases in which the English language is as short as the Mathematical (Pigou, 1925, p. 427; also given in Marshall, 1961, vol. 2, p. 775).

This warning was, however, consistent with Marshall's use of 'the terse, compact, precise language of Mathematics' (Marshall, 1920, p. 545) in cases where English prose was not as terse or compact as an algebraic or geometric presentation. Use of mathematics by Marshall, holder of a first-class honours degree in mathematics, is consistent with a distaste for the use of mathematics by economists who are not mathematicians by nature or training.

The key word in Marshall's reference to the language of mathematics is 'precise'. He recognised instances where mathematics permitted greater clarity and precision than was possible in prose. In the preface to the first edition of the *Principles*, Marshall stated that

> the demand for a thing is a continuous function, of which the 'marginal' increment is, in stable equilibrium, balanced against the corresponding increment of its cost of production. It is not easy to get a clear full view of continuity in this aspect without the aid either of mathematical symbols or of diagrams (ibid., p. x).

At the end of Book VI, Chapter II, he urged the reader on to Notes XIV–XXI, as only the language of mathematics permitted grasping the problem of mutual interdependence (ibid., p. 545).

A famous passage of Marshall's letter to Bowley of 27 February 1906 states that:

> I went more and more on the rules—(1) Use mathematics as a shorthand language, rather than as an engine of inquiry. (2) Keep to them till you have done. (3) Translate into English. (4) Then illustrate by examples that are important in real life. (5) Burn the mathematics. (6) If you can't succeed in 4, burn 3. This last I did often (Pigou, 1925, p. 427; also given in Marshall, 1961, vol. 2, p. 775).

The publication of the unburnt Mathematical Appendix and of the statement of the need for mathematics to understand the complexity of mutual interdependence indicate that Marshall did not apply these rules to general equilibrium. Marshall also relied on mathematical formulation to test the consistency of theories. As he explained to J. B. Clark in a letter of 2 July 1900,

> my acquaintance with economics commenced with reading Mill, while I was still earning my living by teaching Mathematics at Cambridge; and translating his doctrines into differential equations as far as they would go; and, as a rule, rejecting those which would not go. On that ground I rejected the wage-doctrine in Book II, which has a wage-fund flavour: and accepted that in his Book IV; in

which he seemed to me to be true to the *best* traditions of Ricardo's method (I say nothing in defence of Ricardo's positive doctrine of wages) ... (Pigou, ibid., pp. 412–13; also given in Marshall, ibid., pp. 8–9).

Had Marshall been as averse to mathematical economics carried out by competent mathematicians as Coase and Brems suggest, he would hardly have opened his 1881 review of that abstract and rigorously mathematical volume, F. Y. Edgeworth's *Mathematical Psychics*, by proclaiming:

> This book shows clear signs of genius, and is a promise of great things to come ... [T]he moral sciences are various and vast; and a goodly volume might be filled with a mere enumeration of the openings which they offer for the use of mathematical language and mathematical method (Whitaker, 1975, vol. 2, p. 265).

After hailing the book's 'brilliancy, force, and originality', Marshall expressed concern that abstract mathematical reasoning not lose its links with 'statistical enquiries—a consideration of the first importance', but concluded in favour of the value of Edgeworth's methods: 'If, however, Mr Edgeworth can prevent his theories from becoming too abstract he may do great things by them' (ibid., pp. 267–68).

Marshall's Mathematical Appendix has been largely ignored. His name is absent from the index of Walsh and Gram's book on the history of general equilibrium theory (1980), and the chapter on Marshall in Negishi (1989), a work devoted to mathematical reformulation of past economic theories, does not refer to the Mathematical Appendix. Among the four volumes of articles reprinted in Wood, 1982, the Mathematical Appendix is the subject of only one paper, by J. M. Buchanan and C. Platt, correcting an error in Marshall's two-sentence Note XIX, and an appendix to an article by Milton Friedman, in which he examines Notes II and VI with regard to what is held constant in deriving the Marshallian demand curve (Wood, 1982, vol. 3, no. 88 and no. 59, pp. 199–205).

Apart from the half-sentence from Schumpeter's *History of Economic Analysis* (1954) quoted in the opening paragraph of this paper, the presence of a system of equations of general equilibrium in Marshall's Note XXI has been pointed out in a paragraph in Friedman's article in 1949 (Wood, 1982, vol. 3, no. 59, p. 196) and in a brief discussion in Gerald Shove's centenary paper on Marshall in 1942 (Wood, 1982, vol. 2, no. 38, p. 136–37).

More recent works on the development of general equilibrium, texts on the history of economic thought, and articles on Marshall's method tend to ignore Notes XIV and XXI, and to depict Marshall as a partial equilibrium theorist who had no part in general equilibrium analysis and saw no important role for mathematics in economics. An examination of Notes XIV and XXI, however, shows that this view of Marshall is untenable.

## Bibliography

Brems, H. (1975), 'Marshall on mathematics', *Journal of Law and Economics*, vol. 18, no. 2, pp. 583–85. Reprinted Wood, 1982, vol. 1, no. 22.

Cassel, G. (1932), 'The mechanism of pricing', in his *The Theory of Social Economy*, translated to English by S. L. Barron, London: Ernest Benn, as reprinted in H. Townsend, ed., *Price Theory*, Harmondsworth: Penguin, 1971.

Coase, R. H. (1975), 'Marshall on method', *Journal of Law and Economics*, vol. 18, no. 1, pp. 25–31. Reprinted Wood, 1982, vol. 1, no. 21.

Ekelund, R. B., Jr, and Hebert, R. F. (1990), *A History of Economic Theory and Method*, New York: McGraw-Hill, third edition.

Marshall, A. (1879), *The Pure Theory of Foreign Trade: The Pure Theory of Domestic Values*, originally printed for private circulation, Cambridge: H. Sidgwick. Reprinted, Clifton, N. J.: Augustus M. Kelley, 1974 and Whitaker, 1975, vol. 2, pp. 111–236.

Marshall, A. (1890), *Principles of Economics*, London: Macmillan, first edition.

Marshall, A. (1920), *Principles of Economics*, London: Macmillan, eighth edition (reprinted with same pagination in vol. I of Marshall, 1961 and with different pagination in A. Marshall, *Principles of Economics*, London: Macmillan, 1949 with a comparative index of new and old page settings).

Marshall, A. (1961), *Principles of Economics*, C. W. Guillebaud, ed., London: Macmillan for the Royal Economic Society, ninth (variorum) edition, two volumes, vol. 1–text; vol. 2–notes.

Negishi, T. (1989), *History of Economic Theory*, Amsterdam, New York, Oxford and Tokyo: North-Holland.

Newman, P. (1965), *The Theory of Exchange*, Englewood Cliffs, N. J.: Prentice-Hall.

Pigou, A. C., ed. (1925), *Memorials of Alfred Marshall*, London: Macmillan.

Schumpeter, J. A. (1954), *History of Economic Analysis*, E. Schumpeter, ed., New York: Oxford University Press.

Walras, L. (1954), *Elements of Pure Economics*, translated to English by W. Jaffé from the French definitive edition of 1926, Homewood, Ill.: Irwin; and London: George Allen and Unwin. Reprinted Philadelphia: Orion, 1984.

Walsh, V. and Gram, H. (1980), *Classical and Neoclassical Theories of General Equilibrium*, New York and Oxford: Oxford University Press.

Weintraub, E. R. (1985), *General Equilibrium Analysis: Studies in Appraisal*, Cambridge: Cambridge University Press.

Whitaker, J. K., ed. (1975), *The Early Economics Writings of Alfred Marshall 1867–1890*, London: Macmillan for the Royal Economic Society, two volumes.

Whitaker, J. K. (1987), 'Marshall, Alfred 1842–1924', in J. Eatwell, M. Milgate and P. Newman, eds, *The New Palgrave: A Dictionary of Economics*, London: Macmillan, New York: Stockton Press and Tokyo: Maruzen Co., vol. 3, pp. 350–63.

Wood, J. C., ed. (1982), *Alfred Marshall: Critical Assessments*, London: Croom Helm, four volumes.

# 4. Smooth operator: how Marshall's demand and supply curves made neoclassicism safe for public consumption but unfit for science *

*Philip Mirowski*

*Natura non uncta deficit*

Occasions in commemoration of landmarks such as Marshall's *Principles* are most appropriate times for weighing and evaluating the significance of classic texts for our own situation, as well as reviewing the assessments of the intervening years. The problem in the case of Marshall is that many of those intervening *pronunciamentos* are, shall we say, of a peculiarly 'wet' character when it comes to the issue of his theoretical achievements. Marshall's students began this habit by introducing a note of lubricity into their assessments. Keynes has the famous passage where he attributes to an unnamed reviewer delight in the 'humanising which the dismal science received at his hands', only to follow it with the warning that:

> The lack of emphasis and of strong light and shade, the sedulous rubbing away of rough edges and salients and projections, until what is most novel can appear as trite, allows the reader to pass too easily through. Like a duck leaving water, he can escape from this douche with scarce a wetting (Pigou, 1925, pp. 47–48).

The asperges continued with Langford Price's *Memoirs*, which among other things expressed dismay at Marshall's prediction that in a few

---

* I would like to register my thanks to the reference librarians of the manuscripts archive at the London School of Economics, the Leeds Brotherton Library, the Manuscripts Division of Columbia University Library, and Trinity College Library, Cambridge University, for access to their holdings of a folder of Edgeworth correspondence, the Langford Price Memoirs, the Henry Ludwell Moore and Edwin Seligman papers, and the William Whewell papers, respectively.

years Pigou would be 'known as the greatest economist since Adam Smith'.[1]

Upon venturing outside the immediate circle of Marshall's Cambridge, things become even more damp. Schumpeter, for instance, normally quick off the mark to praise any neoclassical theorist, calls the period after 1885 'The Marshallian Age' but qualifies the remark profoundly with the *caveat*:

> abroad, Marshall's work never succeeded as had A. Smith's . . . the economists of all countries who were open to economic theory at all had by 1890 evolved or accepted systems that, however inferior in technique, were substantially like Marshall's in fundamental ideas (Schumpeter, 1954, pp. 833–34).

The disdain of Walras for Marshall's theoretical prowess is well known (Walras, 1965, letter 1123); I think less often noticed is Edgeworth's drier irony towards the Marshallian organon, found, for instance, in his Palgrave entry on 'Supply–Curves'.

Marshall has not fared better with more modern commentators outside the University of Chicago orbit. Frisch (1950, p. 495) began his paper on the Marshallian theory of value with the moist preamble: 'Like all human work, Alfred Marshall's theory of value had its definite shortcomings'. Whitaker, who has spent much of his life improving our access to and understanding of Marshall's writings, detected the mugginess; 'there is an awkwardness and hesitancy about Marshall's efforts at mathematical economics that argues against his ever having breathed freely on the pinnacles of abstraction' (Whitaker, 1975, p. 5). Hicks, upon reading Whitaker's collection of Marshall's early writings, noted that:

> We can see the outline of an early Marshall who is really pre-Jevons, and much more like Mill than he is like Jevons. Consumer's rent, to take a leading example, begins as the difference between value in use and value in exchange, much as in Mill; it is, initially, a sum of 'money' not of 'utility'. It only takes on the latter form when Marshall goes Jevonian, perhaps not until 1880. It might have saved later writers a lot of trouble if this transmogrification had not taken place (Hicks, 1983, p. 336).

The view from across the waters was not much kinder: 'Marshall was so afraid of being unrealistic that he merely ends up being fuzzy and confusing—and confused' (Samuelson, 1972, p. 24), and:

> After the Anglo-Saxon world had come to digest the contributions of Leon Walras, Knut Wicksell and Irving Fisher, it is realized that Alfred Marshall's reputation—deservedly great—was overrated in the 1900–30 period. If the world

excessively overvalued Marshall, Oxbridge outrageously treasured his writings (Samuelson in Feiwel, 1989, pp. 125–26).

But Oxbridge did not pull its punches, either:

[Marshall] worked out his short period for forward movements with great lucidity and then he filled the book with tear gas, so that no one would notice that he had fudged the whole of the rest of the argument (Robinson, 1973, p. 259). Marshall had a foxy way of salving his conscience by mentioning exceptions, but doing so in such a way that his pupils could continue to believe in the rule (Robinson, 1979, p. 169).

I think we can all agree these are not the sort of pious pleasantries which one might expect to grace the progenitor of what, after all, is still the standard introductory textbook pedagogy in orthodox neoclassical economics departments. Now, not everyone would douse Marshall so relentlessly; I have already mentioned the erstwhile fondness for him in the near neighbourhood of the shores of Lake Michigan. He also seems to be the favourite of numerous neoclassical economists who are disaffected in various ways towards some of the more jarring and awkward aspects of the neo-Walrasian synthesis, such as its intractably static character, its unapologetic abstraction, and its banishment of the entrepreneur (and perhaps even the trade coordinator and the firm). In other words, the Marshallian heritage is still the subject of live controversy a century later, with some claiming that his is the only legitimate line of neoclassical theory, a sort of social physics with a human face; whereas others disparage it as only suitable for the care and watering of undergraduates.

I propose to clarify Marshall's importance for the history of neoclassical theory by concentrating on the chequered history of the apparatus of the curves of demand and supply. The problem, as in so many of the narratives of the history of economic thought, is the absence of a coherent conceptualisation of the incidence of continuity and discontinuity within and between research programmes. Alfred Marshall loses some of his reputation for idiosyncrasy only when situated within the larger context of problems in British natural science (Wise, 1989) and Cambridge mathematics (Richards, 1988) in the Victorian period. His achievement is brought into focus by making a sharp distinction between neoclassical economics, which constituted a profound 'epistemological rupture' with the previous classical theory of value, and the curves of demand and supply, which in many respects did not. Hence Marshall was not really responsible for the curves of demand and supply, but he did attempt to reconcile them with the impending 'Marginalist Revolution', which accounts for his fame. However, this reading leaves open the possibility that the 'Laws of Demand and Supply' were not really central to neoclassical theory, but were rather superficial appendages, and hence became expendable once the scientific core of the programme re-asserted itself over the past half-century (Mirowski, forthcoming).

This reinterpretation of the legacy of Marshall will itself be conducted within the narrative frame of a potted history of supply and demand. We shall begin with a bird's eye view of the meaning of supply and demand in the half-century prior to 1890; then move on to discuss the work of the neglected William Thornton and the sorely maltreated Fleeming Jenkin. From there we examine the work of Stanley Jevons as an index of the extent of the rupture with classical political economy; and then finally evaluate the contribution of Marshall as one who wished to smooth over the rift.


## I. Decontextualising price and quantity

One of the most important benefits of the great flowering of the profession of the history of science in *fin-de-siècle* culture has been the progressive realisation that the structure of explanation across such diverse disciplines as physics and economics bears closer family resemblance than previously suspected. Two very significant shared metaphors for our present purposes are:

A. the image of the conserved embodied substance (Mirowski, 1989, chs 2 and 4); and
B. the image of equilibrium as the balance of forces (Wise, 1989).

In the sphere of natural philosophy, the notion of the conserved substance dates at least from Descartes' treatment of motion as an embodied entity passed from one body to another; it also makes its appearance in the theory of heat under the guise of 'caloric', in electricity, as flows of an electrical 'fluid', and so forth. On the other hand, the ideal of balance was pervasive in the Enlightenment discourse, from the law of the lever to Lavoisier's chemical equations, Hutton and Playfair's geology and Condillac's treatment of algebra. These two generic metaphors could be mixed and matched in various permutations and contexts; but it is not our intention to demonstrate their appearance in natural science in this venue. It will suffice to note that anyone who dealt in one or both metaphors would immediately be recognised as engaging in the formal discourse of explanation characteristic of the natural sciences in that period. Indeed, the metaphors of the embodied substance and the balance of forces were the primary *loci* for the mathematicisation of the disciplines cited.

What has only recently been noticed is that these same two metaphors constituted the core of value theory in classical political economy as well. The 'natural' ground of value in the classical period always assumed the format of [A,B], whether the embodied substance was called *blé*, 'corn', or 'labour'. The stable natural determinants of value behind the blooming, buzzing, phenomenological confusion of money prices were treated as if they were generated in 'production', conserved in 'exchange' and destroyed in 'consumption'.[2] 'Natural price' was the direct expression of this underlying determinism. However, the observed 'market price' was often thought to diverge from this underlying natural state; and it was at this point the alternative metaphor of the balance of forces was brought into play. 'Competition' in almost every case was conceptualised as the collision of opposed forces, which in the political liberty of the well-governed state resulted in the eventual convergence or 'gravitation' of market to natural price.

I use the terminology of 'metaphor' here because there did not exist full identity of the [A,B] structure from one writer to the next. In particular, Wise (1989) has done us the service of insisting that the classical political economists were particularly unfettered in their use of the metaphor of balance, rhetorically sliding between two radically different constructions of the meaning of the opposition of forces in the arena of market prices. On the one hand, the classical political economists frequently portrayed market price as a deterministic oscillation around a central natural value. This is, of course, the full 'gravitation' metaphor; the causes of the fluctuations are predominantly the same as the causes of natural price in the first place; the image is modelled upon the harmonic oscillations used to approximate solutions to the three-body problem in Newtonian mechanics. On the other hand, competition was also portrayed as taming the numerous 'accidental' disturbances to market price which could not be analytically encompassed because their motives were deemed outside the realm of economic (or even rational) explanation. In this version, the opposing disturbances were regarded as roughly symmetrical; hence an average of market prices would be expected to indicate the true natural price. The rhetorical freedom grew out of the structure of the coupled [A,B] metaphors: [A], the natural value substance, provided the anchor for the system, while different versions of [B] allowed various authors to exercise their imagination in absorbing as much (or as little) of the dynamics of social interaction in the marketplace as they wished.

While much of this must sound familiar and possibly trite to historians of economic thought, it is imperative to sort out these structural metaphors because of extreme confusion prevalent in the literature about what does and does not constitute an anticipation of the subsequent neoclassical research programme.[3] The operation of 'supply and demand' as opposing forces in the marketplace which result in an 'equilibrium' in the presence of a healthy atmosphere of competition is indeed the gist of metaphor [B], and as such it is an integral part of the research programme of *classical* political economy. The opposed forces are identified with the opposed interests of the two sides of the market, and their interplay is expected to result in convergence to the underlying natural value determinants *in both versions*; be it deterministic oscillation or the cancelling-out of numerous disturbing factors. Supply and demand as an argument was absolutely central and indispensable to the structure of classical political economy, because it was the *locus* of temporal/dynamic reasoning in value theory. This intrinsically dynamic cast of classical 'supply and demand' will shortly play an important role in our narrative.

One important bit of evidence for the thesis that 'supply and demand' was a peculiarly classical notion is that the language of 'supply and demand' was pervasive in 19th-century political economy, a fact which we shall document below. But the mere appearance of the words, which, after all, would qualify any parrot as an economist, are not enough to understand the subsequent role of Marshall in the history of economic thought. It will behove us to pay close attention to the changing face of supply and demand over the 19th century if we are to understand the vexed issue of the putative 'continuity' of classical and neoclassical economic theory. Here the rhetorical wavering concerning the exact meaning of supply and demand comes into play: I want to suggest that the analytical underdetermination of the [B] supply and demand metaphor was largely responsible for the internal breakdown of the [A] substance metaphor over the course of the century, and that this happened through the progressive decontextualisation of price and quantity from other classes of oscillations or disturbances which had previously been lumped together under the rubric of supply and demand. In a nutshell, reducing supply and demand to deterministic functions of price and quantity led to a situation where natural price could no longer be equated with their equilibrium, destroying the entire analytical structure. What Marshall did was not so much to preserve the structure as to propose to shore up a dilapidated, jerry-built metaphor upon a new natural determinant, the recently borrowed physics model of constrained optimisation over a conservative vector field (Mirowski, 1989). But since the problems of convergence and temporal dynamics were not strengthened or fortified by this amendment, the entire structure remains to this day precariously perched upon sand (Mirowski, 1990a). In other words, not only are the Marshallian scissors superfluous to neoclassical value theory; they give rise to intractable contradictions within that framework—contradictions wrought by Marshall's own particular contribution to the neoclassical research programme. This goes some way towards explaining all the 'wet' quotes that preface this paper: scissors cut paper, but paper wraps stone, and stone blunts scissors; only water dissolves all three.

## II. From Smith to Mill

The first usage of 'supply and demand' as opposed forces in the marketplace appears to be found in James Steuart; but the responsibility for its promulgation seems to rest squarely with Adam Smith (Thweatt, 1983). There it was used as the governor of market price in contrast to the determinants of 'natural price'. The actual referent of supply and demand in the *Wealth of Nations* was vague; but it seems that by the early 19th century a habit had arisen of appealing to the 'proportion of demand to supply' when discussing market price. In certain instances, such as the writings of Malthus, this was mooted as a self-sufficient theory of price. However, since demand was thought by most to be comprised of a large number of imponderable influences not amenable to scientific analysis, and in any event since Malthus' concept was as vague as Smith's, the preferred usage was that of Ricardo, which subordinated supply and demand to the natural prices described in our [A, B] schema above.

It is important to note that in that era one could readily cite the 'firmly established doctrine that the value of all commodities depends on the supply and demand', and in the same breath also assert an embodied substance theory of value. Hence, in Jane Marcet's little textbook for children published in 1827, one would find on page 314 that, 'the proportion of the supply to the demand . . . regulates *market price*'; and yet find on page 317 that: 'You must, however, recollect that it is the cost of production of a commodity which constitutes its exchangeable value; the proportion of supply and demand should be considered as only accidentally affecting it'. This is most certainly derived from Ricardo; but one can also find it in McCulloch, who in 1825 argued that: 'Buying and selling are in commerce, what action and reaction are in physics, always *equal and contrary*' (McCulloch, 1825, p. 135); and yet also that the 'average real value of all sorts of commodities will be precisely proportioned to, or coincident with, the common and average quantities of labour required for their production' (ibid., p. 224).

It seems that in the early 19th century one could simply assume that a reference to supply and demand would be understood as a synecdoche, the part which stood for the whole metaphorical complex. C. F. Bastable, looking back from the end of the century, claimed in an address to Section F of the British Association for the Advancement of Science in 1894 that: '"The recognized principles of political economy" or "the immutable laws of supply and demand" were phrases that occurred as readily to a journalist in the sixties as "the exploded doctrine of laissez faire" does to the leader-writer of today' (in Smyth, 1962, p. 127). This can be observed not only in political economy, but also in literature; for instance, in Dickens' *Hard Times*, 1854:

> But she knew from her reading infinitely more of the ways of toiling insects than of these toiling men and women. Something to be worked so much and paid so much, and there ended; something to be infallibly settled by the laws of supply and demand; something that blundered against those laws and floundered into difficulty. . . (Dickens, 1971, p. 160).

It also seems that, to a certain extent, this reflected the self-images of the period in that the fundamental natural determinants of price were almost taken for granted, whereas the transitory accidents of the market were subject to deliberate planned response. This can be observed in the 1820s in the instructions of Owens and Son of

Manchester to their partner in Philadelphia to apportion their cotton purchases to price fluctuations according to an explicit price-quantity schedule (Clapp, 1962); or in the wagers of the major brewing families of London over the prices of hops and barley in the prospective harvest.[4] Supply and demand in this context would thus refer simultaneously to underlying natural forces and to schedule-like adjustments in the face of inevitable accident and unforeseen circumstance.

What was good enough for quotidian discourse was not good enough for science, however. The [A, B] metaphoric complex which was used with great frequency in the early 19th century did not seem to be resulting in a quantitative model as it had done in other fields; even though words which suggested mathematical structures such as 'proportion' and 'equality' kept surfacing with regularity. Hence it was not so very unusual that a number of mathematically inclined individuals such as William Whewell and Antoine-Augustin Cournot sought to formalise the imprecise vernacular in the third and fourth decades of the century. The consequences of their activities, until recently treated as some sort of unproblematic foreshadowing of later neoclassical theory, actually were nothing of the sort. Rather, I should like to argue that this sort of work precipitated a severe internal crisis within classical political economy.

The reason this transpired was that the mere fact of formalising supply and demand according to 19th-century canons of scientific reasoning caused them to become decontextualised from their underlying metaphorical basis. Partly because of its psychological overtones, 'demand' began to be severed from any connection with natural price; but more profoundly, the condition of the *clearing of a market* began to assume much greater significance than it did in the context of classical theory. In a substance theory of value, market clearing at a point in time bore little relevance for natural price, primarily because the underlying determinants of value were conceptualised as persisting through time, independent of contingent market activity (Mirowski, 1989, chs 4 and 5). But to formalise supply and demand as functions in equilibrium inadvertently raised the touchy issue of what was to be considered as invariant in the marketplace; through the stress on market-clearing, the mathematics itself riveted attention on the underlying determinants of the respective curves and their temporal integrity.

What appears to have happened in the 1820s and 1830s is that the drive to construct formal models of supply and demand began to foster a third connotation of those terms without explicit admission of licence. Neither the purely deterministic oscillations around natural price nor the average taken over an arbitrary set of imponderable accidents were the paths chosen for mathematical formalisation (although models of both were already available in the physical sciences). Instead, a third coy option materialised, which was to model supply and demand themselves as deterministic functions with little or no reference to natural price or value theory; to simply abjure any attempt to justify seriously the stability of the functional forms, thus leaving room to readmit the language of 'accident' if so desired; and to associate equilibrium with the occurrence of market clearing at a point in time, which was purportedly identical with the intersection of the demand and supply functions in an abstract price-quantity space. This was the legacy of Cournot and Whewell, and not the 'mathematical statements of price flexibility, demand elasticity, and the Giffen paradox' (Henderson, 1973).

Whewell's method of achieving this innovation was relatively straightforward: just redefine demand to mean a fixed sum of money irrevocably devoted to the purchase of the commodity in question. Why should a fixed sum be doggedly devoted to a particular purchase? The requirements of mathematical formalisation loomed larger than the canons of logic in this particular instance:[5]

> *Supply* is of itself a quantity and offers us no difficulty in measuring it theoretically: but *demand* is of a more intangible and fugitive nature. It consists originally of moral elements as well as physical: of the vehemence of desire, and the urgency of need which men have, as well as the extent of their means . . . [Tooke] supposed (merely as a means of reducing the question to calculation) that men set aside a *certain sum* to purchase a given article, and that sum measures the *demand* . . . Now this mode of beginning the reasoning answers extremely well the purpose of avoiding all indefiniteness (Whewell, 1971 [1829], pp. 9–10).

The structure of the argument then became: the demand curve in price-quantity space was formalised as a rectangular hyperbola (as a consequence of the fixity of expenditure), while supply at a point in time would be conceptualised as equal to a constant quantity; their intersection would identify equilibrium price. While Whewell felt he must acknowledge that the 'approximation is a very loose and inaccurate one', he also felt impelled to make some gesture to link this curious construction of the meaning of supply and demand to the classical value framework, which was nowhere to be found in the mathematics.

> Price is determined by the conflict of supply and demand; price is also determined by the cost of production, in which latter expression demand is not mentioned: how then do these agree? In answer to this it is to be observed, that the former is the immediate, the latter the permanent, determinant of price (ibid., p. 12).

This superimposition of time frames in the text without expressing it in the mathematics was illegitimate, as Whewell must have known, since he repudiated it in his very next paper:

> In order however that solutions of this nature may have any value, it is requisite that the principles, of which we estimate the operation, should include *all* the *predominant* causes which really influence the result . . . The quantities which we neglect must be of an inferior order to those which we take into account; otherwise we obtain no approximation at all. We may with some utility make the theory of *tides* a question of equilibrium, but our labour would be utterly misspent if we should attempt to consider such a principle a theory of *waves*. It appears to be by no means clear that the irregular fluctuations and transitory currents by which the elements of wealth seek their natural level may be neglected in the investigation of the primary laws of their distribution (ibid., 1971 [1831], p. 13).

The comparison held particular poignancy for Whewell, since his main mathematical claim to fame was his treatment of the theory of tides (Becher, 1971). It was a commonplace in the 19th century to compare supply and demand to the ripples of disturbance upon the surface of a body of water; but Whewell understood that this conflated the two versions of the [B] metaphor, namely, periodic wave motion and random disturbance. Since Whewell did not accept the classical substance theory of value, he knew there was no legitimate mathematical approximation to wave motion around equilibrium; and because there also was no legitimate mathematics of random shocks at that time, he had no alternative but to repudiate his own model of supply and demand.[6]

Cournot's 1838 *Researches into the Mathematical Principles of the Theory of Wealth* is another example of the same decontextualisation process being worked out in a slightly different cultural arena. Cournot is often credited with innovation of the curves of demand and supply; and indeed, there is a graph of downward-sloping *loi de débit* and an upward-sloping function in the price/quantity plane (Cournot, 1897, p. 92). But, just as with Whewell, attention to detail will reveal that the grounds for formalisation were equally precarious and vacillating. It is frequently overlooked that Cournot was explicitly anti-utilitarian, viewing such notions as 'ill-suited for the foundation of a scientific theory' (ibid., p. 10). He refused to give any justification whatsoever for his 'law of sales', other than to hint that its continuity (required for differentiation) was due to a sufficiently large number of customers. At least Whewell had the good sense to posit a fixed sum of money devoted to specific purchases, whereas there is no reason at all to accept Cournot's assertion of a differentiable function deterministically relating price to quantity. Mathematics is not intrinsically self-justifying; and neither are ambagious evocations of 'science'. The reason for the yawning *lacuna* was probably the problem of straddling the two previous connotations of supply and demand:

> the price of an article may vary notably in the course of a year, and strictly speaking, the law of sales may also vary in the same interval, if the country experiences a movement of progress or decadence. For greater accuracy . . . the curve which represents the function F [should] be itself an average of all the curves which would represent this function at different times of year (ibid., p. 52).

Were supply and demand law-governed or not? Cut adrift from any particular theory of value, Cournot and all the mathematics in the world were incapable of answering the question, opting rather to avoid it by means of baseless retreat to the previous metaphor of random imponderable disturbances. The prospect grew downright forlorn once the pervasive interdependence of markets was acknowledged (ibid., p. 127).

And yet, the drive to formalise supply and demand continued unabated, mainly through the efforts of engineers and others acquainted with increasing abstraction from context in mathematical physics in the mid-19th century. Jules Dupuit in 1844 also inscribed a downward-sloping function relating price to quantity in order to solve various practical problems of pricing public tolls and taxes. However formidable it looked as geometry, even Dupuit had to acknowledge that it was hopeless as science:

> Suppose that we have two columns of figures showing the number of articles consumed according to each market price from zero, at which consumption is largest, right up to the price which causes all consumption to cease. This series of relationships is not known for any commodity, and it can even be said that it will never be known since it depends on the volatile will of human beings; it is today no longer what it was yesterday. It is thus of no avail to try to determine

this relationship exactly by experience or by groping experiment (Dupuit, 1952, p. 103).

Given the palpable lack of enthusiasm on the part of many of the early protagonists of this movement, we may be prompted to ask why the drive to formalisation maintained its momentum throughout the 19th century. First and foremost, I would suggest that the very obscurity of its referent—in the sense that the three different connotations of the terms coexisted peacefully throughout the mid-century—combined with its impeccable credentials as a central theme in classical political economy rendered it an extremely adaptable and acceptable doctrine. Everyone knew that there were two sides to every exchange, and like Tweedledum and Tweedledee, supply and demand were good enough names for the indefatigable opponents in the marketplace. But there was also another consideration, that supply and demand seemed intrinsically quantitative, and therefore held out the bright and shining promise of mathematical formalisation to those so inclined. But formalisation meant forcibly imposing deterministic functions upon the price-quantity plane, precisely in an area where classical political economy did not expect any such laws. This, in turn, had all sorts of unsavoury consequences: it abstracted price away from the classical substance theory of value; it created great confusion about the relevant time frames in a doctrine which had previously been used to account for the dynamics of adjustment; it surreptitiously began to reinterpret equilibrium in the marketplace as market clearing at a point in time; and, not least, led to some embarrassing statements about the appropriate empirical referent of this dubious 'science'.

This situation was not a happy one, and it was not helped by John Stuart Mill's attempt to render the laws of value complete and uncontentious by fiat. While he merely ratified the Whewell-Cournot line that, 'the proper mathematical analogy is that of an equation' (Mill, 1899, p. 432), he also attempted to reconcile it with the thrust of classical political economy and with his 'three categories' of the law of value, relegating supply and demand to the case where production could be expanded at increased cost (ibid., p. 428), and subordinating the whole to the classical natural price (ibid., p. 439). But this was merely a slapdash expedient; and it was William Thornton's frontal attack upon the analytical structure of supply and demand in 1869 which brought matters to a head.

## III. Thornton and Jenkin and Jevons

William Thomas Thornton (1813–1880) is one of the more important figures in the history of English political economy, although he is rarely accorded the attention he deserves in histories of the subject. Often mentioned as the person responsible for Mill's recantation of the wages fund doctrine, he should also be credited with motivating (directly or indirectly) most of the major protagonists of the neoclassical movement in England, including, of course, Alfred Marshall. His attack on Mill's version of supply and demand was praised by MacLeod, noted by Jenkin as the starting-point for his own work on wages and trade unions, discussed by Jevons in both his *Theory of Political Economy* and in his posthumous *Principles*, noted by Marshall in his review of Jevons' *Theory* (Black, 1981, p. 143) and in his 1876 essay on Mill's theory of value:

> Mr. Thornton's work is not free from faults; but he has not received his due meed of gratitude for having led men to a point of view from which the practical importance of the theory of market values is clearly seen (Whitaker, 1975, vol. 2, p. 263).

But beyond these vague and unspecific acknowledgements, I should like to argue that Thornton sagely put his finger on what was incoherent about the mid-century evolution of the doctrine of supply and demand, and that this set in train the following concatenation of events. First it provoked the engineer Fleeming Jenkin to reformulate the orthodox mid-century interpretation of supply and demand in a geometrical format resonant with the state of mathematical education in Victorian Britain; this in turn, so rattled William Stanley Jevons that, in mortal fear of being scooped as the progenitor of a mathematical political economy, he rushed to pen *The Theory of Political Economy* in 1870 in order to assert his own version of the theory of value; and then Marshall, reading Thornton, Jenkin and Jevons in near proximity on the heels of these events, believed he had found all the components of a reconciliation of supply and demand (and therefore, in the specific sense discussed above, classical political economy) with the newer doctrine of the marginal utility theory of value.

Thornton marks a turning-point in the history of economic thought because he systematically attacked both components of the [A, B] metaphor. He simply dismissed the embodied substance theory of value as 'that pure abstraction of the mind' (Thornton, 1870, p. 45).

He then devoted the bulk of his attention to the B component of the theory, first spelling out with admirable succinctness the decontextualisation of supply and demand in the price-quantity plane (ibid., p. 50), only then to demolish thoroughly any claim for its status as a 'law'. Indeed, the best way to understand Thornton's onslaught is to recognise that he rejected the entire tradition of western value theory, which strove to ground economic value in natural invariants (Mirowski, 1989, ch. 4):

> Price is scarcely ever mentioned without provoking a reference to the 'inexorable', the 'immutable', the 'eternal' laws by which it is governed; the laws which, according to my friend Professor Fawcett, are 'as certain in their operation as those which control physical nature'. It is no small gain to have discovered that no such despotic laws do or can exist; that, inasmuch as the sole function of scientific law is to predict the invariable recurrence of the same effects from the same causes, and as there can be no invariability where—as in the case of price—one of the most efficient causes is that ever-changing chameleon, human character or disposition, price cannot possibly be subject to law (Thornton, 1870, p. 82).

We cannot do full justice to the complexity of Thornton's complete argument here; it must suffice merely to sketch out the structure of his attack upon the classical version of demand and supply. The overarching theme of all his remarks is that no real market transactor is stupid enough or passive enough simply to acquiesce in the abstract market-clearing price (ibid., pp. 63fn., 73). Indeed, the institutional structure of the market organisation is the most important determinant of market prices; he bolsters this assertion by a comparison of the Dutch vs. English auctions, which result in different 'equilibria', even given the same objective circumstances, same transactors, etc. (ibid., p. 56 *et seq.*) For these and other reasons, demand should not be conceptualised as a single-valued function of price (ibid., p. 60). The most important aspect of a market is the temporal pattern of price-setting; the fact that market-clearing takes time inherently violates the presumption that the entire target stock will be sold at a single unique price (ibid., pp. 64–65). Here in a single gesture he demonstrated the incoherence of writing demand and supply as decontextualised functions of price, either at a point in time or as some 'average', and then asserting that they could be the basis of a serious dynamical theory of price. Far from being a fusty antiquarian issue, it is still relevant to the modern neoclassical fascination with the 'law of one price' (Mirowski, 1986, chs 4 and 6).

For Thornton, even the connotation of supply and demand as a congeries of random but offsetting influences held no promise, since 'the variations of demand from week to week, and from day to day, would defy all calculation' (Thornton, 1870, p. 66fn.). The notion of the two sides of the market as personifications of opposing forces in the Newtonian mode was also forlorn: 'There is no regularity about competition—competition is not regulated at all' (ibid., p. 80). Nevertheless, if one were a committed utilitarian, there were a few throwaway phrases that could be read as offering a slender palm of conciliation, such as: 'The upper of these limits [of price] is marked by the utility, real or supposed, of the commodity to the customer; the lower by its utility to the dealer' (ibid., p. 76). These phrases would shortly loom all out of proportion to their place in the text, especially for Jevons and for Marshall.

As if this were not radical enough to roust the political economists, Thornton then proceeded to apply the lessons of his critique to one of the most burning issues of the day: the role and efficacy of trade unions. If the institutional structure of the market were one of the most salient determinants of the resulting price, and it were also the case that labour time was an unusual commodity in that it could not be readily reserved by the seller, then the existence of trade unions would permanently alter the price of labour by allowing it to be treated on a footing with other commodities:

> [L]abourers may by combining acquire an influence which, if exercised with moderation and discretion, employers will be willing rather to propitiate than to oppose . . . the fact of an increase in the rate of remuneration having been artificially caused, furnishes no reason why in the great majority of cases that increase should not be lasting (ibid., p. 320).

Thornton's deconstruction of the artificial/natural distinction, so very crucial to the self-image of political economy as a science, demanded a response; it was swift in coming. While some rejoinders, like that of Mill in the 1869 *Fortnightly Review*, were relatively ineffectual, those written by souls trained in the natural sciences were mobilised to reassert the primacy of the natural. The key to this revanchist movement was displacement of the discourse in the direction of *geometry*. Whilst geometric diagrams for supply and demand were not unknown on the Continent, they did not make their appearance in England until this juncture. The reasons for this timing are many—that much of the French discussion was located in the *grandes écoles* amongst civil engineers; that mathematics in early 19th-century France was more advanced than that in England, that French physical science was more comfortable with phenomenological description than was the science of the English—but the privileged position of geometry in English Victorian culture now came to the fore.

By mid-century, geometry had come to represent the paradigm of both necessary and self-evident truth in British pedagogy, and not only in such relatively uncontroversial areas as surveying and the physics of motion.

> The transcendental truth mathematics was believed to describe had long stood as an exemplar of the perfect truth to which the human intellect aspired. It was a particularly central issue in theology . . . In the 1860s and 1870s, the cultural context of geometrical development was still the unitary view of truth articulated by men like Herschel and Whewell (Richards, 1988, pp. 104, 103).

In such a milieu, simply to restate the recently decontextualised supply and demand relations in geometric form could serve as a powerful response to the brash challenge of a Thornton. This was not because 'mathematics renders assumptions and logical steps more transparent' or any other such silly homily; but rather because the displacement of discussion into a geometric discourse could subtly reassert the putative timeless or 'natural' character of the supply and demand relationship and present it as if it were a self-evident abstract truth. Geometry entered English political economy at precisely the point where images of natural order were put at risk; it was the cultural significance of the geometry that mattered, and not the precise model format. The impression that one could build price theory up from basics in the image of Euclid was much more important than any particular proposed formalisation. One can observe this in the three different formats promulgated by Jenkin, Jevons and Marshall.

In the case of Fleeming Jenkin, the response to Thornton was constructed much along the lines of the earlier work by Cournot. In his article of 1870 'The Graphic Representation of the Laws of Supply and Demand, and their Application to Labour',[7] it is Thornton who is repeatedly reprimanded with geometry, but not, we might observe, with actual market observation. Much like Cournot, Jenkin rested content to posit continuous curves in the price-quantity plane without any satisfactory justification for their stability, continuity or integrity. One observes this most directly when he denies Thornton's analysis of the Dutch and English auctions by insisting his ideas must be expressed with demand and supply curves, against which, as we have seen, Thornton would have most strenuously demurred.

Jenkin begins and ends the essay by invoking natural law: 'The laws of price are as immutable as the laws of mechanics' (Jenkin, 1887, p. 93); and indeed, they should be constructed in their very image. The laws of both supply and demand are asserted to be grounded in psychology; but at the very outset the quest for natural laws goes awry:

> The law thus stated assumes that each man knows his own mind, that is to say, how much of each commodity he will then and there sell or buy at each price, and that the condition of his mind shall not vary . . . But, in practice men's minds do not remain constant for 5 minutes together (ibid., pp. 78–79).

Costs of production are brought in as another candidate for the determination of the shape and slope of the supply curve; and: 'In the long run, the price of the manufactured article is chiefly determined by the cost of its production' (ibid., p. 89), but the exact relationship to psychology is left unexplored. And finally, the political threat to the *status quo* is deflected by means of the assertion that: 'The cost of production of labour determines wages, but is itself determined by men's expectation of comfort' (ibid., p. 102); but if workmen should combine in trade unions, they will only succeed in reducing employment and the production of wealth.

Whilst much in this article anticipates Marshall (even down to identical niceties of phrasing), I do not think it at all accurate to say that Jenkin gives the 'first clear statement in English writing of the concept of supply and demand as functions of price' (Black, 1987, p. 1007). The baseless bravado of inscribing decontextualised demand and supply schedules had a long history in the 19th century, as did vague justifications nodding in the direction of psychology and costs. Moreover, the penchant for sheepishly admitting the spuriousness of the natural law character of the curves was also simply one more variation on a well-worn theme. The only real novelty was the actual geometry; but this was not trivial.

William Stanley Jevons certainly did not think it trivial. In 1868 Jenkin sent Jevons his earlier article on trade unions, and Jevons responded with a copy of the précis of his theory of value which had appeared in the *Journal of the Royal Statistical Society*. Significantly, Jenkin was then prompted to pen a letter to Jevons disputing his 'fluxion theory of exchange' (Black, 1977, vol. 3, p. 166 *et seq.*).

Jenkin's objection seemed to be that price ratios would not be determinate in a bilateral exchange predicated upon two different utility functions, given fixed endowments of the goods to be traded. (Edgeworth made precisely this same point 13 years later.) Then Jenkin proceeded to write his *Graphic Representation* paper described above, *abjuring all dependence upon mathematical specifications of utility*. When Jevons happened upon a copy of this paper 'in wh[ich] no reference was made to my previous', he was shocked and galvanised into action: 'Partly in consequence of this I was led to write and published the Theory in 1871' (ibid., p. 166).

Why would Jevons feel threatened or pre-empted by Jenkin's paper, especially when Jenkin made no use of the constrained maximisation of utility and Jevons had no supply and demand curves in his *Theory of Political Economy*? An answer which transcends the simplistic reaction that both works are part of the same neoclassical research programme has been initiated by White (1989a); but now we may situate this *curiosum* in the larger cultural context. First and foremost, Jevons felt threatened by Jenkin because both were engaged in the project of the construction of a *mathematical* political economy which would subsume what both were calling 'the laws of supply and demand'. Both allowed that 'demand' should be grounded in utility or psychology; and both were advocates of the natural law character of price determination. Both were concerned that Thornton's challenge should be answered. Finally, both were determined to redirect economic discourse into a geometrical mode. But they differed on almost everything else; and that goes some distance in explaining Jevons' sudden mobilisation to write his *Theory of Political Economy*.

Superficial similarities in geometry and terminology did not mask profound differences in their respective approaches. For Jenkin, the 'laws of supply and demand' referred directly to the theory of price-setting embodied in the price-quantity diagram, whereas for Jevons, the 'laws' bore a connotation alien to modern usage. In Jevons' mind, scientific laws 'were a set of observation statements or propositions devoid of theoretical content' (White, 1989a, p. 428); one observed this in his *Principles of Science*, and also in his later attack upon Thornton whose writings, he asserted, were

> ... based upon a misapprehension of the nature of these so-called laws. They are in no sense ultimate, natural or invariable laws, but are only expressions of the general course of phenomena exhibited in commerce when there are many buyers and many sellers. They are laws of aggregate supply and demand, but an

aggregate is a sum of separate quantities, so that the natural law in order to be manifested in the aggregate must be manifested in the elementary quantities (Jevons, 1905, p. 57).

Hence Jevons believed that the true natural law character of prices could only be revealed by total reduction of all phenomena to individual utility, which meant direct imitation of physics. 'Utility . . . is the alpha and omega of the science, as light is of optics or sound of acoustics' (ibid., p. 6). But whereas Jenkin merely wanted laws of supply and demand to resemble those of mechanics, Jevons proposed literally to reduce empirical supply and demand to the laws of energetics: 'The notion of value is to our science what that of energy is to mechanics' (ibid., 1905, p. 50; Mirowski, 1989, ch. 5). This explains such otherwise cryptic comments as: 'A mere quantity of goods does not constitute supply until it is offered for sale—that is to say, until the quantity is connected with a mental feeling' (Jevons, 1905, p. 55).

Although there are minor resemblances of geometry, supply and demand did not mean much of the same thing for Jenkin and Jevons. The only 'scissors' to be found in the *Theory of Political Economy* (Jevons, 1970, p. 140) are not identified as a supply and demand diagram, and this is due to the fact that they represent two utility curves for the same trading body. Jevons' contempt for any reconciliation of supply and demand with cost of production theories is well known (Jevons, 1905, p. 63); this would have been another source of friction with Jenkin. But most importantly, the subsidiary status of the laws of supply and demand were further diminished in Jevons' opinion by doubts concerning their empirical integrity, doubts absent in the paper by Jenkin:

> It would be a matter of great importance, if it were practicable, to ascertain statistically the exact law of the variation of price of the more important commodities. Assuming the demand to be constant, in the sense that there is a constant population of purchasers with fixed tastes, we should make the supply of the commodity . . . the variable, and then ascertain the changes of price, the variant. . . . The laws will not be laws of any generality; they will, in fact, be little more than compendious statements of numerical results . . . But it may seem rather needless to consider what these laws should be, inasmuch as we have not got them, and have no present prospects of getting them. . . . The difficulties in the way of such empirical determination of laws are so formidable that I entertain little hope of successful investigations being made for many years to come . . . there are complicated reactions among the variations of separate markets which defy statistical analysis. Many years ago, about the years 1861– 62, I spent a good deal of labour in endeavouring to arrive at a rough

determination of the laws of price of a few commodities specifically selected for that purpose (ibid., 1905, pp. 146–47).

Thus neoclassical price theory, the theory of constrained optimisation over a conservative vector field, was for Jevons an avenue of escape from the fruitless dialogue over the supposed laws of supply and demand from Whewell to Mill to Thornton to Jenkin. While one might attempt to fit a curve (but *not* demand and supply curves) to some collection of numbers such as the King-Davenant corn price data (Jevons, 1970, pp. 18–83), the exercise gave no added insight into the scientific causes of price movements, which were exhaustively described by the theory of utility/energy. Jevons, ever the lone wolf, was proposing to do away with all the existing connotations of supply and demand: with law-like oscillations around the embodied substance (*nota bene* his dismissal of the labour theory of value comes directly after his discussion of the King-Davenant data in *Theory of Political Economy*); with counterposed and offsetting random disturbance; and with decontextualised schedules floating in aggregate price-quantity space. Jevons innovation of neoclassical price theory was intended to be a rival to the 19th-century tradition of supply and demand functions which we have sketched in this paper, and not its culmination, as has been suggested by many historians of economic thought, taking their cue from Alfred Marshall.

## IV. Marshall (finally)

Never again will a Mrs. Trimmer, a Mrs. Marcet, or a Miss Martineau earn a goodly reputation by throwing [the principles of economics] into the form of a catechism or of simple tales (Marshall in Pigou, 1925, p. 296).

If the reader can forgive the circumlocution of sections I–III, the time has now arrived to render unto Marshall the things that are Marshall's. It seems that much of what passes as Marshallian in the modern economics literature is not in fact traceable to Marshall; and further, much that is now deemed 'Marshallian' has little or no logical connection to the core programme of neoclassical price theory. I do not intend this to be understood in the conventional antiquarian sense that one claims to find ever-earlier 'precursors' of some doctrine, or else quibbles over whether 'Mr X' was *really* an 'Xian'. Instead, it should now become clear that the supply and demand organon had little to do with the formal structure of neoclassical price theory; and neither was Marshall responsible for any substantive theoretical innovation in the theory of value.

Marshall is best understood as one more figure in the mathematical/ engineering tradition of Cournot and Jenkin. His early manuscript, 'Essay on Value', contains their geometric curves of demand and supply, but also evinces little interest in what lay behind the curves (Bharadwaj, 1978b). Variations in demand are simply associated with variations in the number of buyers (Whitaker, 1975, vol. 1, p. 122), even though this displays rather less rigour than Whewell's attempt to derive the slope from a fixed sum of expenditure. Similarities of language, particularly in attributing supply to ill-defined cost-of-production considerations which converge to classical doctrine in the long run, merely echo Mill and Jenkin. All of this would be second nature to anyone steeped in Cournot, Jenkin and the rest. This was noticed by many others in his own lifetime, to whom Marshall violently insisted that he had not read Jenkin prior to his own 'discoveries'.[8] As has often been noted, it was only after reading Jevons' *Theory of Political Economy* and becoming a convert to the energetics revolution that he made any attempt to justify the slope and structure of the demand curve through what remained, at best, a sort of half-hearted utilitarianism.[9] A more technical evaluation of the jerry-built structure of the constant marginal utility of money, the notion of consumer's surplus, the treatment of production, and all the rest can be found in Mirowski (1989, ch. 6).

There are a plethora of reasons why the Marshallian demand and supply functions are inconsistent with neoclassical theory; the simplest way to make this case is to examine any modern advanced text of neoclassical general equilibrium and notice that they are essentially absent.[10] Another, more involved, method is to realise that the sum total of Marshall's 'innovations' undermines the very meaning of equilibrium which was brought over from physics at the  inception of the neoclassical school. The mid-19th-century notion of equilibrium as embodied in the mathematics of the field describes a situation which is conservative and path-independent. All of Marshall's literary attempts to infuse realism into supply and demand involved the introduction of differential time frames, path-dependence, and irreversible change. Now, one might fervently believe that social life is closer to biological evolution than the fall of a stone, but one should then renounce neoclassical value theory as a consequence, and not somehow pretend that the mathematics of constrained optimisation in the appendices had any logical connection to the notoriously evanescent geometry in the main text. Moreover, as Wicksteed claimed long ago, the two curves do not strictly 'live' in the same price-quantity plane from a neoclassical vantage point; but then again, mere mathematical consistency was never a Marshallian strong point.

Even Marshall's penchant for seeing biological metaphors in his curves had no foundation in the mathematics. The supposed applications of Taylor's Theorem to the webbing between a duck's appendages was a figment of his imagination (Marshall, 1920, pp. 841–42); as was the purported connection between differentiable functions and smooth evolution. The recourse to biological metaphors was itself an opportunistic manoeuvre, grounded more in the contingent circumstances of British academy than in the structure of the argument. In an incident in 1877 which deserves greater attention from historians of economics, the statistician and eugenicist Francis Galton spearheaded a drive to oust Section F (Statistics and Political Economy) from the British Association for the Advancement of Science on the grounds that the economists were not comporting themselves in a scientific manner. In 1878, J. K. Ingram's presidential address to Section F (in Smyth, 1962) mounted a defence which claimed that political economy resembled biology in many respects, and therefore should be accorded the same courtesy as the field wherein Galton enjoyed his primary identity. Marshall's subsequent fascination with biological metaphor not only served to blunt the criticism that neoclassical economics was an improper bowdlerisation of physics, but also smoothed over the incongruity that a brace of curves originally intended to decontextualise price and quantity was now supposedly the vehicle for the reintroduction of context.

The (perhaps unpopular) point to be made here is that Marshall should not be regarded as a discoverer of anything nor an original theorist of any stripe in the light of the history of neoclassical theory; he was, as the quote heading this section suggests, first and foremost a textbook writer, a populariser and synthesiser of contradictory doctrines. The appropriate points of comparison are Jane Marcet, Henry Fawcett and Harriet Martineau rather than Walras, Jevons and Edgeworth. Marshall marks the watershed in the pedagogy of English economics, away from the Socratic dialogue or narrative parable and towards an imitation of science as he understood it. The hallmark of this new *genre* was geometry; and the rest was the usual textbook practice of presenting the jumbled motley of the discourse of a profession as if it were unified, internally consistent and profoundly self-assured, not to mention resonant with the larger cultural currents of the day.

Geometry was the shibboleth which attracted Marshall to the demand/supply tradition; and it was geometry which was the vessel in the watering of neoclassical theory in order to render it palatable for English tastes. He signalled his predilection in his otherwise grudging review of Jevons' *Theory*:

> We owe several valuable suggestions to the many investigations in which skilled mathematicians, English and continental, have applied their favourite method to the treatment of economical problems. But all that has been important in their reasonings and results has, with scarcely an exception, been capable of being described in ordinary language: while the language of diagrams, or, as Professor Fleeming Jenkin calls it, of graphical representation, could have expressed them as tersely and as clearly as that of the mathematics. The latter method . . . is not intelligible to all readers. The book before us would be improved if the mathematics were omitted, but the diagrams retained (Black, 1981, vol. 7, p. 146).

What was true in 1870 was still true in 1880, except for the fact that Marshall privately admitted that the smooth surfaces of the geometry often served merely as a pedagogical device:

> I think there is room for question whether utilitarians are right in assuming that the end of action is the sum of the happiness of individuals rather than the vigorous life of the whole. As regards the application of practical rather than analytical reasoning in economics, I have not such decided views as you suppose. When tackling a new problem, I generally use analysis, because it is handier: and in the book which I am just going to begin to write I shall retain (in footnotes) a little mathematical analysis for questions which I can't reduce under the grasp of curves. But partly because curves require a special training, partly because they bear more obviously on the science of statistics—I intend never to use analysis when I can use geometry . . . My experience of the exact treatment of supply and demand in inference has been disappointing. The intricacies of the question are so numerous, the difficulties connected with the time element so great, that I have never got any curves relating to it which have satisfied me for many months after I first drew them.[11]

But geometry itself did not render either neoclassicism or the supply and demand organon an empirical or statistical proposition; indeed, when individuals such as Henry Moore began to fit geometrical curves to real data, Marshall actively discouraged their work (Mirowski, 1990b). Since geometry did not and could not solve any of the knotty problems in political economy, the question arises why the strident insistence upon its central place in the curriculum? We have already touched upon the place of geometry in Victorian Britain as the epitome of self-evident truth and clarity in thought; but the situation at Cambridge was even more peculiar. As another Wrangler reminisced:

> In patriotic duty bound, the Cambridge of Newton adhered to Newton's fluxions, to Newton's geometry, to the very text of Newton's *Principia*: in my own Tripos of 1881 we were expected to know any lemma in that great work by its number alone, as if it were one of the commandments or the 100th Psalm. Thus English mathematics were isolated: Cambridge became a school that was self-supporting, self-content, almost marooned in its limitations (Forsyth, 1935, p. 167).

Marshall, Second Wrangler in 1865, was a product of this system, which valued rational mechanics over mathematical breadth, down-to-earth geometry over continental analysis, and regimented conformity and timeless truths over originality. Marshall would have recognised the physics which inspired the novel neoclassical theory, but only just; he certainly was unprepared to innovate along those lines, unlike an Edgeworth (with his vastly superior familiarity with advanced mathematics and the continental literature) or a Pareto. Edgeworth saw his counterpart with great clarity: 'He would prune whatever was ambitious in mathematical expression or mechanical analogy' (in Pigou, 1925, p. 68). It was this persona of the dour schoolmaster, pruning-shears in one hand and scissors in the other, which brought about the textbook reconciliation of the classical trope of supply and demand with the neoclassical image of free-floating energy in commodity space.

## Notes and references

[1] Langford L. Price, Memoirs and Notes on British Economists, 1881–1947, p. 15, MS 107, Brotherton Library, University of Leeds. Price also relates the following anecdote, which gives some insight into Marshall's character (p. 12):

> I heard that at that time when Marshall was Principal of University College, Bristol, William Ramsay, then a Professor there, solemnly summoned one morning and received with a very grave face, thought that he was going to have intimation of some intended dismissal from his post or something similarly serious. But he was only asked his opinion about the proper place of a new umbrella stand.

That Marshall was humourless when it came to economics would be a characterisation which he himself would probably accept. For example, in a letter to Edgeworth dated 6 June 1896, delivering a reprimand on the 'best way to conduct a Journal', he wrote: 'By the end of your letter I am able to see more fully the dry and caustic humour of your notice: but I don't think the ordinary readers will: & I dislike jokes in an Economic Journal' (Letter in Edgeworth/Marshall correspondence, deposited in the London School of Economics Library, manuscript department).

2 This gross caricature must be fine-tuned depending upon the author in question. For instance, in Adam Smith, only 'unproductive' pursuits destroyed value. For more on this and other distinctions, see Mirowski (1989, ch. 4).

3 One particularly glaring exemplar of this problem appears in the work of Samuel Hollander, where any appearance of something that might be construed as Marshallian supply and demand is immediately identified as an anticipation of the neoclassical organon, to the extreme extent of claiming that there has been only one coherent unified research programme in the entire history of economic thought (Hollander, 1987). It will become obvious that the major thesis of this paper directly questions such practices. But at the opposite end of the spectrum, such otherwise discerning historians as Bharadwaj (1978a) assert that supply and demand explanations were the thin wedge used to insinuate neoclassical theory into classical discourse. This, too, is denied herein. If in this respect I can make some small contribution to transcending the Hollander/neo-Ricardian debate over value theory which has raged for more than a decade now, I shall undoubtedly be promoted in my next life to something more exalted: perhaps a dentist.

4 'At our Rest Dinner in July 1822 whilst we are conversing on the probable prices of Barley and Hops for the following year, it was suggested and agreed to that at our future annual Rest Dinners each of us should put down in writing what we considered would be the prices of Barley & Hops on the first Monday in January in the ensuing year . . .' Greater London Record Office, Acc 73.36 B/THB.

5 That the requirements of formalisation motivated Whewell to a greater degree than any others is not just suggested by the quotation, but also by a notebook on political economy, manuscript number R.18.8 in the Whewell papers in the Trinity College Library, Cambridge. There, in a section which seems to be a sketchbook for the 1829 article, he makes a list of various possible equilibrium concepts which might be applied to mathematical formalisations of political economy.

6 In Whewell's 1862 *Six Lectures on Political Economy*, on p. 51 he explicitly repudiates mathematical models of supply and demand, which should quash all such claims such as that in Henderson (1973) that he should be regarded as any species of precursor of neoclassicism.

7 This essay was originally published in *Recess Studies*, edited by Sir Alexander Grant and published in Edinburgh in 1870. The version here cited is drawn from Jenkin's collected papers.

8 One example should suffice. In 6 April 1896, Marshall wrote to Edwin Seligman that: 'On p. 156 you seem to think I was helped out by Fleeming Jenkin's paper. It is a matter of no moment but as a fact my obligations are solely to Cournot; not to Fleeming Jenkin or Dupuit. I had given the main substance of my doctrines in lectures a year or two before he read his paper at Edinburgh' (Dorfman, 1941, p. 407). Seligman, in reply, tried to placate him on this point, only to discover that the matter was of greater moment than a man with an average sense of humour might allow. Marshall wrote in another letter of 10 July (and not 21 October as stated in Dorfman) 1896: 'You say you think it was "natural" to assume that I had borrowed my theory of taxation in relation to consumer's rent—

or some part of it—from Fleeming Jenkin. Will you kindly forgive my saying plainly that it seems most unnatural' (ibid., pp. 407–408).

Although Whitaker (1975, vol. 2, p. 241) writes: 'It is unfortunate that evidence on dating is insufficient to justify Marshall's claim that he anticipated Jenkin, but there is nothing in the annotations making such a claim inherently implausible', this should be counterbalanced by evidence such as Foxwell's letter to J. M. Keynes, 24 April 1925 (J. M. Keynes papers, Cambridge): 'I happened to come across [Jenkin's 1870 paper] in the Easter vacation of 1870, when I was attending Marshall's lectures on diagrammatic economics, & I shall never forget his chagrin as he glanced through the article as I showed it to him. There was nothing in Cournot which so closely agreed with Marshall's general approach to the Theory of Value & particularly to his statement of the equation of supply & demand'. While the decontextualised 'diagrammatic' approach could be attributed to Cournot, much of the actual structure of argument came from Jenkin. How anyone could get away with claiming he had invented something which had been published 20 years prior to his own book, and which many knew he had seen at that time, is simply a testament to the power of Cambridge in constructing its own genealogy as part and parcel of its orthodoxy.

[9] Marshall to Edgeworth, 8 February 1880, London School of Economics Miscellaneous Collection, folder 470: 'As to the interpretation of the Utilitarian dogma, I think you have made a great advance: but I still have a hankering after a mode of exposition in which the dynamical character of the problem is made more obvious; which may in fact represent the cultural notion of happiness as a process rather than a statical condition'. That the energetics was more important than the utilitarianism has not been previously noted; one would begin to illustrate this thesis by examining Herbert Spencer's *First Principles* and Benjamin Kidd's *Social Evolution*, two works Marshall admitted were important to his intellectual development. Both deal in the mid-19th-century fascination for the conservation of energy, and both reveal the ties to evolution and biological metaphor so prominent in Marshall's thought.

[10] See, for instance, Kreps (1990, p. 37): 'Because Marshallian demand plays a very limited role in the remainder of this book . . . we will give the subject relatively short shrift here'.

[11] Letter of Marshall to Edgeworth, 28 March 1880, London School of Economics Miscellaneous Collection, folder 470.

## Bibliography

Bagehot, W. (1953) [1880], *Economic Studies*, Stanford: Academic Reprints.

Becher, H. (1971), *William Whewell and Cambridge Mathematics*, unpublished Ph.D. thesis, University of Missouri.

Bharadwaj, K. (1978a), *Classical Political Economy and the Rise to Dominance of Supply and Demand Theories*, New Delhi: Orient Longmans.

Bharadwaj, K. (1978b), 'The subversion of classical analysis', *Cambridge Journal of Economics*, vol. 2, pp. 253–72. Also given in Wood, 1982, vol. 3, no. 94.

Black, R. D. C., ed. (1977), *Papers and Correspondence of W. S. Jevons*, vol. 3, London: Macmillan for the Royal Economic Society.

Black, R. D. C., ed. (1981), *Papers and Correspondence of W. S. Jevons*, vol. 7, London: Macmillan for the Royal Economic Society.

Black, R. D. C. (1987), 'Fleeming Jenkin', in J. Eatwell, M. Milgate and P. Newman, eds, *The New Palgrave: A Dictionary of Economics*, London: Macmillan, New York: Stockton Press and Tokyo: Maruzen Co.

Brownlie, A. and Lloyd Prichard, M. (1963), 'Professor Fleeming Jenkin 1833–1885: pioneer in engineering and political economy', *Oxford Economic Papers*, 15, pp. 204–16.

Cairnes, J. E. (1874), *Some Leading Principles of Political Economy Newly Expounded*, New York: Harper.

Clapp, B. W. (1962), 'A Manchester merchant and his schedules of supply and demand', Economica, vol. 29, pp. 185–87.

Cournot, A.-A. (1897) [1838], *Researches into the Mathematical Principles of the Theory of Wealth*, translated to English by N. T. Bacon, New York: Macmillan.

Dickens, C. (1971) [1854], *Hard Times*, New York: Signet.

Dorfman, J. (1941), 'The Seligman correspondence', *Political Science Quarterly*, vol. 56, pp. 407–409.

Dupuit, J. (1952), 'On the measurement of the utility of public works', *International Economic Papers*, 2, pp. 83–110.

Ekelund, R. and Shieh, Y. (1989), 'Jevons on utility, exchange, and demand theory', *Manchester School*, vol. 57, pp. 17–33.

Feiwel, G., ed. (1989), *Joan Robinson and Modern Economic Theory*, New York: New York University Press.

Forsyth, A. R. (1935), 'Old Tripos days at Cambridge', *Mathematical Gazette*, vol. 19, p. 167.

Frisch, R. (1950), 'Alfred Marshall's theory of value', *Quarterly Journal of Economics*, vol. 64, pp. 495–524. Reprinted in Wood, 1982, vol. 3, no. 61.

Henderson, J. (1973), 'William Whewell's mathematical statements of price flexibility, demand elasticity and the Giffen paradox', *Manchester School*, vol. 41, pp. 329–42.

Hicks, J. R. (1983), *Classics and Moderns*, Oxford: Basil Blackwell.

Hollander, S. (1987), *Classical Economics*, Oxford: Blackwell.

Jenkin, H. C. F. (1887), *Papers Literary, Scientific, etc.*, S. Colvin and J. Ewing, eds, London: Longmans, Green.

Jevons, W. S. (1905), *The Principles of Economics*, H. Higgs, ed., London: Macmillan.

Jevons, W. S. (1970) [1871], *The Theory of Political Economy*, Baltimore: Penguin.

Kreps, D. (1990), *A Course in Microeconomic Theory*, Princeton: Princeton University Press.

Macleod, H. (1884), *An Address to the Board of Electors to the Professorship of Political Economy in the University of Cambridge*, London: Blundell.

Maloney, J. (1985), *Marshall, Orthodoxy, and the Professionalisation of Economics*, Cambridge: Cambridge University Press.

Marcet, J. (1827) [1816], *Conversations on Political Economy*, London: Longman, Rees, Orme, Brown & Green, sixth edition.

Marshall, A. (1947), *Principles of Economics*, London: Macmillan, eighth edition.

Mason, R. (1989), *Robert Giffen and the Giffen Paradox*, Totawa, N.J.: Barnes & Noble.

McCulloch, J. R. (1825), *Principles of Political Economy*, Edinburgh: Black.

Mill, J. S. (1899) [1848], *Principles of Political Economy*, New York: Colonial Press, two volumes.

Mill, J. S. (1967) [1869], 'Thornton on labour and its claims', in J. M. Robson, ed., *Collected Works of John Stuart Mill*, Toronto: University of Toronto Press, vol. 5.

Mirowski, P. (1986), 'Mathematical formalism and economic explanation', in P. Mirowski, ed., *The Reconstruction of Economic Theory*, Norwell: Kluwer.

Mirowski, P. (1988), *Against Mechanism*, Totawa, N. J.: Rowman & Littlefield.

Mirowski, P. (1989), *More Heat than Light: Economics as Social Physics*, New York: Cambridge University Press.

Mirowski, P. (1990a), 'The rise and fall of the equilibrium concept', *Recherches Economiques de Louvain*, vol. 55, pp. 1–22.

Mirowski, P. (1990b), 'Problems in the paternity of Econometrics: Henry Ludwell Moore', *History of Political Economy*, vol 22.

Mirowski, P. (forthcoming), 'The how, the when and the why of mathematics in neoclassical economics', *Journal of Economic Perspectives*.

Mummery, A. F. and Hobson, J. A., (1956) [1889], *The Physiology of Industry: Being an Exposure of Certain Fallacies in Existing Theories of Economics*, New York: Kelley & Millman.

Newman, P. K. (1960), 'The erosion of Marshall's theory of value', *Quarterly Journal of Economics*, vol. 74, pp. 587–601. Reprinted in Wood, 1982, vol. 3, no. 75.

Pigou, A. C., ed. (1925), *Memorials of Alfred Marshall*, London: Macmillan.

Richards, J. (1988), *Mathematical Visions: the Pursuit of Geometry in Victorian England*, New York: Academic Press.

Robinson, J. V. (1973), *Collected Economic Papers*, Cambridge, Mass.: MIT Press, vol. 4.

Robinson, J. V. (1979), *Collected Economic Papers*, Cambridge, Mass.: MIT Press, vol. 5.

Samuelson, P. A. (1972), *Collected Scientific Papers*, Cambridge, Mass.: MIT Press, vol. 3.

Schabas, M. (1989), 'Alfred Marshall, Stanley Jevons, and the mathematization of economics', *Isis*, vol. 80, pp. 60–73.

Schumpeter, J. A. (1954), *History of Economic Analysis*, E. Schumpeter, ed., New York: Oxford University Press.

Smyth, R., ed. (1962), *Essays in Economic Method*, London: Duckworth.

Stigler, G. (1941), *Production and Distribution Theories*, New York: Macmillan.

Thornton, W. (1870), *On Labour*, London: Macmillan, second edition.

Thweatt, W. (1983), 'Origins of the terminology 'supply and demand', *Scottish Journal of Political Economy*, vol. 30, pp. 287–94.

Walras, L. (1965), *Correspondence of Leon Walras and Related Papers*, W. Jaffé, ed., Amsterdam: North Holland, three volumes.

Whewell, W. (1829), 'Mathematical exposition of some doctrines of political economy', *Transactions* of the Cambridge Philosophical Society. Reprinted in Whewell (1971).

Whewell, W. (1831), 'Mathematical exposition of some of the leading doctrines in Mr. Ricardo's *Principles of Political Economy and Taxation*', *Transactions* of the Cambridge Philosophical Society. Reprinted in Whewell (1971).

Whewell, W. (1967) [1862], *Six Lectures on Political Economy*, New York: Kelley.

Whewell, W. (1971), *Mathematical Exposition of Some Doctrines of Political Economy*, from the *Transactions* of the Cambridge Philosophical Society, reprinted New York: Augustus Kelley.

Whitaker, J. K., ed. (1975), *Early Economics Writings of Alfred Marshall 1867–1890*, New York: Free Press, and London: Macmillan for the Royal Economic Society, two volumes.

Whitaker, J. K. (1987), 'The continuing relevance of Alfred Marshall', in R. D. C. Black, ed., *Ideas in Economics*, London: Macmillan.

White, M. (1989a), 'Why are there no demand and supply curves in Jevons?', *History of Political Economy*, vol. 21, pp. 425–56.

White, M. (1989b), 'Invention in the face of necessity: Marshallian rhetoric and the Giffen goods', unpublished paper, Monash University.

White, M. (1989c), 'Cuckoo or bowerbird? Jevons, physics and the marginalist revolution', unpublished paper, Monash University.

Wise, M. N. (1989), 'Work and waste: political economy and natural philosophy in 19th century Britain', *History of Science*, vol. 27, pp. 263–301.

Wood, J. C., ed. (1982), *Alfred Marshall: Critical Assessments*, London: Croom Helm, four volumes.

# 5. Marshall on taxation

*Peter D. Groenewegen*

Taxation was a subject which occupied Marshall throughout his active life as an economist, though he never wrote a general treatise on taxation and failed to complete the segment on tax foreshadowed for Book X of Volume 2, of the *Principles*. The importance he attached to taxation is reflected in his teaching at Cambridge, Bristol and Oxford which invariably devoted lectures to this subject. Unfortunately, few of these lecture notes are extant, and much of the 'oral tradition' on Marshall's tax views has been lost for posterity (an exception is reproduced in Whitaker, 1975, vol. 2, pp. 379–85).

However, some of that 'oral tradition' did get into Marshall's published work. Interesting fragments on taxation dating back to the first five years of his economic studies are preserved among the Marshall papers and collected in his early writings (ibid., pp. 279–80, 285–302). Some of these fragments were used in the preparation of the *Principles*. Marshall published two specific pieces on taxation. His *Memorandum on the Classification and Incidence of Imperial and Local Taxation*, delivered in 1897, was subsequently published in 1899 as part of the Royal Commission on Local Taxation's *Report* and reprinted in Marshall's *Official Papers* (Marshall, 1926). Much of this went into the *Principles* from the fifth edition onwards. Marshall's views on national taxation for post-war reconstruction were published during the first world war (Marshall, 1917, reprinted in part in Pigou, 1925, pp. 347–52). Marshall's *Principles* includes additional material on taxation to that already mentioned, as does, to a lesser extent, the subsequent *Industry and Trade* (Marshall, 1923b [1919]). Finally, some interesting tax views are preserved in Marshall's correspondence as edited by Pigou (1925).

In contrast to much of Marshall's economics, his views on taxation have received little attention by way of systematic treatment. The four volumes of critical assessments of Marshall (Wood, 1982) do not contain a single paper devoted to his taxation economics. Reisman's book (1987, pp. 170–82) is a useful exception; Whitaker (1987, pp. 354, 359) contains brief observations on Marshall's analytical contributions to tax theory as does Musgrave's famous text and brief, doctrinal public finance history (1959, especially pp. 137, 141, 162, 287; 1987, pp. 26, 39). During the 'age of Marshall' from 1890 to 1920, the journal literature took his views on taxation into account (examples include Cassel, 1901, p. 485; Sanger, 1901, pp. 327, 331; Bickerdicke, 1902; Wedgewood, 1912, p. 394), though to a lesser extent than would have been expected. His cautious support for taxing decreasing returns industries in order to subsidise industries subject to increasing returns assisted in sparking the famous cost controversies of the 1920s. Ultimately, much of Marshall's taxation economics was transmitted to a wider audience via its elaboration by Pigou (1912, part IV); and subsequently Pigou (1928) in a manner Marshall himself did not always favour.

This paper examines Marshall's taxation economics, by placing the tax views of his *Principles* in the context of his other available tax writings. This seems the best way to link Marshall on taxation with the publication centenary of his *Principles* commemorated by this collection of essays. In addition, it gives recognition to what is an undeservedly neglected aspect of his work.

The argument is divided as follows. First, Marshall's general views on tax principles are examined, including those on optimal taxation. Second, Marshall's views on the relative merits of particular forms of taxes are discussed. Third, his theory of tax incidence is briefly reviewed. By way of background, the British tax system for 1870–1920 is first briefly surveyed. The paper ignores Marshall's detailed analysis of taxes on imports and exports, a topic to which he devoted much space in later books (Marshall, 1917, pp. 329–45; Marshall, 1923, Book III, chs VIII–XI) and in earlier defences of free trade (Marshall, 1926 [1903]; cf. the manuscript on foreign trade in Whitaker, 1975, vol. 2, especially ch. III, sections 3.3, 5.2). A final section draws some conclusions.

I

During the greater part of Marshall's lifetime the British tax system consisted of relatively few taxes and stayed fairly stable until the problem of World War I finance induced significant changes. Broad details of the British revenue system from 1870 to 1920 are summarised in Table 1. The first and most important taxes were customs and excise duties, but their relative revenue importance gradually declined from 1870 onwards. The exigencies of first world war finance speeded this gradual process and by 1920 they raised less revenue than income tax. Even by 1870, customs and excise duties had already been effectively reduced to the function of raising revenue from a number of important consumption goods. Apart from alcoholic beverages and tobacco products, these included coffee, tea, sugar, cocoa, dried fruit, playing cards and, from 1909–19, motor spirits. At the start of the 20th century, demands for increasing their protective use became more fervent, particularly with Chamberlain's 1903 pronouncements which Marshall (1903) strongly criticised.

Next in importance as tax revenue sources and rising to dominance during the final years (from 1917) of the first world war, were property and income tax. Initially imposed in England from 1798 to 1816 as a special war tax, income tax was reintroduced as a peace tax (to finance fiscal reforms in commodity taxation) from 1842. Rates rarely exceeded 5 per cent and averaged 2.5 per cent for much of the 19th century. Generous tax thresholds excluded most ordinary wage and salary earners from income tax liability. Its sub-classification of income into five schedules covered owners of land, including houses (schedule A), farmers, including owners in occupation (schedule B), fund holders in the domestic debt (schedule C), profits and professional and other gains, including interest on overseas government debt and company income (schedule D) and income from public office including state and municipal enterprises (schedule E). This explains why it was known as income and property tax. Progressive income tax rates were not introduced until 1909 with Lloyd George's 'People's Budget'. This imposed a sur- or super-tax on what were considered to be very high incomes, something of which Marshall later strongly approved (Marshall, 1917, pp. 519–21).

Death duties were the third most important group of taxes. Prior to 1870, these were classified as stamp duties; subsequent reforms enabled their separate listing. In 1894, Britain's first application of the principle of graduation was in estate duty: initial rates rose in smooth steps from 1 per cent (for estates between £100 and £500) to a maximum of 8 per cent on estates in excess of £1 million. Up to the first world war, death duties contributed a significant proportion of tax

Table 1. United Kingdom—principal government revenue items 1870–1920, including local rates

| | Customs and excise | | Stamp duties | | Land and assessed taxes | | Property and income tax | | Death duties | | Local rates[a] | |
|---|---|---|---|---|---|---|---|---|---|---|---|---|
| | £ m. | % | £ m. | % | £ m. | % | £ m. | % | £ m. | % | £ m. | % |
| 1870 | 43.3 | 58.8 | 4.0 | 5.4 | 4.5 | 6.1 | 10.0 | 13.6 | 4.8 | 6.5 | 17.0[b] | 23.1 |
| 1880 | 44.6 | 60.8 | 4.2 | 5.7 | 2.7 | 3.7 | 9.2 | 12.6 | 6.2 | 8.5 | 22.5 | 30.1 |
| 1890 | 47.6 | 50.3 | 5.0 | 5.3 | 3.0 | 3.2 | 12.8 | 13.5 | 9.1 | 9.6 | 27.7 | 29.3 |
| 1900 | 61.4 | 47.3 | 8.5 | 6.5 | 2.5 | 1.9 | 18.8 | 14.5 | 18.5 | 14.3 | 40.7 | 31.3 |
| 1910 | 61.3 | 46.5 | 8.1 | 6.1 | 0.7 | 0.5 | 13.3 | 10.1 | 21.8 | 16.6 | 63.3 | 48.1 |
| 1920 | 283.1 | 21.1 | 22.6 | 1.7 | 2.6 | 0.2 | 316.9[c] | 23.7 | 40.9 | 3.1 | 105.6 | 7.9 |

[a] Local rates, a tax levied by local government, were recorded separately from central government revenue. The percentage column indicates the relative size of rate revenue in terms of current imperial (national) revenue. It should also be noted that these local rate data cover England and Wales only.

[b] Not given in source, because unavailable—recorded here as mid-point between 1868 and 1871 collections.

[c] Surtax in 1920 contributed a further £42.2 million making a total percentage contribution of 26.8 to gross income of the government.

*Source:* Calculated from Mitchell, B. R., *Abstract of British Historical Statistics*, Cambridge: at the University Press, 1962, pp. 393–95, local rates, pp. 414–15.

revenue, occasionally exceeding income tax collections in importance. However, after the war, their importance gradually declined.

Stamp duties were also a significant source of revenue during Marshall's lifetime. Most stamp revenue was raised from duties on deeds and other instruments of property transfer, receipts, and bills of exchange and promissory notes. Financing the war reduced the importance of these taxes for revenue purposes, whose use in any case was strongly condemned (cf. Bastable, 1895, p. 541). The traditional land tax introduced at the end of the 17th century had largely been redeemed during Marshall's lifetime (for details see Hook, 1905). Land value was taxed under Schedule A of the income tax by way of rent. It was likewise taxed on transfer at death, and, particularly important in the context of Marshall's view on taxation, it was taxed together with improvements, by the local rate. A land development tax was introduced in 1909 and accounts for most of the revenue listed under land tax after that date.

Although included in Table 1, local rates were generally listed separately from imperial (or national) taxation. Table 1 shows their rising importance as a tax from the 1890s. This growth was particularly strong during the first decade of the 20th century, and may explain why Marshall incorporated the lengthy treatment he had devoted to the subject in his submission to the Royal Commission on Local Taxation (Marshall, 1926 [1897]) with the pages of the 1907 fifth edition of the *Principles* (Marshall, 1961, vol. 2, p. 798). Varying from a third to a half of central government revenue, the incidence of rates had become a pressing problem, deserving detailed treatment in a text on economics. The local rate base was the annual rental value of the real property, levied on the occupier. This made its base similar to the inhabited house duty in so far as domestic residential rates were concerned. This latter tax, in its modern form (as compared to 17th century usage), dated back to 1851, and raised from £1.5 to £3 million over the half-century ending 1920.

In spite of the general stability of British taxation during the greater part of Marshall's lifetime, some substantial change did occur. The adoption of graduated rate scales for estate duty in 1894, and subsequently for income tax, was one such change; the growing burden of property taxation in the form of local rates and estate duties was another. The predominance of commodity taxation ended during the first world war to be replaced by that of income tax. The potential for growth in tax revenue which an emergency like war could generate was also demonstrated, thereby shattering traditional beliefs in normal tax burdens in terms of national output. Marshall's writings on taxation comment on many of these changes.

## II

In his lectures (see Whitaker, 1975, vol. 2, p. 382), Marshall invariably referred favourably to Smith's famous four canons of taxation, as he did indeed elsewhere in his early writings (ibid, pp. 71–72, 82). He was also familiar with these Smithian principles as elaborated by McCulloch (1852, pp. 16–39) and John Stuart Mill (1848, Book V, chapter II), the latter used as text for his public finance lectures until the availability in the 1890s of more specialised texts (Bastable, 1892; Plehn, 1896). More modern expressions of tax criteria in terms of equity, efficiency and simplicity, were also known to Marshall. He explicitly discussed the first, and was clearly fully aware of the importance of the other two. In particular, Marshall recognised the interdependence of such tax criteria. For example, Marshall argued that *equity* in taxation was most advanced where

> taxes favoured the development of the energies and inventiveness of the people; which have hindered them the least in the selection of those routes for the satisfaction of their wants; which . . . have given a preference to taxes which were productive and elastic, in proportion to the army of officials needed to levy them; which have avoided vexatious meddlings, and which have been most definite and certain, and free from surprises and opportunities of corruption (Marshall, 1926 [1897], p. 339).

The one explicit reference to tax equity in the *Principles* (Marshall, 1920, pp. 799–800) derived from the fuller treatment of the subject in his *Memorandum* for the Royal Commission on Local Taxation (Marshall, 1926 [1897], pp. 336–39). This defined equity in terms of the now generally accepted views on vertical equity but modified them by reference to what Marshall called 'obligations of duty'. This qualification was particularly important in connection with taxes which Marshall described as 'remunerative' or 'beneficial'. These were taxes where benefiting property owners should pay according to the benefit received, for example, a tax to defray the expenses of drainage. Benefiting property owners could then be simply assessed on the joint-stock principle of tax distribution, that is, 'on their proportional share in the common venture'. By contrast, 'onerous'

taxes, or those imposed to finance more general public responsibilities, required different rules for an equitable distribution. They
were to be apportioned, not in proportion to net income, but in such a
way 'that the poorer classes should contribute a smaller percentage of
their revenues than the middle classes; and these, again, a smaller
percentage than the richer classes' (ibid., p. 337). Where more than
one onerous tax was used, their burden should be assessed on aggregate to see that it conformed to this rule; separate examination of the
distribution of tax burden was not appropriate. Marshall concluded
that net income was therefore the best tax base from the equity point
of view. However, this conclusion applied only to 'onerous' taxation,
and was modified by the efficiency losses generated from net income
taxation which Marshall ascribed to its detrimental treatment of
savings. Marshall saw fully equitable taxation as unattainable.

The notion of graduated taxation as a means of enhancing public
well-being had been defended in the *Principles* from the fifth edition
(Marshall, 1961, vol. 1, p. 719; vol. 2, p. 719), but as a principle of
taxation it had been recognised from the third edition of the *Principles*
in a note on Bernoulli's law of declining marginal utility of money
income (ibid., vol. 1, p. 135fn., vol. 2, p. 266). Marshall's earlier
lecture notes defended non-proportional taxation on strict Millian–
Benthamite lines. These emphasised a need to exempt 'necessary
income' and supported the proposition that temporary income from
personal exertion should be taxed less heavily than more permanent
property income[1] (in Whitaker, 1975, vol. 2, pp. 383–84). Marshall's
strongest support for graduated taxation was given in his contribution
on post-war tax policy. There he argued, that after exemptions of
'necessary income', income tax shares 'must be graduated very
steeply' (Marshall, 1917, p. 319).[2] In that context, he confirmed his
1897 opinion that only income and property taxes could be graduated.
This conformed to the by then prevailing Treasury practice, on which
he commented favourably in 1907 (in Pigou, 1925, pp. 327–28). In
private he appears to have been more pessimistic about the likely
effects of taxation on income distribution, as he wrote on 24 January
1900 to Bishop Wescott (ibid., p. 386).

A final practical comment by Marshall on equity concerned
inequitable consequences from using specific instead of *ad valorem*
rates in excise duties. This induced inverse graduation in commodity
taxation, not only because expenditure on excisable commodities was
a larger proportion of income for the poorer classes in the community,

but because 'the finer and costlier sorts are . . . taxed at nearly the same rate per pound or gallon as the cheaper sorts' (Marshall, 1917, pp. 327–28). Wine, tea, coffee and tobacco products like cigars were commodities to which this applied. Post-war tax reform was an opportunity for redressing this inequity, Marshall suggested (ibid., p. 328), but entailed a cost in 'opening the door to fraud and contention'. Equity objectives were constrained by efficiency, administrative and compliance costs,[3] a further example of Marshall's stress on the interdependence of tax criteria.

Marshall's discussion of efficiency considerations in taxation rank among his major contributions to economics, but are still inadequately acknowledged in the literature.[4] An early mathematical note on the influence of taxation includes quite explicit reference to measuring the dead-weight welfare loss from an indirect tax by the area of the familiar triangle of lost consumer surplus (in Whitaker, 1975, vol. 2, pp. 179–80). In his comments on this paper, Whitaker (ibid., vol. 1, p. 39; vol. 2, p. 281), draws attention to the fact that it was written before Dupuit's work had become known in England, and that Marshall himself in this context only acknowledged Cournot, von Thünen and Bentham (Marshall, 1961, vol. 2, p. 263).

Marshall subsequently elaborated his argument on the excess burden of commodity taxation. A draft document presenting an 'abstract theory of a General Uniform Tax', dated by Whitaker at 1873 or 1874, not only presents the familiar diagram but also the condition for minimum excess burden in terms of tax rates and elasticity of demand (Whitaker, 1975, vol. 2, pp. 297–99). From this, it was an easy step to argue that 'the fittest subjects for taxation are those luxuries which are almost necessaries. Whatever share of taxation the poor man is to bear is as well levied on his tobacco, alcohol and sugar as on anything else.' Welfare losses from taxation were next raised in his *Pure Theory of Domestic Values* (Marshall 1930 [1879], pp. 25–32; see also Whitaker, 1975, vol. 2, pp. 77–78) and finally in the *Principles of Economics* (Marshall, 1961, vol. 1, pp. 467–70) from the first edition onwards. Remarks in the *Principles* (Marshall, ibid., p. 467, fn. 1) repeat the view that minimum excess burden depends on elasticity of demand, hence suggesting a rule of taxing necessaries rather than 'comforts'. This conclusion is qualified by a need to take other considerations, particularly ability to pay, into account.[5] The use of the excess burden analysis to establish the superiority of income tax over excise of the 1870s foreign trade manuscript (Whitaker, 1975, vol. 2, pp. 71–72), is not repeated in the *Principles*, perhaps reflecting that Marshall changed his mind on this subject.

In an appended note to the 1873–74 manuscript on the theory of a general uniform tax Marshall hinted at more substantial difficulties for analysis when it was conducted in terms of variable labour supply. This hint was never developed further. Marshall (1917, p. 322) argued that 'excessive taxes on large incomes may check energy and enterprise' and that in this way 'the problems of a steeply-graduated income tax run into those of graduated taxes on capital'. More importantly, a tax on income, whether graduated or not, is inimical to saving, because it involves the double taxation of that saving: first as income; second, and fully in the long run, as tax paid on the yield from the assets in which the savings are invested.[6]

Marshall also believed that 'heavy taxes on capital . . . tend to check its growth and to accelerate its emigration' (ibid., p. 322). Marshall, however, changed his mind about the extent of this affect perhaps in response to the growth in capital taxation after Harcourt's graduated estate duty of 1894. Detrimental accumulation effects from all capital taxation had been confidently asserted in lectures of the early 1880s (Whitaker, 1975, vol. 2, pp. 381–82), and was repeated in 1897 where Marshall ascribed the same results to 'all taxes on profits' (Marshall, 1926 [1897], pp. 356–57). An addition to the fifth edition (Marshall, 1961, vol. 1, p. 713–14; vol. 2, p. 717) qualified this view. It suggested that diminishing the 'evil of great inequality of wealth' which did 'not sap the springs of free initiative and strength of character, and would not therefore materially check the growth of the national dividend' would be a 'clear social gain'. Perhaps the estate duties England had by then been levying for over a decade were assisting achievement of this goal. Finally, in response to a request from Lord Reay on his reactions to the 1909 People's Budget, Marshall wrote (12 November 1909) that he had changed his mind on detrimental effects of death duties. 'Now I think they are on the whole a good method of raising a rather large part of the national revenue; because they do not check accumulation as much as had been expected, and a small check does not seem to me now as great an evil as it did then [ i.e. 15 years ago]' (in Pigou, 1925, p. 463). By 1917, Marshall was therefore willing to advocate further 'moderate increase' of estate duties as a useful contribution to additional post-war tax revenue requirements, but nevertheless continued to warn that all 'taxes on capital must be handled with caution'. (Marshall, 1917, pp. 322–23).

Only brief reference needs to be made to Marshall's famous policy of taxing diminishing returns industries and subsidising the output of increasing returns industries with the proceeds. The consequences in theory were increased welfare from enhanced consumer and producer surpluses. However, Marshall was careful to describe this as a 'simple plan' fraught with practical difficulties, to which he generally drew attention (Marshall, 1961, vol. 1, pp. 472–73, but cf. Marshall, 1923b [1919], p. 405, fn. 1 which did not). Given its development in the 1870s, (Marshall, 1930 [1879], ch. II, especially pp. 32–34), this material was included in the *Principles* from the first edition.

It has already been mentioned that Marshall was well aware of the importance of administrative considerations in taxation. His frequent warnings that theoretical tax principles are difficult to apply is one manifestation of this. Application of proposals like the one mentioned in the previous paragraph which in theory conferred great economic benefit on the nation even when all administrative costs were fully considered, assumed a great deal about the quality of government. Detailed knowledge of the operation of markets plus an ability to predict accurately cost changes from changes in output were crucial pre-conditions to successful implementation; probity of officials in implementing the measure, was another (Marshall, ibid., pp. 33–34). Marshall was always very conscious of the need to minimise collection costs, an objective he argued was more easily realised by direct taxation. He likewise worried about excessive compliance costs imposed on taxpayers by any particular tax regime (Marshall, 1917, p. 326). Generally speaking, Marshall did not deal in much detail with these issues, but as implied in earlier references to Marshall's emphasis on the interdependence of tax criteria, he appears to have been fully cognisant of the limitations which tax administration could place on tax reform. Furthermore, as a firm supporter of Smith's canons, convenience combined with the avoidance of complexity and uncertainty in tax regulation were principles which Marshall would not have ignored when suggesting tax proposals, as his most detailed discussion of this in the 1870s trade manuscript in fact suggests (in Whitaker, 1975, vol. 2, pp. 71–84).

## III

Aspects of Marshall's views on the tax criteria are further illuminated by his preference ordering of tax instruments. This was explicitly included in his *Memorandum* to the Royal Commission on Local Taxation, and repeated in his perspective on post-war tax policy twenty years later.

Despite its many deficiencies Marshall expressed a clear preference for the taxation of net income from the early 1870s (ibid., vol. 2, pp. 81–82, 86), largely for reasons of equity. At one stage in the 1870s, he also defended this preference on excess burden grounds (ibid., vol. 2, pp. 72–73). A reason he initially advanced against income tax was the fact that concern over privacy made it difficult to implement equitably, particularly for the 'trading classes'. The major problem with income taxation arose from the difficulty of exempting saving systematically in order to tax only direct consumption expenditure. This was the tax system most economists preferred, if only it were practical[7] (ibid., vol. 2, pp. 233–34). Ignoring small variations in presentation, Marshall remained faithful to this proposition (Marshall, 1926 [1897], p. 338; Marshall 1961, vol. 1, p. 802; Marshall, 1917, pp. 318–23). A graduated income tax was best, but this judgement needed qualification because of the inefficiency consequences of its double taxation of saving and, to a lesser degree, disincentive effects on effort from very steep graduation. Equity gains could be further reduced by administrative problems.

Marshall expressed a strong second preference for property taxation, particularly in the form of estate duties. As he explicitly recognised later in his life, its detrimental effects on accumulation had been overstated. Equity was the major consideration and, as already mentioned, Marshall regarded inequality in the ownership of wealth more socially harmful than that of income. Following a more muted presentation in 1897 and in the *Principles* derived therefrom (Marshall, 1926 [1897], pp. 362–64; 1961, vol. 1, pp. 136–37), his 1917 paper suggested specific taxes on property which was used for 'extravagant display' and which, furthermore, could act as a proxy for unnecessary consumption expenditure. These suggestions included a steeply graduated tax on housing. Marshall saw housing as a particularly good index of ability to pay, and one which, in addition, did not bear excessively on saving as compared with a graduated income tax. Graduated taxes could likewise be levied on hotels and restaurants, domestic servants, and, an indication of Marshall's awareness of current developments, on motor car ownership. A tax on cars was useful as a tax on wealth from which pleasure of display derived, something he identified as a generally useful source of revenue,[8] and also because car travel imposed great discomfort on other people when it took place on 'a dusty road at thirty miles per hour'.

Marshall strongly condemned taxes on transfers, like stamp duties. They lowered mobility of goods and factors of production, the items on which they were invariably levied. Marshall's views on this subject echoed contemporary opinion (Marshall, 1926 [1897], pp. 355–56; cf. Bastable, 1895, p. 541).[9] Likewise, Marshall condemned taxes on particular expenditure forms as generally inferior, despite the exceptions noted in the previous paragraph, and the major exception of taxes on 'stimulants'. The last, together with taxes on housing were regarded as particularly useful because even if levied at high rates, they caused minimal excess burdens, as Marshall had attempted to show in the early 1870s (Whitaker, 1975, vol. 2, pp. 299–301; Marshall, ibid., pp. 338–39).

Local rates were regarded as more useful by Marshall and ranked after 'the alcohol taxes, the death duties and the income tax' (Marshall, ibid., p. 363). Like all taxes, they had their faults, particularly because they sometimes induced detrimental effects on building and population movements. As shown subsequently, Marshall argued such effects to be slight. He also saw local rates as an eminently suitable local tax, not because of its immobile tax base, but, because as 'beneficial' taxes, (which made up the greater part of rate revenue) they benefited local property owners directly.

In this context it may be noted that Marshall's *Memorandum* for the Commission on Local Taxation comes closest to treating fiscal federalism issues, so prominent in current public finance analysis. Its final paragraphs (ibid., pp. 363–64) raise issues of local tax assignment and intergovernmental grants and develop additional government structures designed to enhance the efficiency of service delivery. These show Marshall's support for an extension of local government responsibilities, facilitated by inserting a provincial tier between the imperial (central) and 'local' levels, which yields a more even distribution of rich and poor in sub-national jurisdictions. In tax assignment, Marshall opposed 'the allocation of central [i.e.

'onerous'] taxes to local purposes', but recognised in this context that 'poor relief, asylums, police and education' had national as well as local objectives (Marshall, ibid., p. 389). However, Marshall admitted local government rights to 'experiment' with methods of revenue raising, including local access (subject to central government control) to licence fees from the sale of alcohol and taxes on vehicles including motor vehicles (Marshall, ibid., pp. 359, 363–64; but cf. Marshall, 1917, pp. 324–25 which assigned some of these taxes nationally as useful ability-to-pay taxes based on the 'display of wealth'). Although Marshall also supported more extensive use of rates, possibly assisted by central withdrawal from the inhabited house duty to make room for rate increases, he generally preferred to finance the greater part of expanded local and provincial government activities from central government grants. Central grants were particularly useful to ensure that local government performed its more national duties with 'vigour and intelligence' (Marshall, 1926 [1897], pp. 359, 363; cf. Sanger, 1901, p. 327).

Marshall's tax preferences reflected the bias of his times. Over his lifetime, he revealed increasing support for the use of steeply graduated taxes on income and property (especially estate duties) in line with the actual developments which were taking place in the British tax system. His support for the direct consumption expenditure tax reflected contemporary views, especially that of Mill (1848, pp. 814–17). Marshall showed little sympathy for indirect commodity taxes and taxes on transactions like stamp duties, excepting taxes on alcohol for social, moral and efficiency reasons.[10] Marshall also regarded local rates and other land taxes quite highly, with improvements to be taxed with the land itself. Despite public opposition to Henry George's general views (Marshall, 1969 [1883], where a policy of increased land taxation is defended on pages 205–07), Marshall on various other occasions fully supported land tax on 'the public value of land . . . which arises from position, extension, its yearly income of sunlight and heat and rain and air' (Marshall, 1926 [1897], p. 341; cf. Marshall, 1961, vol. 1, p. 433; vol. 2, p. 437, inserted from the fifth edition and incorporating large parts of the former source).

## IV

Marshall's frequent references to taxation issues in the *Principles* had a specific pedagogical purpose. This was explicitly stated in his *Memorandum* for the Royal Commission on Local Taxation (Marshall, 1926 [1897], p. 340) in a passage reproduced in the *Principles* from the fifth edition onwards (Marshall, 1961, vol. 1, p. 413; vol. 2, p. 432), which can be quoted in full:

> For indeed a great part of economic science is occupied with the diffusion throughout the community of economic changes which primarily affect some particular branch of production or consumption; and there is scarcely any economic principle which cannot be aptly illustrated by a discussion of the shifting of some tax 'forwards', *i.e.* towards the ultimate consumer, and away from the producer of raw material and implements of production; or else in the opposite direction, 'backwards'.

This statement reveals Marshall as a true follower of Ricardo who had also used tax incidence analysis as a major application of his theory of value and distribution. In fact many of Marshall's illustrations of the theory of value drawn from the incidence of taxation were initially inspired by his close study of Ricardo and Mill on the subject.[11] However, the more Marshall departed from their theories by developing his own theory of distribution, the more he questioned their traditional incidence results. A fragment on profits tax, dated 28 May 1884, clearly shows this. Its objective was identifying problems to be solved when explaining the demand for factors of production, an important step in his development of the distribution theory for the *Principles* (Whitaker, 1975, vol. 2, p. 335).

The intensity of Marshall's initial study of tax incidence is visible in his foreign trade manuscript of the early 1870s (especially ibid., p. 85). The page cited refers to the important but 'incomplete' work on the subject 'by the two great schools of abstract economics: that founded in France by Quesnay and that founded in England by Ricardo' but Smith's 'more careful work, . . . directed towards the discovery of the difficulties which still surround these doctrines. . .', was by then already preferred by Marshall. When combined with Malthus's work (for an explanation see Marshall, 1961, vol. 1, p. 475fn.) their views contained two important results on tax incidence:

The first is that a tax on wages or on necessaries tends to check the growth of the labouring population; to increase the competition of capitalists for workmen and diminish the competition of workmen for hire. So that the taxes, which have for many generations been levied on the working classes have had the effect of rendering less than they would otherwise have been the benefits which the rich and in particular the landowners derive from their property. The second result is that whatever diminishes the rate of profits tends to check to some, though not necessarily to a great extent, the accumulation of capital; and therefore of the means of supporting labour. Taxes on the rich fall to some extent on profits, so that the taxes which have for many generations been levied on the rich, have had the effect of making the position of the working classes less desirable than it otherwise would have been. (in Whitaker, 1975, vol. 2, p. 85).[12]

Marshall's treatment of tax incidence is most succinctly set out in his *Memorandum* for the Royal Commission on Local Taxation (Marshall, 1926 [1897], pp. 340–44, 352–57).[13] Shifting of tax burdens is implicitly analysed in terms of elasticities of supply and demand. Only a tax assessed on the pure monopoly as a unit or on its net profits cannot be shifted (cf. Marshall, 1961, vol. 1, pp. 481–84; vol. 2, p. 534, material dating substantially from the first edition). Other taxes on monopolies can be shifted.[14] The incidence of taxes on profits is in general much more complex. Marshall explains this by the fact that profits are a composite form of income comprising 'some interest on capital, some earnings of ability and work, and, often, some insurance against risk', components which vary considerably in relative importance between industries and, within an industry, between firms of different size and different location (Marshall, 1926 [1897], pp. 356–57). Despite this complexity, the classical proposition that taxes on profits fall on capital, and are therefore widely diffused throughout the community, remains valid.

The importance of elasticity of supply and demand (and hence time period) to tax incidence analysis is illustrated by Marshall in a famous example of a sudden and heavy tax on printing (ibid., pp. 341–42; much of which reproduced in the *Principles* from the fifth edition onwards; Marshall, 1961, vol. 1, pp. 414–15; vol. 2, p. 432). Elasticity of demand and supply considerations cause the tax to fall initially on those working in the industry whose skills tend to be specific to the activity taxed. Only if the tax is local can such employees escape its impact through emigration. The longer run enables some forward shifting of the tax. If instead the tax is imposed on printing presses, tax effects on price and output are delayed until old presses have to be replaced. If applied to the use of presses, tax on old presses is paid from quasi-rents and not shifted. When applied to new presses, tax raises marginal costs, lowering the supply of printing and raising its price until the use of the new presses at the margin pays the tax in order to return the customary net profit for the industry. In conformity to Marshall's views on the pedagogic value of tax incidence examples, this particular case illustrated the qualities of the concept of quasi-rent including the considerations of time it introduced to the analysis of marginal cost in relation to value.

The analysis of monopoly tax incidence (Marshall, 1926 [1897], pp. 240–41) was likewise intended to illustrate intricate aspects of marginal cost in relation to value; this time from the side of rent and effects thereon from taxes on land (cf. Marshall, 1923b [1919], pp. 824–27). A tax on pure economic rent or its 'original' and 'inherent' value, like a tax on the net profit of monopoly, cannot be shifted. However, the shifting of a tax levied on land or its produce is possible when designed to discourage cultivation or investment in improvements like farm buildings. The former case is complex and depends on whether the analysis is conducted in terms of agricultural produce as a whole (the classical economists' generic 'corn') or a specific product of the land. In the first instance, the extent to which the tax can be shifted depends on the relative supply of 'corn' grown at the margin of cultivation; the lesser (greater) the quantity grown in this circumstance, the more (less) of the tax falls on the farmer (and, ultimately, the landlord) and the less (more) on the consumers of corn. The slope of the supply curve over the relevant range determines this result, *ceteris paribus*. A tax on a specific commodity like hops is shifted to consumers depending on its elasticity of supply and demand. Inelastic demand and elastic supply, for example, may induce a price rise approximating the tax and hence its substantial shift to consumers. Similar results are derived for the short period to explain the incidence of taxes affecting returns to farm buildings and, quasi-rents in general (Marshall, 1961, vol. 1, pp. 432–38).

Marshall's analysis of the incidence of local rates reflects many of these issues. An example is his distinction between the effects of a local and a national tax, the former potentially leading to population movements. If rates are 'beneficial', the net benefit of the tax exceeds its burden and population shifts (or other detrimental consequences) are unlikely. Similar reasoning is relevant for explaining the incidence of rates on building values. Incidence of domestic rates between owner and occupier depends on progress of the district: in a declining locality, incidence is likely to be on the owner rather than the occupier; *vice versa* for a progressing district. Rates on business premises are passed forward to customers depending on supply and demand elasticities. A degree of spatial monopoly (dealing 'in things which cannot be easily got from a distance') facilitates forward shifting. Long- and short-run consequences are also carefully distinguished. Switching the rate base from improved capital values to site values initially raises the value of expensive buildings in districts where rates are heavy and lowers the value of obsolete buildings on large sites. After a time, buildings reflect site values and rate burdens: hence new building shifts to the suburbs where vacant building land is now paying higher rates. Marshall warns at the outset that this incidence analysis of rates embodies only 'general tendencies'; precise consequences of a rate change depend on the specific features of each particular case (ibid., Appendix G especially pp. 795–99).

Marshall's incidence analysis made a number of important contributions of which the distinction he made between long- and short-run effects was the most important, as Musgrave (1987, p. 39) has argued. Furthermore, his use of demand and supply elasticity in tax incidence analysis enabled more precise results about shifting of specific taxes to be obtained. Both these contributions rely on innovative features of his theory of 'value', explaining why he thought tax incidence analysis particularly useful for illustrating such concepts in the *Principles*.

## V

Marshall's analysis of taxation is instructive on several counts. First, his theoretical discussion, particularly with respect to tax incidence, sheds light on the more innovative aspects of his theory of value. Examples are his notions of supply and demand elasticity so crucial to more precise determination of where tax burdens will eventually be placed. Given the time dependence of elasticity, short-period effects must be separated from longer-period effects. Tax incidence examples were therefore also very useful to illuminate the concept of quasi-rent.

Secondly, Marshall's opinions on tax policy were invariably extremely cautious. One manifestation of this is that they tended to follow rather than lead public opinion. His growing support for the principle of graduation is an example, reflecting as it did contemporary estate duty and income tax practice. Another example of that caution is his explicit reluctance to move from theoretical principles to practice. His warnings about the difficulties in attempting to reap the welfare benefits from taxing a decreasing costs industry to subsidise increasing returns industries from the revenue so raised illustrate this clearly. Marshall's doubts about availability of the essential information to implement the measure effectively absolve him from Clapham's criticism (1922) of using 'empty economic boxes'. His failure to publish his findings on excess burden and optimal taxation point in a similar direction, as do his many warnings against simplistic assessment of taxes in terms of single criteria like equity.

Marshall's taxation writings also provide interesting perspectives on the history of economic thought. His strong preference for Smithian incidence analysis, incomplete and imprecise though this analysis was relative to the more precise but abstract findings from the schools of Quesnay and Ricardo, is a further pointer to the high esteem in which he held the author of the *Wealth of Nations*. As noted, Marshall's interest in taxation also demonstrates his acquaintance with Whewell's work at an early stage of his career

Finally, the taxation material provides further reasons for regretting the fact that Marshall never completed his second volume of the *Principles* in which tax principles and their application would have been fully elucidated. Fortunately, enough is available to indicate the lines on which Marshall would have developed these views. In addition, his incorporation of much tax material with the later editions of the *Principles* which explicitly abandoned reference to a second volume, enabled diffusion of this tax material to a wider audience. That audience in connection with taxation, was, however, surprisingly small.[15] Many of Marshall's insights into tax theory, like his important work on monetary theory and policy, had therefore to be retrieved long after they were initially made.

## Notes and references

[1] After noting the evasion possibilities from income splitting inherent in a linear income tax of the type discussed, Marshall illustrated this proposition by giving the following formula for a graduated income tax

$$c. \sqrt[3]{\frac{n-a}{100} \cdot \frac{n}{100}}$$

where 'c' is an appropriate constant, 'n' is income and 'a' is 'necessary income' which, for illustrative purposes, Marshall took to be 100 (in Whitaker, 1975, vol. 2, p. 383). The Mill-Benthamite origins of this approach to non-proportional income tax can be seen in Mill (1848, pp. 809, 813). Marshall's early concern with income tax evasion is illustrated by a quotation from the Inland Commissioners for 1869 given in Palgrave's *Local Taxation* (1871, p. 78), which he copied into his copy of Mill's *Principles* (Bk. V, ch. III, § 5, p. 500). This read as follows: '40 per cent of persons assessed had understated their incomes to such an extent that a true return would give an addition of 130 per cent'. Marshall's copy of Mill's *Principles* (the 'people's' edition of 1865) is preserved in Cambridge University Library (manuscript collection, Marshall, d.61).

2 Marshall (1917, p. 318) described this plea for steeply graduated income and property taxation as a product of 'constructive ethics', a position he identified as being 'in full swing' before the start of the first world war, perhaps an oblique reference to the 1909 budget proposals and the support these generated in the country.

3 This matter had earlier been broached in the unfinished manuscripts of the early 1870s relating to the theory of foreign trade (Whitaker, 1975, vol. 2, pp. 83–84) in which Marshall particularly dwelled on the administrative problems associated with *ad valorem* taxes on commodities like wine and cigars.

4 See for example, Musgrave (1987, p. 26) who is not aware of Marshall's early work on the subject, and Auerbach (1987, p. 61) who omits any mention of Marshall in this context.

5 As Whitaker (1975, vol. 2, p. 188) points out, the 'factual' accuracy of this proposition is flawed by its misleading welfare implication arising from the assumptions required to aggregate losses of consumer surplus across all the separate commodities. Constancy of marginal utility of money income in the measurement of consumer surplus for a particular commodity is a major obstacle to such aggregation but there are others as well, as Marshall himself fully realised (see *Principles*, 1961, vol. 1, pp. 131–32 and 842). Both of these references date substantially from the third edition, perhaps explaining why Marshall did not qualify his taxation rule which did not appear until over 300 pages later and had originated from the first edition. Marshall may have seen such a qualification as unnecessary in any case because practical applicability of the tax proposition in question was denied in later sentences in the footnote in which it appeared.

6 See Marshall (1917, p. 213). A note gives an arithmetical illustration: 'Suppose a tax of, say, a shilling in the pound [five per cent] is levied permanently on all income, and £1 000 saved yields, say, 4 per cent permanently: then that £40 of annual income will yield permanently £2 as tax; and the present value of that permanent yield will be £50—the exact amount of the original tax'.

7 Marshall, (1926 [1897], p. 338) suggests partial exemption of savings for a limited period of years as an experimental remedy to the double income tax on savings which might be usefully tried on a small scale. His discomfort with this suggestion is indicated by the typical Marshallian qualification: 'Any such plan must necessarily proceed on broad lines, and ignore the lighter considerations of equity when seeking to adjust the weightier; and it would need to be introduced gradually and tentatively'. The 1917 discussion of tax policy did not develop the notion of an income tax experiment of this kind.

[8] The last enables Marshall to plead likewise for a tax on the ownership of jewellery which would extract revenue from the pleasure of owning such pieces of property. He may therefore have had some sympathy with the notion of regular wealth ownership taxes, as currently levied in various OECD countries. A tax on such an item of display would have reduced the attractiveness of holding such sterile forms of investment, but Marshall did not develop this aspect of the matter (Marshall, 1917, p. 325). Marshall likewise supported the introduction of a tax on advertising on social grounds, partly for the public good of diminishing the growing influence of advertising managers on the editorial policy of the periodical literature. (ibid., p. 325, cf. 1926 [1897], p. 364). Marshall's rationale for a tax on advertising was therefore different from that of Kaldor and Neild (1962) which was designed to reverse the drift towards concentration of ownership in the media.

[9] Marshall's criticism of stamp duties sits uneasily with his remarks (1926 [1897], pp. 358–59) that England is a country 'which has rid herself . . . of all taxes which are in themselves mischievous. . .'.

[10] Minimisation of excess burden had been the justification of alcohol taxation in the early 1870s (Whitaker, vol. 2, p. 299) but Marshall's judgement thereon is not confirmed by more recent estimates of the dead-weight welfare loss of this type of tax. R. A. and P. B. Musgrave (1984, p. 307) report the excess burden of excises on liquor as 28 per cent of revenue, far greater in relative terms than that imposed by the work-leisure, or saving-consumption choices induced by the income tax.

[11] (Marshall, 1961 vol. 1, p. 413; vol. 2, p. 432, cf. Musgrave, 1987, p. 39.) Marshall's Appendix L, 'Ricardo's Doctrine as to Taxes on Improvements in Agriculture' (Marshall, 1961, vol. 1, p. 833) is a good example. This had originally appeared in the first edition as a lengthy textual note to Book VII, chapter 10 (see Marshall, 1961, vol. 2, p. 829). The issue of taxes on improvements in agriculture had been intensively studied by the young Marshall as some detailed annotations in his copy of Mill's *Principles* demonstrate. One of these comments, incidentally (on the blank page facing p. 507) refers to Whewell's work in the *Transactions*, 1829, p. 108 (Whewell 1971, pp. 17–18), thereby providing proof that at an early stage of his studies, Marshall had been familiar with Whewell's mathematical economics, contrary to what Whitaker (1975, vol. 1, p. 45, fn. 26) seems to imply.

[12] cf. Marshall's notes on Turgot and Ricardo on the subject (in Whitaker, 1975 vol. 2, pp. 252–53, 257–59). Turgot's work appears to have been the only writing by a member of Quesnay's school with which Marshall was familiar. It may also be noted that results like those quoted in the text featured in Marshall's surviving lecture notes on taxation (ibid., pp. 381–85).

[13] Much of the incidence material of this memoir was incorporated in the *Principles* from the fifth edition onwards, in part in Book V, chapters IX–XI, in part in Appendix G. Not all of Marshall's tax incidence theory in the *Principles* derived from this source. Examples include the incidence analysis of a tax on monopoly (as shown below) and that on the improvement of land in Appendix L. Tax incidence material was also included in Marshall (1919): for example, on incidence in general, pp. 410–11; on monopoly tax shifting, pp. 411–12, 824–27 (the last of which leads into land taxation); incidence of local rates, pp. 818–19. In the context of monopoly tax incidence Marshall briefly discussed incidence of a tax on 'joint products': lessening of sale of the first of these products induced by the tax would lower the supply of the second automatically (p. 414, fn.1).

[14] Because they affect price or output decisions; Marshall (1961, vol. 1, p. 856) presented a mathematical proof of this, whose final form comes from the second edition. It is as elegant as that offered a few years later by Wicksell (1896).

[15] This was implied in the first section of this chapter by the relatively small number of tax papers in the *Economic Journal* in which his work was directly cited. Even some of his more favourite students failed to cite him on the subject. A good example is Chapman (1912 and 1913), though the latter paper, on pp. 34–35, almost paraphrases Marshall's original support for progressive taxation in terms of a 'hierarchy of wants'-type argument (Marshall, 1961, vol. 1, pp. 134–37).

## Bibliography

Auerbach, A. J. (1987), 'The theory of excess burden and optimal taxation', in A. J. Auerbach and M. Feldstein, eds, *Handbook of Public Economics*, Amsterdam & New York: North Holland, vol. 1, ch. 2.

Bastable, C. F. (1895) [1892], *Public Finance*, London: Macmillan, second edition.

Bickerdicke, G. F. (1902), 'Taxation of site value', *Economic Journal*, vol. 12, no. 4, December, pp. 472–84.

Cassel, G. (1901), 'The theory of progressive taxation', *Economic Journal*, vol. 11, no. 4, December, pp. 481–91.

Chapman, S. J. (1912), 'The incidence of some land taxes and the dispersion of differential advantage', *Economic Journal*, vol. 22, no. 3, September, pp. 489–92.

Chapman, S. J. (1913), 'The utility of income and progressive taxation', *Economic Journal*, vol. 23, no. 1, March, pp. 25–35.

Clapham, J. H. (1922), 'Of empty economic boxes', *Economic Journal*, vol. 32, no. 3, September, pp. 305–14.

Colwyn Committee (1927), *Report of the Committee on the National Debt and Taxation*, Cmnd 2800, London: HMSO.

Hook, A. (1905), 'The present position of the land tax', *Economic Journal*, vol. 15, no. 3, September, pp. 374–80.

Kaldor, N. and Neild, R. R. (1962), 'A proposal for a levy on the advertising revenue of newspapers', in N. Kaldor, ed., *Reports on Taxation*, London: Duckworth, 1980, pp. 115–23.

Marshall, A. (1897), *Memorandum to the Royal Commission on Local Taxation on the classification and incidence of imperial and local taxes*. Published in the Commission's *Report*, Cmnd 9528 of 1899 and reprinted in Marshall, 1926, pp. 327–64.

Marshall, A. (1903), *Memorandum on the Fiscal Policy of International Trade*, published 1908 as House of Commons Paper no. 321. Reprinted in Marshall, 1926, pp. 365–420.

Marshall, A. (1917), 'National taxation after the war', in W. H. Dawson, ed., *After-War Problems*, London: George Allen and Unwin.

Marshall, A. (1923a), *Money, Credit and Commerce*, London: Macmillan.

Marshall, A. (1923b) [1919], *Industry and Trade*, London: Macmillan, fifth edition.

Marshall, A. (1926), *Official Papers by Alfred Marshall*, J. M. Keynes, ed., London: Macmillan for the Royal Economic Society.

Marshall, A. (1930) [1879], *The Pure Theory of Foreign Trade. The Pure Theory of Domestic Values*, No. 1 in a series of Reprints of Scarce Tracts in Economic and Political Science, Aldwych: London School of Economics. Originally printed for private circulation by H. Sidgwick, Cambridge, 1879 and more recently reprinted, Clifton, N.J.: Augustus Kelley, 1974.

Marshall, A. (1961), *Principles of Economics*, C. W. Guillebaud, ed., London: Macmillan for Royal Economic Society, ninth (variorum) edition in two volumes; vol. 1–text; vol. 2–notes.

Marshall, A. (1969) [1883], 'Three lectures on progress and poverty', edited with an introduction by G. J. Stigler, *Journal of Law and Economics*, vol. 12, no. 1, April 1969, pp. 181–226. Reprinted in Wood, 1982, vol. 4, no. 109.

McCulloch, J. R. (1852) [1845], *A Treatise on the Principles and Practical Influence of Taxation and the Funding System*, London: Longman, Brown, Green and Longmans, second edition,

Mill, J. S. (1965) [1848], *Principles of Political Economy, with some of their Applications to Social Philosophy*, in *Collected Works of John Stuart Mill*, University of Toronto: Toronto University Press, vol. 3.

Musgrave, R. A. (1959), *The Theory of Public Finance*, New York: McGraw-Hill.

Musgrave, R. A. (1987), 'A brief history of fiscal doctrine' in A. J. Auerbach and M. Feldstein, eds, *Handbook of Public Economics*, Amsterdam & New York: North Holland, vol. 1, ch. 1.

Musgrave, R. A. and P. B. (1984), *Public Finance in Theory and Practice*, New York: McGraw Hill, fourth edition.

Palgrave, R. H. Inglis (1871), *The Local Taxation of Great Britain and Ireland*, London: The Statistical Society of London.

Pigou, A. C. (1912), *Wealth and Welfare*, London: Macmillan.

Pigou, A. C., ed. (1925), *Memorials of Alfred Marshall*, London: Macmillan.

Pigou, A. C. (1928), *A Study in Public Finance*, London: Macmillan.

Plehn, C. C. (1911) [1896], *Introduction to Public Finance*, New York: The Macmillan Company, third edition.

Reisman, D. (1987), *Alfred Marshall: Progress and Politics*, London: Macmillan.

Sanger, C. P. (1901), 'The report of the local government commission', *Economic Journal*, vol. 11, no. 3, September, pp. 321–33.

Wedgewood, J. C. (1912), 'The principle of land value taxation', *Economic Journal*, vol. 22, no. 3, September, pp. 388–97.

Whewell, W. (1971) [1829], 'Mathematical exposition of some doctrines of political economy', from the *Transactions* of the Cambridge Philosophical Society, Cambridge, reprinted New York: Augustus M. Kelley.

Whitaker, J. K., ed. (1975), *The Early Economic Writings of Alfred Marshall, 1867–1890*, London: Macmillan for the Royal Economic Society, two volumes.

Whitaker, J. K. (1987), 'Alfred Marshall 1842–1924', in J. Eatwell, M. Milgate and P. Newman, eds, *The New Palgrave: A Dictionary of Economics*, London: Macmillan, vol. 3, pp. 350–63.

Wicksell, K. (1896), 'Taxation in the monopoly case', *in Finanztheoretische Untersuchungen*, Jena: Gustav Fisher, ch. 2, Appendix. Reprinted in R. A. Musgrave and C. S. Shoup, eds, *Readings in the Economics of Taxation*, London: Allen and Unwin, 1959, Reading 16, pp. 256–57.

Wood, J. C., ed. (1982), *Alfred Marshall: Critical Assessments*, London: Croom Helm, four volumes.

# 6. Marshall on free trade

*Phyllis Deane*

## I. Marshall's early views on free trade and protection

By 1867, when Alfred Marshall began to study political economy and became 'a wanderer in the land of dry facts: looking forward to a speedy return to the luxuriance of pure thought',[1] British commercial policy was firmly committed to a free trade stance. The shift in political opinion that induced the most advanced industrial nation in the world to dismantle a complex system of protective tariffs in the first half of the 19th century can be traced back to the 18th century when first the Physiocrats and then Adam Smith gave their intellectual cachet to the idea of trade liberalisation. However, the symbolic breakthrough in the movement towards full free trade came in 1846 with the repeal of the Corn Laws—a measure of agricultural protection that had been a hot political issue for a whole generation. The end of a tax which had raised the price of the poor man's loaf in order to maintain the incomes of farmers and landlords was an event of major social significance. More significant still was the fact that it did not, after all, have the disastrous consequences for British agriculture that opponents of repeal had predicted. Indeed it was followed after a short interval by the Great Victorian Boom and by an international trend towards trade liberalisation. To most educated contemporaries, and especially to the policy makers and political economists who pontificated on commercial policy, there seemed little doubt that the British experiment with free trade had achieved the kind of legendary success that could underwrite a universal doctrine.

As he was to recall in a letter written to Seligman in April 1900, Marshall's original plan for his first book, formulated as early as 1873, was to write a policy-oriented monograph on *International Trade with reference to Protection etc* and it was as part of his research for that project that he visited the United States in 1875 'chiefly in order to understand enlightened Protectionism on the spot' (Whitaker, 1975, vol. 2, p. 3). He was deeply impressed by what he learned in the course of this visit and referred to it often in later years. For example, his presidential address in 1890 to Section F of the British Association for the Advancement of Science described his American field trip thus:

> I discussed the Protective policy with several of its leading advocates, I visited factories in almost every first class city, and compared as well as I could the condition of the workers there with that of similar workmen at home, and I . . . said to myself as I went: 'The adoption of Free Trade, as soon as its first disturbances were over, would strengthen this firm and weaken that'; and I tried to strike a rough balance of the good and evil effects of such a change on the non-agricultural population. On the whole it seemed to me that the two were about equally balanced, and that the abandonment of Protection would injure the lower rather than the higher class of manufacturing industries (Pigou, 1925, p. 262).

Such an approach to the policy issue was an enormous contrast to that of Marshall's predecessor in the Cambridge Chair of Political Economy, Henry Fawcett, who claimed in 1878 that 'scarcely anyone could be found in England who would express doubt as to the great advantages which free trade confers' (Fawcett, 1878, p. 14). Indeed, the main thrust of Marshall's address was towards making the point that modern economic scientists based their arguments on impartial reasoning and thorough empirical enquiry, in contrast to yesterday's political economists or to dogmatic socialists. He wanted to impress on his British Association audience that 'the economists of today abhor creeds and catechisms'. He criticised English political economists for failing to address 'the problems of cosmopolitan economies' (i.e., to consider the relevance of the actual economic circumstances of countries at different stages of industrial development, and with different patterns of production and trade) when advocating free trade. For example:

> It is a constant source of wonder to Englishmen that Protection survives and thrives, in spite of the complete refutations of Protectionist arguments with which English economists have been ready to supply the rest of the world for the last fifty years or more. I believe that these refutations failed chiefly because some of them implicitly assumed that whatever was true as regards England, was universally true; and, if they referred at all to any of the points of difference between England and other countries, it was only to put them impatiently aside, without a real answer to the arguments based on them. And further, because it was clearly to the interests of England that her manufactures should be admitted free by other countries, therefore, any Englishman, who attempted to point out that there was some force in some of the arguments which were adduced in favour of Protection in other countries, was denounced as unpatriotic (Pigou, 1925, pp. 258–59).

Significantly, however, Marshall did not disagree with the conclusions of English economists such as Fawcett who beat a dogmatic drum for free trade. They were absolutely right in his view to reject the case for a protective policy at home as being based on 'false reasoning'. Their error lay in being too dismissive of the arguments for protection put forward by eminent American or German economists. In the fragment that survives of a section entitled *Protection to Native Industries*, drafted for his projected early monograph on foreign trade, he echoed Mill in rejecting the case for protecting English industries:

> There is not in England any body of men considerable either on account of their numbers or their intelligence who hold that England at present can with advantage adopt a system of Protection duties. England's industries generally are in an advanced condition; she is dependent on foreign supplies of agricultural produce and the raw materials of manufacture; she has special facilities for acting as a depot for the commerce of the world. The adoption of a Protectionist system could confer on her scarcely any of the benefits which it may confer on other countries; and the injures which it would inflict on her would be exceptionally numerous and far-reaching. For these reasons it is inexpedient that a discussion of the Protectionist system should have special reference to the conditions of England (Whitaker, 1975, vol. 2, p. 98).

And he went on to say that he intended to consider the pros and cons of protection only in relation to American industries. Even for the United States his self-consciously open-minded, on-the-spot enquiries into 'enlightened Protectionism' led him inexorably to the same policy conclusion though his reasoning hinged more on moral or social than on narrowly economic considerations. For example, after telling his British Association audience in 1890 that the economic arguments for and against free trade were 'about equally balanced', he concluded:

> Taking account therefore of the political corruption which necessarily results from struggles about the tariff in a democratic country, and taking account also of the interests of the agricultural classes, I . . . decided that, if an American, I should unhesitatingly vote for Free Trade (Pigou, 1925, p. 263).

The message of Marshall's presidential address to Section F reflected a set of ideas on economic freedom and economic science that were developed more systematically and in broader perspective in his *Principles of Economics*, the first edition of which had appeared only a few weeks before. Most of the rather few references to the doctrine of free trade that occur in the *Principles* are in the introductory chapter and two related appendices. Appendix A is a teleological history of economic civilisation culminating in the first industrial revolution and the free politico-economic system of modern Britain, for example, 'the same causes which enabled England and her colonies to set the tone of modern politics, have also set the tone of modern business. The same qualities which gave them political freedom gave them also free enterprise in industry and commerce' (Marshall, 1949, p. 617).

Marshall then went on in Appendix B to inquire how the form of that problem (with which economic science has now to deal) 'has been fashioned by the process of events and the personal peculiarities of great thinkers' (ibid., p. 623). It was Adam Smith who 'developed the Physiocratic doctrine of Free Trade with so much practical wisdom and with so much knowledge of the actual conditions of business, as to make it a great force in real life'; but the Ricardian school lapsed into insular narrowness; and Marshall cited List who

> showed that the Ricardians had taken but little account of the indirect effects of free trade. No great harm might be done in neglecting them as far as England was concerned; because there they were in the main beneficial and thus added to the strength of its direct effects. But he showed that in Germany, and still more in America, many of its indirect effects were evil; and he contended that these evils outweighed its direct effects. Many of his arguments were invalid, but some of them were not; and as the English economists scornfully refused them a patient discussion, able and public-spirited men impressed by the force of those that were sound, acquiesced in the use for the purposes of popular agitation of other arguments which were unscientific but which appealed with greater force to the working classes (ibid., p. 633).

In sum, the image of modern economic science that Marshall wanted to impress on his audience was his vision of a developing field of knowledge in which the professional analyst needs to be formally explicit concerning the specific assumptions and the conditional clauses governing its laws; for example: 'Almost every scientific doctrine when carefully and formally stated will be found to contain some proviso to the effect that other things are equal, but in economics it is necessary to specify the assumptions and conditioning clauses more frequently because the material world which economists study varies over time and space'; and because 'its doctrines are more apt to be quoted by persons who have had no scientific training and who perhaps have only heard them at secondhand and without their context'. Finally: 'Though economic analysis and general reasoning are of wide application, yet every change in social conditions is likely to require a new development of economic doctrines' (ibid., pp. 30–31).

Indeed up to the early 1900s, Marshall saw no need to rehearse at length the case for full free trade in Britain. His main concern was to distance himself from the dogmatism associated with orthodox free trade doctrine, and to demonstrate that the new generation of economists (of which he was the doyen) were 'more scientific and much less dogmatic than those good and great men who bore the brunt of the battle with the difficulties of economic problems' (ibid., p. 632). In a postscript to his British Association address, after announcing that 'for England, Protective policy would, I believe, be an unmixed and grievous evil', he judiciously conceded the possibility that—under certain conditions—there might be a case for some of the

> many and ingenious schemes that have been propounded for 'Retaliation' on those countries that impose high duties on imports for England, or for taxing imports from foreign countries, in order to allow some differential advantage to the goods of our colonies, on condition that they grant corresponding advantages to English goods' (Pigou, 1925, p. 263).

He added, however, that 'there seems at present to be no probability that the proposed conditions will be realized in practice' (ibid., p. 263).

Even as late as 1901 when Marshall commented in a letter to *The Times* on the Chancellor of the Exchequer's budget proposal to levy an export duty on coal, he was careful to detach himself from those who condemned it on general economic principles.[2] The issue hinged, he insisted, on a balancing of the costs and benefits indicated by an unavoidably intricate analysis of the incidence of import duties: 'And it is not by trained economists—not even by those who are the most ardent free-traders—that the defence of free trade is based on absolute *à priori* reasoning. On the contrary, it is based on a study of details' (ibid., p. 320–21). He identified three kinds of 'frontier taxes which may be economically defensible', *viz.* (1) non-differential import duties raised for revenue purposes, (2) duties on imports designed to protect infant industries, and (3) 'special export duties on commodities with which foreigners cannot easily dispense . . .'. The first of these was unobjectionable; the second—though not inadmissible on principle—he would not defend because he believed that there were other ways of achieving the same end. As for the third, he seemed equivocal: 'On the one hand, our coal is a chief foundation of our industrial well-being; we are wasting our children's inheritance; and there is much to be said for taking toll from coal in order to lessen our National Debt' (ibid., p. 322). Against these considerations he recognised the technical difficulties of levying such a toll and dangers of retaliation by other countries. But he added:

> It is now five and twenty years since I first thought of writing to advocate an export duty on coal, but was restrained by this last consideration; and I have often taken up the question since. My doubts have never been resolved; but I admire the courage of the Chancellor (ibid., p. 322).

## II. The debate on tariff reform

Within the next year, however, the tariff issue erupted into British political debate as part of a campaign for imperial preference orchestrated by the ebullient Colonial Secretary—Joseph Chamberlain. In 1897 Chamberlain had presided over a meeting of the Conference of Colonial Prime Ministers held in conjunction with Queen Victoria's diamond jubilee[3] and floated, among various ideas for cementing ties with the Commonwealth, the notion of an imperial *Zollverein*. While the mother country was committed to an uncompromisingly free trade policy stance, however, and the colonies had reasons for protecting their infant industries, even the most modest proposal for a scheme of imperial preference was unlikely to get off the ground. Then, by chance, in the aftermath of the Boer War when the Chancellor of the Exchequer was desperately seeking new sources of revenue to balance his 1902 budget, and when imperial sentiment had been freshly aroused by the wartime co-operation of British and colonial forces in Africa, the imposition of a corn registration duty opened up a small door for imperial preference.

It was not a new tax. Peel had first imposed it (again for revenue purposes) when he repealed the Corn Laws and it was retained until 1869. For Hicks-Beach, the Chancellor presenting the 1902 budget, its virtues were that it was cheap to collect, predictable in its immediate consequences and easy to justify as an emergency measure to relieve the burden of unpopular income and stamp taxes. Though condemned by Cobdenites and the Manchester School of Commerce, it was not generally seen as a breach of free trade principles until the Canadian Prime Minister saw it as the thin end of an imperial preference wedge. On 12 May, when the finance bill was still being debated in the Westminster parliament, Laurier informed his own parliament that he proposed to raise with the British government the question of remission of the corn duties in favour of Canada on his forthcoming visit to London. That was to be a few weeks later at the third Colonial Prime Ministers' Conference scheduled to coincide with the coronation of Edward VII. Chamberlain responded immediately to the Canadian advance. His speech to his Birmingham constituents a few days later described graphically an empire under pressure from an unprecedented level of commercial rivalry, from hostile tariffs and subsidies and from powerfully wealthy foreign trusts and combinations. He concluded:

> If by adherence to economic pedantry, to old shibboleths, we are to lose opportunities of closer union which are offered to us by our colonies, if we are to put aside occasions now within our grasp, if we do not take every chance in our power to keep British trade in British hands, I am certain that we shall deserve the disasters which will infallibly come upon us (Amery, 1951, p. 16).

When, as Colonial Secretary, Chamberlain presided a few weeks later at the 1902 Colonial Conference he found the assembled premiers lukewarm about most forms of closer union, but sympathetic towards a programme of imperial preference beginning with a remission of the United Kingdom corn duties. Accordingly he raised the proposal for discussion at the October meeting of Cabinet where the battle for free trade was joined. Balfour, the prime minister, reported to the King on the Cabinet meeting that he himself was inclined to favour Chamberlain's proposal, but added 'it raises very big questions indeed—colonial and fiscal—and the Government which embarks upon it provokes a big fight' (ibid., p. 17). When it was discussed again at the November Cabinet meeting the Chancellor, Charles Ritchie, articulated the opposition in a Cabinet memorandum which rejected the 'imposition of a charge on the taxpayers of the United Kingdom in order to benefit our kith and kin beyond sea' and branded any form of imperial preference as a breach of free trade principles. According to Balfour's letter to the King, the November Cabinet meeting resulted in a decision to maintain the corn duty at the next budget, and to remit it in favour of the British Empire: but there were no formal Cabinet minutes and subsequent reports are conflicting. In any case, Ritchie's 1903 budget abolished the one duty that had opened up the possibility of implementing a policy of imperial preference and the split in the Cabinet became a matter of public scandal.[4] Chamberlain of course was furious. On 15 May, in another rousing speech to his constituents, he launched what was to be his last radical campaign and set off a national debate which dragged even the academic economists into the political arena.

Chamberlain had already one academic supporter committed to the imperialist cause well before 1903. That was Hewins, who was Director of the London School of Economics from its foundation in 1895 to 1903, when he resigned to become Secretary to the Tariff Reform Commission—a privately founded body set up to collect information of propaganda value to the Tariff Reform League. Hewins boasted in his autobiography that the L.S.E. was

> the first institution to organise a course of lectures and research courses of the University type on a large scale on the policy and administration of the British Empire. As for my own lectures, they were for me the means by which I came to see clearly the scientific basis of economic policy (Hewins, 1929, p. 29).

Hewins was commissioned by Gustav Schmoller of the University of Berlin to write an article on 'Imperialism and its probable effect on the commercial policy of the United Kingdom' for *Schriften des Vereins für Sozialpolitik* published in 1900.[5] He was also invited by *The Times* in June 1903 to 'write some controversial articles' to fuel the debate on tariff reform that had been raging in newspapers and journals since Chamberlain delivered his 'Save the Empire' speech in the preceding month (ibid., p. 66).[6]

Hewins' articles for *The Times*—there were sixteen in all—were published at intervals from June to September under the title 'The Fiscal Policy of the Empire' and signed 'An Economist'. Marshall, as the most authoritative academic economist, was formally invited to reply—but refused. In a letter to Brentano dated 17 July 1903, when the articles were appearing in *The Times*, Marshall wrote: 'I have ventured to write him some remonstrance: but I have declined to answer him' (McCready, 1955, p. 261).[7] By this time, however, Marshall had already accepted an invitation from Ritchie's private secretary at the Treasury to write a paper for the Chancellor giving his considered views on 'the fiscal problem'.[8] In his letter of 17 July to Brentano, Marshall justified his refusal to argue with Hewins through the pages of *The Times* on two grounds: first because 'he has not committed himself to supporting Chamberlain: . . . He keeps on assuring us that he is not a protectionist, but a most divinely enlightened free trader'; and second because

> though writing as 'an economist', he is even more dogmatic and omniscient in his capacity of statesman than in that of economist. And his later letters, while

professedly talking sheer economics, assume premises which he considers himself to have established as a politician. So if one answers him, one must mix up politics and economics.

The second reason seems to have been the most important of the two, for Marshall went on to say that 'economists of the chair, who make it a duty to bring out arguments, which tell against their ultimate conclusion, as faithfully as those which tell for it' were not as well fitted for a public argument as 'the better class of newspapers and members of Parliament' (ibid., p. 261).

When he wrote to Brentano on 17 July Marshall (who was then spending the vacation in Austria) had not yet seen the seventh of Hewins' articles; that had appeared in *The Times* of the preceding day. His next letter to Brentano on 20 July reflects a much higher temperature level. He fumed at 'An Economist's' 'monstrous' use of the statistical evidence on the price effects of 19th-century corn duties in England, France and Prussia, describing his argument as

> most objectionable and if I had access to my books I should I think write to the *Times* about it. But you could do it much better than I; for you can read between the lines of the statistics. I can do that for England, of course, but not for Prussia (ibid., p. 262).

However, by this time Brentano himself had been commissioned to write an article for the *Fortnightly Review* giving a German free trader's view on Chamberlain's Birmingham speech of 15 May and Balfour's contribution to the House of Commons debate of 28 May (Brentano, 1903, p. 215). He poured scorn on 'Balfour and Chamberlain, the docile pupils of our [German] Protectionists' but upset Marshall by concluding his article with a rather curious passage suggesting that if the British adopted a policy of 'countervailing bounties against export premiums of that kind which was adopted by the Brussels Sugar Convention . . . it would be a death blow to all Protective policy and an impulse towards the universal introduction of Free Trade' (ibid., p. 221). This provoked a pained lecture in Marshall's letter of 24 July, where he pleaded with Brentano not to 'help destroy English free-trade, in your anxiety to stop a system which I admit to be most injurious to the country which adopts it; but not to the country to which it sells' (McCready, 1955, p. 264).

Meanwhile in Britain, where a cascade of letters to the editor, articles, pamphlets, speeches and books, was fuelling public debate, Edgeworth—in consultation with leading 'economists of the chair' such as Bastable, Cannan, Nicholson and others—was drafting an

authoritative joint letter to *The Times*. Marshall—who first declined
to draft it, then hoped to be let off the hook of adding his signature by
the vagaries of the post to Austria and his own objections to the first
draft—was eventually goaded into signing a revised draft by 'the most
glaring economic falsities' currently being put about in millions of
leaflets circulated by Chamberlain's Tariff Reform League.[9] The
Manifesto of the Fourteen Economists (as the joint letter came to be
known) appeared in *The Times* on 15 August 1903 and was reprinted
in the *Economic Journal* later the same year (*Economic Journal*,
vol. 13, 1903, pp. 446–48).[10] It claimed to express the opinion of the
signatories 'on certain matters of more or less technical character
connected with the fiscal proposals which now occupy the attention of
the country.' But the trouble was that the complex set of issues raised
in the current debate were neither largely technical nor narrowly
economic. They were fundamentally political. In so far as they *were*
technical (e.g., in the sense that they hinged on detailed analysis of the
incidence of tariffs or export duties) the economist could not offer
either definite or general conclusions without making assumptions of a
statistical or political or sociological nature that were outside his
professional competence of knowledge. Marshall's original instinct
was sound. To argue with Hewins it was necessary to 'mix up politics
with economics', a task for which the new generation of economic
scientists (such as Edgeworth, Pigou or Marshall himself) were not
well equipped. In the event, the Manifesto had a very poor press. As
Professor Coats has shown in two classic articles,[11] it engendered more
ridicule than respect, and the fact that leading academic economists
were divided among themselves on the issue of free trade did nothing
to enhance their credentials among the educated public. It seems that
this joint declaration had as little impact on either the public at large or
the policymakers as the short statement signed by 364 professional
economists nearly eight decades later. Each of course provided a
convenient Aunt Sally for contemporary political speechmakers.[12]

## III. Marshall's *Memorandum on the Fiscal Policy of International Trade*

Marshall's personal contribution to the debate on tariff reform that led
up to the Cabinet crisis of September 1903 was contained in the paper
on the fiscal problem that he wrote at the invitation of the Treasury

and completed in August. The original version, written in greater haste than suited its author, remained on Treasury files, unpublished, until 1908 when Lloyd George (then Chancellor of the Exchequer) used it for a speech on the finance bill in June and subsequently requested its publication as a House of Commons Paper (Marshall, 1926).

In his prefatory note on August 1903 Marshall insisted that he was writing

> from the point of view of a student of economics rather than as an advocate of any particular policy. I have not held back my own conclusions on the questions to which my attention was directed. But I have endeavoured to select for prominence those considerations which seem at once important and in some danger of being overlooked, whether or not they tell for or against my conclusions (ibid., 1926, p. 367).

To this he added a post-script to preface the revised 1908 version and to explain the delay in publication:

> The haste with which it was written and its brevity are partly responsible for its lack of arrangement and for its frequent expression almost dogmatically of private opinion, where careful argument would be more in place. It offends against my rule to avoid controversial matters; and, instead of endeavouring to probe to the causes of causes, as a student's work should, it is concerned mainly with proximate causes and their effects (ibid., p. 368).[13]

Marshall confronted two questions in his *Memorandum* to the Treasury. The first (discussed in Part I) called for an analysis of the incidence of import duties, a problem which he thought too complex to be dealt with outside 'the student's closet' but on which he nevertheless tried to justify his opinion that 'in nearly all cases they are borne almost exclusively by the consumer' (ibid., p. 370). The nub of his argument was that:

> a country cannot expect to throw any considerable share of the burden of her tariff on other countries, unless she is in a position to dispense with a great part of the goods which she imports from them; while she is at the same time in possession of such large and firmly established partial monopolies that those countries cannot easily dispense with any part of their imports from her. So far as the latter condition is concerned, England was in a strong position early in the last century. But not even America is in a strong position now; while England and Germany are, as it seems to me, in weak positions (ibid., p. 372).

He went on to buttress this view with: (i) a laborious 'partial theoretical solution of the problem' which he was probably right to presume that most of his readers would find too difficult to grasp;[14]

(ii) a selection of 'representative cases' from the real world; and (iii) an empirical analysis of German and British 19th-century experience of the effects of tariffs on prices and real incomes.

The second question which Marshall confronted was 'how far, and in what directions, the circumstances which formerly made Free Trade the best policy for this country have been altered?' That was the subject of Part II in which he developed the full force of the rationale for his conviction that:

> the policy [of uncompromising Free Trade] adopted in England sixty years ago remains the best, and may probably remain the best, in spite of increasingly rapid economic change, because it is *not* a device but the absence of any device ... The simplicity and naturalness of Free Trade—that is, the absence of any device—may continue to outweigh the series of different small gains which could be obtained by any manipulation of tariffs, however scientific and astute (ibid., p. 394).

Marshall began by reiterating his rejection of the dogmatic approach to economic principles and warned especially against applying to changing economic situations truths 'which are as universal as the truths of geometry or mechanics', without careful consideration of the respects in which such conditional truths might have been invalidated by the 'subversive changes' of recent decades. He then proceeded to list and evaluate 'some of the changes which may be urged as affording a *prima facie* case for reconsidering the fiscal policy adopted by England sixty years ago'. These were: improvements in other countries; rising tariffs against manufactured exports; the diminishing relative strength of the United Kingdom in the world economy; the increased vulnerability of domestic markets to dumping by giant trusts and cartels; and recent proposals (in England and the colonies) to strengthen imperial unity 'by raising the tariff against foreign goods without lowering it in favour of British goods' (ibid., p. 418).

The conclusion of Marshall's examination of the pros and cons for maintaining, in the conditions prevailing in the 1900s, the United Kingdom's commitment to full free trade, was never really in doubt. One by one he shot down the arguments currently being advanced by the tariff reformers. He dismissed out of hand, for example, the notion that protective tariffs might relieve unemployment in British manufacturing industries by invoking 'the great truth that the importation of goods which can be produced at home does not in general displace labour, but only changes the direction of employment' (ibid., p. 389). He conceded that government was less corrupt and more efficient than it had been when Adam Smith was writing the *Wealth of Nations*, but saw great practical difficulties and still more moral risks in introducing 'an intricate system of combative finance' which might 'bring back into English politics the notion that there is plenty of money to be got by influencing votes in Parliament, and by controlling the public press' (ibid., p. 396–97). This of course was a political rather than an economic argument. Marshall's main economic argument against using tariffs as bargaining weapons (or in retaliation against dumping) hinged on the reasoning developed in Part I which led him to the conclusion that:

> England is not in a strong position for reprisals against hostile tariffs, because there are no important exports of hers, which other countries need so urgently as to be willing to take them from her at considerably increased cost; and because none of her rivals would permanently suffer serious injury through the partial exclusion of any products of theirs with which England can afford to dispense (ibid., p. 408).

But he also insisted that the best way of halting the decline of England's competitive position in the world economy was to stimulate her too-complacent manufacturers into continuously improving efficiency, by 'keeping her markets open to the new products of other nations and especially to those of American inventive genius and of German systematic thought and scientific training' (ibid., p. 409).

Marshall brought essentially the same lines of economic reasoning to bear upon the imperial preference issue. They led him again to the conclusion that for industrialised countries—and especially for 'the oldest of industrial countries'—there was no justification for import duties levied for non-revenue purposes: 'Though they cause new employment to appear in certain directions they will necessarily lessen the National Dividend; and therefore they will necessarily lessen the amount of employment at good wages' (ibid., p. 419).

Even for young countries, where the infant industry argument might justify protective tariffs, he claimed (somewhat vaguely) that there were better ways of government intervention that could help new industrial ventures to overcome their early competitive disadvantages. In the last analysis, of course, the crux of the case for imperial preference was political rather than economic, and in combating the tariff reform schemes currently under discussion Marshall added his characteristic seasoning of moral ingredients to clinch the argument against. For example, in the colonies, even honourable men there are being drawn into slippery paths. They advocate preferential arrangements effected by raising the tariff against foreign goods without lowering it in favour of British goods; and they put in the forefront their zeal for the high ideal of Imperial unity. They look as little as possible at the private gain which may accrue to them from the particular method of promoting that ideal which they advocate (ibid., p. 418).

Moreover, since the aggregate material loss from such schemes was likely on economic grounds to be greater than the aggregate material gain, they are

likely to breed more of disappointment and friction between England and her Colonies, than of good will and the true spirit of Imperial unity. And if approached in a spirit of greed rather than of self-sacrifice, they are likely to rouse animosity in other lands, and to postpone the day at which it may be possible to work towards a federated Anglo-Saxondom which seems to be an even higher ideal than Imperial unity (ibid., p. 420).

Marshall's *Memorandum on Fiscal Policy* stands out amongst his published works as being an essay in persuasion, written in heated haste, and hence without the laborious qualifications and studied impartiality which seemed to him essential to the analytical method of a modern economist. He could not actually bring himself to the point of publication in 1903, but in the Marshall Library collection of his unpublished papers there is a draft preface for it (much corrected and patently unfinished) dated 23 September of that year.[15] In this he agonised over the dilemma facing an economic scientist who felt morally obliged to swerve from his straight scientific path into one of the rougher byways of political economy. For example:

I have made it my rule to avoid taking part in the discussion of a burning political question even if it contains a large economic element. For, however clearly a professional economist may distinguish in his own mind those aspects of the question on which his studies directly bear from those on which he has no special knowledge, the distinction is apt to be ignored by partisans on either side and if he allows himself to be drawn into the heat of the fight he may himself lose sight of the distinction . . . He desires to influence the public. The public will not [take] subtle distinctions or complex reasoning. A full discussion of the economic basis of the problem will repel them and be ineffective.

And he went on to say that what distinguished the political issues then riding high in current debate from any other that had arisen over the past two generations was 'the extent to which the leaders on either side have formally accepted certain distinctly economic statements as a part—not the whole—of the basis of these positions'.

The original memorandum on the fiscal problem had gone to the Treasury in August 1903 with a much shorter prefatory note than the draft dated 23 September, but by the latter date Marshall had read Balfour's *Economic Notes on Insular Free Trade* published a few days previously. That may have been one of the factors discouraging him from publishing his own contribution to the debate. For the Prime Minister's lucid, rational, open-minded discussion of 'some of the more fundamental problems' requiring careful consideration by 'those who desire to arrive at a sober and unprejudiced estimate of our fiscal policy' was a model of its kind (Balfour, 1903, p. 3). Against it, Marshall's own memorandum seems not only stylistically inelegant, but verging on the polemical. The fact is that Balfour's *Economic Notes*, originally written as a discussion paper for a mid-August Cabinet meeting, were not designed to propagate (or to demolish) specific policy recommendations.[16] They represented an attempt to avert political crisis, by elucidating the complex issues and alternative solutions facing his divided administration, and by nudging the uncompromising free traders and the would-be tariff reformers nearer to agreement on a viable policy stance. It deliberately deflated certain of the more doctrinaire axioms currently being slipped into the debate—including some of Marshall's ideological hobby horses. For example—as against the latter's view that one of the virtues of full free trade was its 'simplicity and naturalness'—Balfour dismissed the idea 'that what is economically "natural" as opposed to artificial or contrived is probably expedient'; and to Marshall's favourite 'slippery slope' argument against state intervention in matters of trade, he opposed the commonsensical observation that 'in these days of Factory legislation, Housing legislation, compulsory Education, inspection of Mines and Mercantile Marine Acts, Parliament can hardly assume its own incompetence as a fundamental axiom' (ibid., p. 30).

Balfour's *Economic Notes* posed the question 'whether a fiscal system suited to a free trade union in a world of free traders remains suited in every detail to a free trade nation in a world of protectionists' and his response was economically literate, statesmanlike, well written and above all undogmatic. It was not easy for the scientific economist to reject his arguments on general principles though it was easy enough to differ in detail. Marshall admitted (in his draft preface dated 23 September) that: 'no one, and least of all the academic economist can fail to be attracted by its charm or to concur in the greater part of its arguments. But some of them seem open to objection'. He then fell back on his 'slippery slope' argument: 'The immediate step suggested is small, and might involve no great national risk if it were certain to be the last step. But it is on a slope which experience and reason alike seem to show is steeper and more slippery than almost any other in the region of economic practice'.

In the last analysis all that Balfour was suggesting was that government should take steps to negotiate from strength with commercial rivals who were otherwise able with impunity to raise protective tariffs against British goods. 'The only alternative [to exhortation]' Balfour argued 'is to do to foreign nations what they always do to each other and instead of appealing to economic theories in which they wholly disbelieve, to use fiscal inducements which they thoroughly understand' (ibid., p. 30). And he concluded 'I hold myself to be in harmony with the true spirit of free trade when I plead for freedom to negotiate that freedom of exchange may be increased' (ibid., p. 31).

When Balfour died in 1930, J. M. Keynes, then Secretary of the Royal Economic Society, wrote for the *Economic Journal* an obituary for the last of the Society's original statesmen vice-presidents.[17] Not surprisingly, Keynes—who was never reluctant to mix up politics with economics—read Balfour's *Economic Notes* with sympathetic, if critical interest. He described it as 'one of the most remarkable scientific deliverances ever made by a Prime Minister in office' and added

> I think that economists today would treat Balfour's doubts, hesitations, vague sensing of troubles to come, polite wonder whether unqualified *laisser-faire* is quite certainly always for the best, with more respect, even if not with more sympathy than they did then (Keynes, 1972, p. 44).[18]

And he drew attention to the existence in the Marshall Library in Cambridge of Marshall's personal copy of Balfour's pamphlet, with numerous pencilled marginal comments showing that the academic economist's prevision of the subsequent course of events was less reliable than that of the statesman.[19]

Marshall was in his early sixties when he broke his rule to avoid controversial matters and became a temporary political economist, and it was then, in his *Memorandum on Fiscal Policy* that he expressed his views on free trade most fully, forcefully and candidly. It is noteworthy that these views had not greatly developed—still less changed in any significant aspect—since his early thirties, when he returned from his American enquiries, convinced that free trade was the best policy for England and probably also for the United States. If anything his ideological commitment to uncompromising free trade seems to have been hardened by the heat of the tariff reform debate of 1903.

Five years later, when the revised memorandum was published as a House of Commons Paper—by which time the heat had gone off the issue—Marshall indicated in his prefatory note dated August 1908 that he was then preparing a 'more careful and fuller discussion'. However, there is no evidence in his later writings that any re-thinking took place on the free trade question. His references to it in the main text of his *Industry and Trade* (1919) are so few and glancing that it gives the impression of bypassing the topic. In so far as Appendices D to G[20] bear on the matter they are largely repetitious of earlier writings (e.g., the *Principles* or his presidential address to Section F). The obvious place in which one might expect to find the promised fuller discussion, of course, was Marshall's *Money, Credit and Commerce* (1923) and there are indeed three chapters on import and export duties. Of these, two deal with the question of incidence and the third with protective tariffs. On incidence the discussion is more succinct and better presented than in Part I of his *Memorandum on Fiscal Policy* but the reasoning is the same and a number of crucial passages are repeated almost *verbatim*. It is in the chapter on 'import duties designed to foster particular industries' that the free trade issue surfaces most directly and here again there is extensive repetition of the actual wording of the *Memorandum*—this time of Part II. In sum, it is hard to avoid the conclusion that the *Memorandum* hastily written in the summer of 1903, published with drafting revisions in 1908 and redrafted again for *Money, Credit and Commerce* in 1923, contained the nub and essence of Marshall's views on free trade.

## Notes and references

[1] The passage appears in a draft preface for *Money, Credit and Commerce*. It was quoted by Keynes (1972, p. 171).

[2] The letter was published in *The Times* on 22 April and reprinted (together with a follow-up letter on the same theme that appeared on 9 May) in the *Economic Journal* (1901, vol. 11, pp. 265–67). The letter of 22 April is also reprinted in Pigou (1925, pp. 320–22). The page references here are to the Pigou reprint.

[3] The first had taken place in 1887 on the occasion of Victoria's golden jubilee.

[4] The detailed story of the Cabinet infighting and of Balfour's role in first papering over, and then trying to make political use of the split has been told many times. See, in particular, Amery (1951) and Gollin (1965).

[5] The article, circulated privately in English among statesmen and politicians of Hewins' personal acquaintance in 1900, is published in Hewins (1929, pp. 50–61).

[6] Hewins became Chamberlain's 'economic expert'.

[7] Lujo Brentano was a distinguished free trader and Professor of Political Economy at Munich.

[8] This was his *Memorandum on the Fiscal Policy of International Trade* discussed below.

[9] See Marshall's letter of 18 August to Brentano, justifying his decision to sign. His next letter, however, dated 26 August describes ruefully the attacks on the Manifesto by Foxwell, Hewins and others (McCready, 1955, pp. 265–66).

[10] *Economic Journal* (1903), pp. 446–48. The 14 signatories were C. F. Bastable, A. L. Bowley, Edwin Cannan, Leonard Courtney, F. Y. Edgeworth, E. C. K. Gonner, Alfred Marshall, J. S. Nicholson, L. R. Phelps, A. C. Pigou, C. P. Sanger, W. R. Scott, W. Smart, G. Armitage-Smith. Professors S. J. Chapman and J. H. Clapham afterwards asked to be regarded as in favour but a number of eminent economists (besides Hewins) publicised their disagreement with the Manifesto, including W. Cunningham, H. S. Foxwell, R. H. Inglis Palgrave, L. L. Price, J. Venn and G. U. Yule.

[11] See Coats (1964) and (1968) for articles which put the controversy into perspective of the history of economic thought. A nice illustration of the fun the leaderwriters had at the expense of the signatories of the Manifesto is contained in an extract from *The Times*, quoted by Coats (1964, p. 99), where the spectacle is conjured up 'of these fourteen dervishes emerging from their caves and chanting in solemn procession their venerable incantations against the rising tide of inquiry' adding 'A more scientific conception of their own science . . . would save professors from the painful discovery that they convince nobody who stands in need of conviction'.

[12] The statement signed by 364 economists, including most of the chief economic advisers who had served post-war British governments, was sent (unsolicited) to the Prime Minister and the Chancellor of the Exchequer and appeared in *The Times* and other leading national newspapers on 30 March 1981. It proclaimed the conviction of the signatories that:

> There is no basis in economic theory or supporting evidence for the Government's belief that by deflating demand they will bring inflation permanently under control and thereby induce an automatic recovery in output and employment. Present policies will deepen the depression, erode the industrial base of our economy and threaten its social and political stability. There are alternative policies; and the time has come to reject monetarist policies and consider urgently which alternative offers the best hope of sustained economic recovery.

In 1981 as in 1903, however, those who practised the art of political economy were unimpressed by the collective authority of academic economists.

[13] See Wood (1980) for a detailed discussion of the nature and extent of the revisions.

[14] He summarises the 'partial theoretical solution' thus: '. . . the keynote of our main argument was that the country B whose goods were taxed would seek other

markets for them, until they had risen in value in the taxing country A sufficiently to throw nearly the whole burden of the tax on the consumer' (Marshall, 1926, p. 399).

[15] Marshall Library Large Brown Box, item 24. See also Maloney (1985, pp. 36–37) for a discussion of Marshall's 'habitual indecisiveness on political questions' and for further quotations from this draft preface.

[16] The Prime Minister actually circulated two documents on fiscal policy for discussion at the Cabinet meeting of 13 August. The other (generally referred to as the 'Blue Paper') was closer to Chamberlain's views and raised more powerful and explosive opposition. So Balfour abandoned it. See Gollin (1965) for a detailed account of the Prime Minister's abortive efforts to hold his Cabinet together.

[17] The obituary was originally published in *Economic Journal*, vol. 40, June 1930 and is reprinted in Keynes (1972, Ch. 7).

[18] Here Keynes refers to Pigou's hasty letter to *The Times* in response to the publication of *Economic Notes* (Keynes, 1972, p. 44).

[19] 'Here again one feels—beginning with Balfour's sentence "we must now accept the fact that the most advanced of our commercial rivals are not only protectionist now, but in varying measure are going to remain so" and Marshall's comment, "not certain"—that the statesman's prevision of the subsequent course of commercial and industrial policy had proved more correct' (Keynes, 1972, p. 45).

[20] Marshall (1919), Appendix D, English Mercantilists and Adam Smith; Appendix E, The British Movement towards Free Trade; Appendix F, The Zollverein; and Appendix G, Early Industrial Conditions and Fiscal Policies of the United States.

# Bibliography

Amery, J. (1951), 'Joseph Chamberlain and the tariff reform campaign', in vol. 4 of J. L. Garvin and J. Amery, *Life of Joseph Chamberlain*, London: Macmillan, in six volumes, 1932–69.

Balfour, A. J. (1903), *Economic Notes on Insular Free Trade*, London: Longman Green.

Brentano, L. (1903), 'The proposed reversal of English commercial policy', *The Fortnightly Review*, vol. 74.

Coats, A. W. (1964), 'The role of authority in the development of British economics', *Journal of Law and Economics*, vol. 7.

Coats, A. W. (1968), 'Political economy and the tariff reform campaign of 1903', *Journal of Law and Economics*, vol. 17.

Fawcett, H. (1878), *Free Trade and Protection: An Inquiry into the Causes which have Retarded the General Adoption of Free Trade since its Introduction into England*, London: Macmillan.

Gollin, A. (1965), *Balfour's Burden: Arthur Balfour and Imperial Preference*, London: Anthony Blond.

Gonce, R. A. (1982), 'Alfred Marshall on industrial organization: from *Principles of Economics* to *Industry and Trade*', in Wood, 1982, vol. 4, no. 123.

Hewins, W. A. S. (1903), 'The present state of the case for Mr Chamberlain's policy', *The Fortnightly Review*, vol. 74.

Hewins, W. A. S. (1929), *The Apologia of an Imperialist*, London: Constable.

Keynes, J. M. (1972) [1933], Alfred Marshall, 1842–1924, *Essays in Biography*. Reprinted in D. Moggridge, ed., *Collected Writings of John Maynard Keynes*, London: Macmillan for the Royal Economic Society, vol. 10.

Maloney, J. (1985), *Marshall, Orthodoxy and the Professionalisation of Economics*, Cambridge: Cambridge University Press.

Marshall, A. (1890), 'Some aspects of competition', the Section F Presidential address to the Leeds meeting of the British Association for the Advancement of Science, reprinted in Pigou, 1925, pp. 256–91.

Marshall, A. (1903), *Memorandum on Fiscal Policy of International Trade*, published 1908 as House of Commons Paper no. 321; reprinted in Marshall (1926).

Marshall, A. (1923) [1919], *Industry and Trade*, London: Macmillan, fifth edition.

Marshall, A. (1926), *Official Papers by Alfred Marshall*, London: Macmillan for the Royal Economic Society.

Marshall, A. (1929) [1923], *Money, Credit and Commerce*, London: Macmillan.

Marshall, A. (1949), *Principles of Economics*, London: Macmillan, eighth edition, reset and with a comparative index of new and old page settings.

McCready, H. W. (1955), 'Alfred Marshall and tariff reform, 1903: some unpublished letters', *Journal of Political Economy*, vol. 63, pp. 259–67. Reprinted in Wood, 1982, vol. 4, no. 100.

Pigou, A. C., ed. (1925), *Memorials of Alfred Marshall*, London: Macmillan.

Whitaker, J. K., ed. (1975), *The Early Economics Writings of Alfred Marshall 1867–1890*, London: Macmillan for the Royal Economic Society, two volumes.

Wood, J. C., (1980), 'Alfred Marshall and the tariff reform campaign of 1903', *Journal of Law and Economics*, vol. 23, pp. 481–95. Reprinted in Wood, 1982, vol. 4, no. 122.

Wood, J. C., ed. (1982), *Alfred Marshall: Critical Assessments*, London: Croom Helm, four volumes.

# 7. The spread of Alfred Marshall's economics in Italy, 1885–1925 *

*Mauro Gallegati*

## I. Introduction*

At the beginning of the 20th century the Italian school of economics found itself in a somewhat privileged situation. While Cambridge and Lausanne were the headquarters of partial and general analysis, the *circus* of Vienna was developing the imputation theory, and French and German economists were principally occupied with the theory of cycles and economic history, Italy was at the cross-roads of the new trends. First Pantaleoni and De Viti De Marco, then Mazzola, Pareto and Barone made up the theoretical nucleus of that Italian school which at the time, as Schumpeter (1954, p. 855) says, 'was second to none' in the world.

This is the story of the diffusion of Marshallian theory in Italy from 1885 to 1925. These dates, as ever in such cases, are mere signposts whose choice was dictated by the publication, respectively, of the first review of one of Marshall's works by Dalla Volta, and of the well known essay by Sraffa on the relation between cost and quantity produced. Between these two dates, Marshall's theory spread steadily in Italy and in the years 1904–1912 the Pareto school was formed. The conflicts and compromises between these two expressions of marginalism, which had no counterpart elsewhere in the world, are a main reference of this research. Although Marshall's approach was emphasised, it was set into the frame of reference of the general equilibrium school. This was not only a result of the tendency of some of the 'Italian' interpretations of Marshall to relate the contribution of the *Principles* to that of Walras' *Elements d'économie politique pure*, but also of the particular Italian interest in abstract themes.

* I wish to thank G. Becattini, T. Cozzi, R. Faucci, S. Perri and J. K.Whitaker for their most useful comments. I benefited from the financial support of the Fondazione 'Luigi Einaudi' of Turin.

After a discussion in Section II of pre-Marshallian marginalism in the period 1875–1890, we shall analyse in Section III the contribution of Pantaleoni, the criticisms of the new school and the reception given to the *Principles*. Section IV is dedicated to Pareto, in which the gradual distancing from Marshall under the influence of the Walrasian school is highlighted. The contribution of Barone and, more generally, those of other followers of Marshallian pure theory are highlighted in the following sections. Sraffa's essay is examined in the final section.

## II. Pre-Marshall marginalism

As Barucci (1972) has demonstrated in his essay on the diffusion of marginalism in Italy, starting from 1874 the spread of marginalist ideas was principally due to Walras. However, the attempt to introduce marginalism failed because of the lack of understanding of his correspondents, Errera and Boccardo, and the aversion to mathematical methods on the part of the economists of the *laissez-faire* school.

Around 1875, Italian economists found themselves divided into two schools, which can be defined according to their adoption or not of protectionist policy. On one side we find authors like Scialoja, Lampertico, Luzzati and Cossa who attack the *laissez-faire* principles; on the other are the supporters of Francesco Ferrara, loyal to Smithian doctrine. The new marginalist school entered with extraordinary timing into this climate of heated debate thanks to the translation of Jevons' *Theory of Political Economy* and Walras' *Theorie mathématique de la richesse social,* both published in 1874 in the third series of the 'Biblioteca dell'Economista'. The reception given to these works was rather lukewarm; suffice to recall that Messedaglia, an authoritative exponent of the application of mathematics to political economics, found Walras' contribution 'lacking in innovation'. This was in part due to the chance nature of the publication and to the fact that such essays were presented as the 'application of mathematics to economics', causing their almost instinctive rejection by the followers of the Ferrara school.[1] In this light it is not surprising that the works of Marshall which preceded the *Principles* were almost unknown; there were some exceptions but, notwithstanding the attempts at diffusion by Pantaleoni and Dalla Volta, it is unlikely that Marshall's works became known to the majority of Italian economists until the *Principles of Economics* became available.

Although Italian economists were introduced to marginalism at an early stage, they had to wait for the essays of Pantaleoni to gain an adequate understanding of Jevon's theory. Furthermore, Walras was assimilated only after the appearance of Pareto's works and his popularity was in decline, and Menger was almost unknown. It was only after 1890 that marginalism became the dominant economic school in Italy, thanks to the 'second phase' of its introduction with Antonelli and Pantaleoni's theory of value. After this date Marshall, through Pantaleoni's work, and Walras, through Pareto's, became the seers of the 'new economics'.

This was the situation when Dalla Volta published the first Italian review of one of Marshall's works in October of 1885 (Dalla Volta, 1885).[2] The author of this brief review comments on Marshall's 'uncommon cogency of argument', and though affirming that he does not share all of Marshall's views, clearly appreciates the concept of economic theory 'not as a body of concrete truths, but as a means of discovering concrete truths'. Thus the relationship between Marshall and the Italian economists was established.

The period between the publication of this review and 1900, with the works of Pantaleoni, Barone, De Viti, Mazzola and Pareto, sees the first Italian contributions of an international standard since the time of Ferrara. It also sees the diffusion of the marginalist method into every sector of economics, even if real 'success' for the school was delayed until the first years of the new century.

## III. When marginalism became 'the' economics: the *Principii* of Pantaleoni

Pantaleoni's *Principii di economia pura* was published in 1889. The feature that characterises the *Principii*, in relation to Pantaleoni's previous production, is the presence of Marshall's theory despite his continuing high regard for Jevons. He had been able to consult Marshall's two essays on *Pure Theory* (1879) and to reproduce the diagrams contained in them in his *Principii*.[3]

With the publication of the *Principles* imminent and given the esteem in which he held the Italian economist, Marshall was able to look at these early writings 'with a more relaxed attitude' (Whitaker, 1975, vol. 1, p. 107). The way in which Marshall's *Pure Theory* was used in the *Principii* emerges from the correspondence between

Pantaleoni and Walras. The Italian economist, replying to Walras who found 'assez singulier' the private publication of these essays, states that 'Marshall imprime ses leçons lorsqu'il était très malade et probablement ne croyait plus de pouvoir vivre. Je n'en suis servi seulement après avoir vu M. Edgeworth s'en servir dans sa *Mathematical Psychics*. Alors je lui en ai demandé la permission' (Walras, 1965, vol. 2, p. 323).

The *Principii* constitute a linear and consistent development of the application of the ideas of marginalism to the Benthamite hedonistic principle. The book opens with a statement concerning the application of hedonistic premises to the 'vision' of the classics. In fact, Pantaleoni maintains that 'economic science consists of the laws of wealth, systematically deducted from the hypotheses that men are motivated to act exclusively by the desire to attain the greatest possible satisfaction of their needs with the least possible individual sacrifice'. The context from which the passage is taken reveals, however, how this statement must be read in the light of Marshall's inaugural lecture (Pigou, 1925, pp. 152–74), which assigns to economics the role of a science that studies needs and not, as in Smith, the wealth of nations.

Thanks to Pantaleoni, Marshall became the most authoritative and popular representative of the new school in Italy. As well as interpreting Marshall's contribution as a conciliation between the classical school and marginalism, Pantaleoni attributed to partial analysis a fundamental role in the interpretation of the facts revealed by empirical evidence, that the analytical rigour of Walras' method could not succeed in encompassing. With the new century, the criticism of marginalism abated whilst the contrast widened inside the new school between the Marshallian theory and that of Walras and Pareto. The Austrian synthesis of ideas fell gradually into disfavour, especially with the revision of the concept of hedonism by Pareto, and the progress guided by Einaudi and Montemartini, towards De Viti's financial theory of production.

Though Marshall's *Principles* did not meet with the extraordinary success seen in the Anglo-Saxon countries, it was immediately circulated in Italy, thanks to Pantaleoni's, Cossa's, and Dalla Volta's interest in English authors. This latter, as we have seen, had favourably reviewed Marshall's production, but the review article of the *Principles* (Dalla Volta, 1890) is characterised by its timing and the comparison with the works of Jevons. After briefly 'introducing' Marshall (successor to Fawcett at Cambridge, author of an 'elementary treatise', *The Economics of Industry*, of numerous studies of value and of monetary questions), Dalla Volta states that the *Principles* is 'superior . . . to the great number of pieces published in the last 20 years in England' and to the abstract continental formulations. He also points out how the principal merit of the volume consists in its presentation of an effective synthesis, a reconciliation between the two new schools of economics, 'he contrives to wed classical economics with the school of Jevons and Menger–Böhm'. The review closes with the observation that Marshall abandons the distinction between normal and market value used in the *Economics of Industry*. Dalla Volta, whilst not explicitly linking this change to Marshall's new conception of competition, correctly subjects normal value to the influence of time rather than to that of competition: we read in the *Principles* that 'normal value does not mean competitive' (Marshall, 1890, p. 347).

## IV. The discreet charm of general equilibrium: Pareto's intellectual progression

The fundamental role played by Pantaleoni in the affirmation of marginalism was not completed with the *Principii*, with the work done as editor of the *Giornale degli Economisti* or by his spreading of Marshall's message, but is also evident in Pareto's 'conversion' to neoclassical doctrine. In this section we shall trace Pareto's scientific *iter* in the years from 1891 to the publication of the *Cours d'économie politique*, 1897. This will allow us to analyse his 'vision' of the relationship between partial and general equilibrium, which was later to be adopted by the economists closest to Pareto.

The story has a clear starting-point: Pantaleoni's *Principii*. In a series of letters, written between July and October 1891, Pareto revealed to Pantaleoni that he harboured some doubts about the theory of marginal utility. In his own words, there existed 'no experimental proof that in exchanges the utility curves have a form analogous to those' found in the *Principii* (Pareto, 1960, vol. 1, p. 46). Even admitting the relation between experimental behaviour and abstract theory, once one wishes to effect comparisons between the utility of different individuals, difficulties arise which may be only overcome by postulating the existence of an absolute level of utility. In fact, this consideration hides doubts which are of a methodological nature, founded on the criticism of the neoclassical hypothesis of *homo economicus*. This 'logical abstraction' does not correspond, for Pareto, to the real behaviour of individuals, and brings with it the risk of pushing aside the experimental method of investigation as the basis for the formulation of economic theories. Discussion with Walras did not persuade him to change his mind: 'Walras does not see'—Pareto writes to Pantaleoni—'any soundness in anything apart from the mathematical method . . . whilst for me any method is good if it brings us nearer to the truth' (ibid., vol. 1, p. 58).

The definitive acceptance of the mathematical method and of the principle of equimarginality was intimately connected with the recognition of the accuracy of the methods of Marshall and Walras. At this point—November 1891—Pareto had not yet detected any significant difference between the two systems—as is revealed by a letter of thanks to Pantaleoni for sending him the second edition of Marshall's *Principles* (ibid., vol. 1, p. 67).

The fact that Pareto began to distinguish the peculiar qualities of each method was due to an analysis of the debate between Walras and Auspitz and Lieben. He noted certain differences between partial and general equilibrium, but seemed to attribute them more to a differing degree of approximation to empirical evidence, or to the academic rivalry between Marshall and Walras, than to substantial methodological divergences. Walras 'insists a great deal on his differing opinions with Auspitz and Lieben, because, in his view, one must take into account the prices of all goods. Theoretically he is right but it would no longer be practically possible to solve any problem' (ibid., vol. 1, p. 195).

Pareto's comment and his initial valuation of Marshall's system as an interpretation of empirical evidence are directed to the application of the theoretical system. This is certainly a subject of central importance but corresponds more closely to the research of Auspitz and Lieben than that of Marshall. It is in fact possible to gain the impression, from numerous passages in the *Principles*, that the *coeteris paribus* method essentially constitutes an approximation useful for analysing theoretical problems rather than real issues. This interpretation was to enjoy great favour in the Italian school and would become one of the bases for the development of the first research projects in applied economics as well as for the use of both Marshall's system and at times that of Walras (duly modified), in the study of empirical questions.

Pareto thus connects 'applicable' economics to the analysis of partial equilibrium, through the concept of the constancy of marginal utility of money. The criticism of Marshall's system, levelled directly by way of the dispute with Auspitz in 1892–1893, centres indeed on the theoretical admissibility of this instrument. According to Pareto and Walras, Marshall, like Auspitz and Lieben, confused the price curve with that of total utility. It is clear that if, like Pareto, one does not fully comprehend the reasons for the use of this instrument of economic analysis, the next step is necessarily to impute the existence of this hypothesis to the absence of a clear concept of economic equilibrium. In this way equilibrium can only be general and Pareto considers himself justified in asserting:

> I think Edgeworth is right in saying that there are profound differences between the schools of Cambridge and Lausanne. Marshall has not yet succeeded in understanding economic equilibrium. He merely translates the old ideas into modern language. In this way he has translated Ricardo's notions on rent. The ideas of Walras have enabled economics to take a giant step forward, whilst Marshall has added nothing of great note to our understanding (ibid., vol. 1, p. 417).

Partly through the good offices of Pantaleoni, Pareto became professor at the University of Lausanne in 1893, succeeding Walras. Pareto's move away from the themes of Marshall did not immediately produce a systematic criticism of Marshall's theory. An examination of the correspondence between Pareto and Pantaleoni reveals that the latter was a confirmed defender of Marshall, and analysis of the debate between the two will help us to clarify their approach to the question of equilibrium.

Pantaleoni maintains that Marshall and Pareto, like Edgeworth and Walras, do not have different 'visions' of the economic system. Their principal diversification lies in the degree of approximation; Pareto replies to this review with a letter in February 1897, in which he affirms that he has 'little or nothing' in common with Marshall since the latter ignores the very concept of equilibrium. Pantaleoni only partially accepts the objections of Pareto, making a distinction between the Marshall–Edgeworth approach and that of Walras–Pareto. However, in a review published in April of the same year, he reiterates that 'the fundamental concept of the doctrine of Pareto, is also that of Walras and of Marshall, and of all those who have understood what economic equilibrium means' (Pantaleoni, 1897, p. 365).

Pantaleoni would repeat the same declaration ten years later, insisting on associating Pareto and Marshall as 'leaders' in the area of general equilibrium. It was then that Pareto declared, after having repeated how distant his position was from that of the English economist: 'I don't know why you put me with Marshall. I do not share a single idea of Marshall's. If he says yes I say no, and vice versa' (Pareto, 1960, vol. 2, p. 63). He also listed a series of points of difference between his theory and that of the *Principles*. It ranges from the demand schedule to the constant marginal utility of money, from social laws to collective goods to the superior nobility of collective, as opposed to private, use of wealth. And to Pantaleoni who objects: 'Is it possible to maintain that Marshall is not aware of interdependence?', Pareto replies in the affirmative. In his view, Marshall breaks up general equilibrium into so many partial equilibria; while the true progress of science in general, and of economics in particular, consists of the exact opposite: that of substituting a general vision for a partial one.

Pantaleoni's defence of Marshall does not imply a flat modelling of his own analysis on that of the English economist, as is demonstrated by the former's construction of a 'dynamic' nucleus of pure theory and the formulation of a 'connected costs' hypothesis. Suffice to recall that the Italian economist saw in Marshall a 'new Ricardo',[4] albeit flawed by 'factiousness' for his continuing ignorance of Pareto's work. But this may perhaps be considered an aspect of the 'insularism' of the English economists about which, as early as 1896, Pareto had complained to Edgeworth (ibid., vol. 3, p. 400).

In 1897 the second volume of the *Cours* was published, completing the first stage of Pareto's theoretical research and, at the same time, marking the start of a new period in which the author gradually separated Walras' analytical formulations from his own. It was also the period in which Marshall's ideas, thanks to Pantaleoni and Barone, came to constitute the most popular marginalist stream in Italy, while a school which in some ways took on the characteristics of a sect came to be formed around Pareto.

## V. 'Centres of influence' and the Barone story

There was no Pantaleoni school, at least not in the accepted sense of the word. Pantaleoni was not the leader of a group of scholars who developed and illustrated the theorems constructed by their master, as was the case with Marshall at Cambridge. This peculiarity must be considered when evaluating the influence exercised by Marshall's economics in Italy; though it possessed an authoritative point of reference in Pantaleoni, it depended mainly on individual contributions. In fact, it is possible to identify two distinct centres of influence that housed the major exponents of Marshallian economics—the Roman school headed by Pantaleoni and Barone, and that in Milan and Turin, near the 'Laboratorio'.[5]

In Rome, Pantaleoni, Barone and Ricci showed themselves to be particularly sensitive to the themes of general equilibrium, which they attempted to 'simplify' with the tools suggested by Marshall. To the aforementioned we may also add Fanno, who taught at Genoa. Pantaleoni and Fanno tried to reconcile the classical school with Marshall, while at the same time Barone and Ricci were trying to do so with Marshall and the Walras–Pareto approach. The difference between these two efforts is certainly not marginal, but it must be noted that unlike the Turin school both groups used the same methodology.

Meanwhile in Turin, Einaudi, Jannaccone, Prato, Sella, and in part, Nitti and Cabiati, were Marshallian in their economic analysis and positivist in methodology. The influence of the 'Laboratorio' must be remembered with respect to the evolutionary concept of economics based on biology, which finds an authoritative legitimisation in the fourth edition of the *Principles*. Thus Jannaccone, in his Introduction to the Italian edition of this work, can highlight precisely this continuity of Marshall's thought (and of economic reality), which 'has not the nature of a radical overthrowing of the old doctrines, nor that of a change of method . . . but simply of a more comprehensive penetration into human nature and into social institutions, due to the widening of our scientific horizon through the influence of biological studies' (Jannacone, 1905, p. 53).[6] Though they reach the same conclusion as the 'Roman' group with regard to the interpretation of Marshall, the Turin economists put more emphasis on the idea of an organic rather than a mechanical development of economic forces, a theory susceptible to rigorous analysis through systems of equations but too 'mechanistic' to constitute a profitable analysis of empirical evidence. The most representative choice in this respect was made by Einaudi.

Einaudi seems to consider general equilibrium to be an overly 'cerebral' construction, and this not simply because of his poor command of the necessary mathematic tools. It is a different conception of economic modelling which leads Einaudi towards Marshall's viewpoint, partly because of the relative facility of application of *ceteris paribus*, which allowed one to emphasise only the most significant relationships. This does not, however, prevent him from considering general equilibrium a constant 'admonition' which must always be taken into account and which, in certain cases, may constitute the essential reference of the theory.

In the absence of a school, the propagation of Marshall's ideas depended not only on the work of these two 'centres of influence' but also on the widespread diffusion of the *Principles*, on the co-operation between Pantaleoni and Edgeworth, and on a bare minimum of academic contacts with Marshall himself.

If Pantaleoni's teaching, principally understood to be a 'reconciliation' between classical and marginalist theory, met with a certain degree of success, a real diffusion of Marshall's methods was only achieved through Barone's writings. Schumpeter (1954, p. 858), bemoaning the lack of attention paid by Italian economists to Barone, recalls that fundamental contributions in at least four sectors of economic analysis may be attributed to Barone: (*a*) the comparison between static and dynamic theory; (*b*) the theory of production and distribution; (*c*) the analysis of collective economics; and (*d*) his essays on finance.

Between March and June 1894 the *Economic Journal* was host to a debate between Nicholson and Edgeworth on the theory of consumer's rent. Nicholson asserted the uselessness and technical limitation of this concept which may be inferred only from one particular unjustified premise: the constancy of the marginal utility of money. In September of the same year, Barone, with an essay on this dispute, demonstrated the correctness of Marshall and Edgeworth's position illustrating how 'the calculation of consumer's rent carried out on the assumption of a constant marginal utility is not only extremely useful' (Barone, 1894, p. 412), but also theoretically correct. In a letter informing Walras of the imminent publication of this essay, Barone maintains that he is in a position to pouvoir bientot démontrer . . . que l'exactitude de votre manière de traiter la question de la demande et de l'offre ne porte aucunement à la conséquence que la méthode est inexacte. Marshall vise à des solutions approximatives ayant regard au fait dynamique correspondant à des petites variations des prix; . . . la votre est la solution exacte, la sienne est la solution approximative. Mais votre incrément total d'utilité ne diffère de celui de Marshall que d'une quantité de deuxiéme ordre (Walras, 1965, vol. 2, p. 616).

Comparing Marshall's and Walras' positions, Barone is able to demonstrate that the differences between the total utilities of the curves would only emerge when considering quantities of secondary importance. The theory of a constant marginal ophelimity of money is thus for Barone only an 'ingenious device' that does not alter the results in any substantial way, since these differences are in fact 'of secondary importance'. These conclusions reinforce his views of several months earlier about the application of 'consumer's rent' to finance, and contributed to Barone's opening a new area of research, with an essay in the same year on dynamic analysis.

Barone therefore justifies, within the limits of Marshallian hypotheses, the legitimacy of the consumer's rent theory and its potential usefulness in financial and dynamic applications. Having recognised the greater general relevance of Walras' theory, he maintains that, when dealing with dynamic problems, it is necessary to simplify the systems by the extensive use of Marshallian procedures. These, if interpreted and applied in the right way 'as the nearest approximation of dynamic phenomena, are not only theoretically correct, but also very useful in a practical sense' (Barone, 1894, p. 416), since the complicated 'calculation' that derives from Walras' entire system of equations, could be avoided without altering the results in any significant way.

The second and third points described by Schumpeter did not cause any extended debate. For the theory of production we may, however, recall a relevant development and a criticism. The criticism came from Labriola (1900),[7] on the road to conversion from Marxist analysis to pure theory—who points out, *à la* Hobson, the futility of the question as to whether or not each factor of production receives what it has produced, since it is impossible to attribute a profit quota to each of the 'factors involved in productive cooperation'. The development is found in two works published by Montemartini (1899a, 1899b),[8] who takes up and 'vulgarises' the results obtained by Barone, combining them with those of Clark, and taking into account Hobson's comments.

## VI. Between Marshall and Walras: further contributions to equilibrium theory, 1900–1920

In the years from the publication of the *Principles* to that of *Industry and Trade*, Italian economists published the results of research on theoretical themes which, unlike Jha's conclusions (1963) about English economics in the time of Marshall, did not always show an immediate affinity with empirical evidence. At least nine areas of research may be identified, in order of importance: (*a*) the theory of imperfect competition, monopoly and duopoly; (*b*) dynamic analysis; (*c*) reconciliation between Marxism and marginalism; (*d*) the theory of 'connected' prices; (*e*) analysis of supply and demand curves; (*f*) applications of the theory of income to particular cases; (*g*) the theory of international trade; (*h*) the theory of distribution based on marginal productivity and, finally (*i*) the economic theory of collectivism. This copious production of studies which, apart from areas (*g*) and (*h*), occurred almost entirely after 1900, came after a series of criticism regarding the new economics made between 1890 and 1902. After the turn of the new century this criticism became increasingly feeble, while the marginalist school began to cover all sectors of economic life. We will review the areas (*c*) and (*d*), in which Italian contributions were highly innovative.

Between the two theories of equilibrium, the Italians strove to find an intermediate solution: a theory of 'connected prices'. In his *Lezioni di economia pura* (1904), Pantaleoni illustrates the concept of 'families of goods', for the identification of which it is necessary to recognise five main relationships: instrumentality, complementarity, substitution, competition and joint production. It is evident that these relationships between goods, corresponding to the cases listed by Marshall in Note XXI of the Mathematical Appendix of the *Principles*, enable the partial consideration of the supply and demand of goods, as function of a single price, to be abandoned. At the same time, they only permit the description of the strongest links between goods, without arriving at the Pareto–Walras version, which is certainly more general, but difficult to apply. This theory identifies a sector of collaboration between the two versions of equilibrium on which the Italian tradition would work at length demonstrating 'that the comprehensive but gaunt and colourless idea of the universal interdependence . . . can be brought home and made alive to the many by means of concrete cases about the relations between the values of "competing" or "completing" commodities' (Schumpeter, 1954, p. 996).

The most analytically rigorous example consists of two contributions by Fanno (1914, 1926) on joint-cost supply and on substitute goods. In these works the author, bearing in mind the pronouncements of Pantaleoni and, above all, of Barone on the compatibility of the systems of Marshall and Walras, analyses the functional relationship between the various families of goods. After recognising the analytical rigour of Pareto's formalisation, Fanno then identifies in this excessive degree of abstraction the practical limitation of the general equilibrium theory. This limitation should not however lead to a return to the old theories on the causality of the relationship of value, nor to an 'extensive' application of Marshall's hypothesis of the constant marginal utility of money. It is therefore necessary to locate and analyse only the relationships 'of primary importance' between various goods; one must split up the system of correlations between prices into groups or categories, and then proceed to study each one separately. Fanno thus identifies four main 'groups': (*a*) combined products; (*b*) complementary products; (*c*) rivals with regard to production and (*d*) rivals with regard to demand. Only groups (*a*) and (*b*) are covered in his monograph, but he does establish the basis for 'an organic theory that covers all the facts and puts them down to a single informing principle' (Fanno, 1914, p. 11).

Last but not least, the Italian contribution to the reconciliation between Marxism and marginalism should be considered. In this field Italy demonstrates some rather peculiar elements, basing the reconciliation between the two schools on a renunciation of the quantitative aspect of Marx's doctrine—that is, the theory that labour prices of production are based on the quantity of labour necessary— regardless of the criticism of the opposing school, and preserving a qualitative analysis of the relationship in the production process. In synthesis, we might say that while the 'neoricardians' found themselves more in agreement with Marshall, whose 'genetic' connection with Ricardo they emphasise, the hedonistic Marxists, like Labriola and Leone,[9] adopted Walras' view. Especially for the latter, it was necessary that Marxism be 'reduced' to microeconomics, contrary to the 'aggregate' approach of the most authoritative Marx–Marshallian, Graziadei. Leone, in fact, in a manner similar to that of most of the

Italian revisers of Marxism, had as his main objective the safeguarding of the Marxist category of exploitation above and beyond the theory of labour-value. He combined, in a microeconomic system, Loria's theory of a monopsonist labour market with the disappearance of consumer's rent in the context of a general equilibrium, reaching an analysis of 'exploitation' similar to that which would later be formalised by Pigou (Leone, 1909).

In 1899, after analysing the mechanism of production and the distribution of a surplus in a macroeconomic vision, Graziadei[10] introduced Marshall's apparatus of distribution in order to analyse the division between the individual units of production. The unsatisfactory result of this work does not affect the analysis of the cycle, which Graziadei derived by mixing Marx and Marshall's hypotheses and, above all, by constructing one of the most effective examples of the application of *ceteris paribus* to an empirical situation (Graziadei, 1909).

## VII. On the extent of Marshall's contribution to pure theory: the criticism of Sraffa (and other considerations in conclusion)

By the time *Industry and Trade* (1919) and *Money, Credit and Commerce* (1923) were published, the diffusion of Marshallism in Italy had already passed its peak. At the end of the 1920s, the Pareto school constituted the major component of marginalism, and, soon after, Sraffa was to contribute to the further removal of *ceteris paribus* from pure economics.

Furthermore, the considerable delay that marked the publication of nearly all Marshall's works was even more marked in the case of these final contributions, so that their theoretical content was already widely known at the time of publication. In the absence of the innovative spark required for epoch-making work, they did not stimulate any debate other than the recurrence of old arguments over the many controversial elements that accompanied the spread of Marshall's message. The numerous reviews 'limited' themselves therefore to pointing out the peculiar character of *Industry and Trade*, midway between theory and economic history, and the 'original' formulation of already known doctrines like that of money and the credit cycle, given in *Money, Credit and Commerce*.

Sraffa's criticism (1925, 1926) on the relationship between costs and quantity produced did not cause the 'devastating' effect in Italy that it would have caused in England. The explanation, now banal in the light of what has been said, is that unlike the situation at Cambridge, there was no 'Marshallian dictatorship' in Italy. There are, however, other less obvious reasons for the lack of scandal at Sraffa's comments, which may be attributed to a sort of Italian tradition on the issues of 'empty economic boxes' and on the controversy regarding increasing returns and perfect competition. Moreover, Sraffa's very demonstration of the theoretical inadmissibility of *ceteris paribus* was prompted by Barone's comments and by the criticisms of Ricci. Both the connection between variable returns and 'economic boxes', and that between increasing returns and perfect competition are illustrated in two essays by Pantaleoni (1889, 1904), to whom the Italian school traditionally makes constant reference. Thus, after highlighting the Italian contributions to these two controversies *ante litteram*, we shall then analyse the sources and the extent of Sraffa's criticism.

In the *Principii,* Pantaleoni identifies the origin of the laws of production with technical limits of the production itself. He recalls two classic laws: Smith's division of labour and Ricardo's law of decreasing returns. Having done this, Pantaleoni is able to limit the law of increasing returns to the manufacturing sector and the other to agriculture. According to Pantaleoni, these laws do not contradict each other but, rather, produce cost curves which first decrease and then increase. Because of the particular hypothesis about the curves, no firms would be able to produce at decreasing costs along the curve for an indefinite interval. Once he had assumed the temporary nature of decreasing curves, he no longer had the problem of reconciling perfect competition and increasing returns and moved on to identify products according to the various laws.

But not all industries obey the general law Pantaleoni identified. It is entirely possible, as Jannaccone pointed out in 1914, to find industries which, regardless of the sector, work for periods which are not well defined into operative intervals, under conditions of decreasing costs. After making an effective distinction between the increase-decrease of average and marginal costs along lines similar to those made years later by Sraffa, he asserts that 'production with increasing or decreasing costs is not the prerogative of certain industries and certain categories of goods, . . . but a moment in the life of every firm, no matter what industry it belongs to or the type of goods it produces' (Jannaccone, 1914, p. 102).

This aspect of 'a moment in the life of every firm' would later be examined in greater depth by Foa (1928), who proposed an interpretation according to which it is necessary to abandon the traditional distinction between increasing and decreasing costs, redefining these categories. Once the existence of an 'ideal' amount of production has been established, in which the value of the net marginal product is the same for all resources, and which corresponds to the case of constant returns, Foa recognises 'a relative difference' of a temporal nature between firms which have or have not reached their 'ideal' conditions. The increasing or decreasing returns are thus brought within the 'temporal cycles' that each industry passes through, going from the first to the second in shorter or longer periods for manufacturing industries or agriculture respectively. As Marshall says in the preface to the *Principles*, 'the element of Time . . . is the centre of the chief difficulty of almost every economic problem' (Marshall, 1890, p. vii).

In a letter to J. M. Keynes 6 June 1926, Sraffa wrote: 'I tried to demonstrate that Marshall's assumptions are compatible, in general, only with constant returns . . . . This conclusion was misunderstood as if it implied that constant returns prevail in real life'.[11] In the English essay of 1926, the criticism of the cost-quantities relation is obscured by the analysis of imperfect competition. In 1925, Sraffa criticised two questions internal to marginalist theory. The first, the *ceteris paribus* method, is a peculiarity of the Marshallian approach. The other, the functional link between costs and quantities, is common to both of the versions of neoclassical analysis.

Already in the *Principii*, Pantaleoni asserted the strong relationship between the production level and change in marginal costs, but the variability of returns, he suggested, is a consequence of the hypothesis illustrated above. In fact, if the *ceteris paribus* method is not used, the change in the costs of some industries will influence the structure of costs for the whole system. Such incoherence was not pointed out until Barone's essays on dynamic questions (Barone, 1894). He emphasised Marshall's theoretical mistake concerning supply curves of products, although he maintained the demand curve hypothesis which is based upon the same principles. Sraffa asserted that one cannot adopt the *ceteris paribus* method as an instrument approximate to pure theory to empirical evidence. Instead, he maintains that

that hypothesis is absurd and contradictory to the previous hypotheses, as the increase in the production of a product leads to an increase in cost which has equal importance for that product as for others of that group: so much so that one cannot take it into consideration in the first case and overlook its implication for the others (Sraffa, 1925, p. 212).

Italian economists did not exhaustively consider Sraffa's criticism, but it signalled the end of the innovative moment initiated by the *Principles*. The movement survived in several contributions until the growing importance of cyclical movements, accelerated by the 1929 crash, 'corporativism' and, later, the Keynesian revolution brought to a close the period in which 'all Italian economists turned to the study of special problems postulating *ceteris paribus*' (Einaudi, 1980, p. 104).

## Notes and references

[1] Representative of this position is Martello (1912) who considered Marshall an 'intruder' into the mathematical school.

[2] Dalla Volta was editor of *L'Economista* and Professor of Economics at the University of Florence.

[3] The *Pure Theory* is used by Pantaleoni in the paragraphs devoted to the problem of the (in)stability of positions of equilibrium.

[4] In a letter to F.Y. Edgeworth, preserved at Nuffield College, Oxford, Pantaleoni writes on 15 Nov. 1890: 'I think and say you are the closest approximation of a match for Marshall living in England. You know that to my mind, Marshall is simply a new Ricardo who has appeared in the field'.

[5] The 'Laboratorio di economia politica' was established in Turin in 1893 by S. Cognetti De Martiis. It was a postgraduate centre for the study of empirical evidence with a positivist methodology. Among its students were Jannaccone, Einaudi and Graziadei.

[6] Pasquale Jannaccone (1872–1959) was one of the most eminent Marshallians in Italy. Editor of the 'Biblioteca dell'Economista' and of *La Riforma sociale*, he was Professor of Economics in Siena, Padua and Turin.

[7] Arturo Labriola (1873–1959) was a leading political figure of the socialist movement in Italy. Minister of Labour in Giolitti's government, he was a minor figure in the Italian revision of Marxism.

[8] Giovanni Montemartini (1867–1913) was a scholar of public finance. He was a follower of the Austrian school's doctrine which he tried to compromise with Marx's theory of exploitation.

[9] Enrico Leone (1875–1940) was a follower of Sorel's 'revolutionary unionism'. Editor of *Il Divenire Sociale* and *L'Azione* he was Professor of Economics in Rome and Bologna.

[10] Antonio Graziadei (1873–1953) was one of the leading figure of the Italian revision of Marx's doctrine which he tried to reconcile with the Marshallian system; he was Professor of Economics in Cagliari, Parma and Rome.

[11] The letter of Sraffa is reproduced in Roncaglia (1972, p. 192).

# Bibliography

Barone, E. (1894), 'Sul trattamento di quistioni dinamiche', *Giornale degli Economisti*, vol. 9, no. 5, November.

Barucci, P. (1972), 'The spread of marginalism in Italy, 1871–1890', *History of Political Economy*, vol. 4, pp. 512–32.

Dalla Volta, R. (1885), 'A. Marshall, "The present position of economics"', *L'Economista*, 25 October.

Dalla Volta, R. (1890), 'A. Marshall, *Principles of Economics*', *L'Economista*, 28 September.

Einaudi, L. (1980), 'La scienza economica in Italia. Reminescenze', in M. Finoia ed., *La scienza economica in Italia, 1850–1950*, Bologna: Cappelli.

Fanno, M. (1914), *Contributo alla teoria dell' offerta a costi congiunti*, supplement to *Giornale degli Economisti*, vol. 19.

Fanno, M. (1926), 'Contributo alla teoria economica dei beni succedanei', *Annali di Economia*, no. 3.

Foa, B. (1928), *Di alcune influenze del tempo sul valore*, Milano: Edizioni del Lavoro.

Graziadei, A. (1899), *La produzione capitalistica*, Torino: Bocca.

Graziadei, A. (1909), *Saggio di un'indagine sui prezzi in regime di concorrenza e di sindacato tra gli imprenditori*, Imola: Galeati.

Jannaccone, P. (1905), *Introduzione* to the Italian translation of Marshall's *Principles of Economics*, fourth edition, Torino: Unione Tipografica Torinese.

Jannaccone, P. (1914), 'Teoria e pratica del dumping', in P. Jannaccone, *Prezzi e mercati*, Torino: Einaudi, 1934.

Jha, N. (1963), *The Age of Marshall*, London: Frank Cass.

Labriola, A. (1900), 'Distribuzione del dividendo e produttività marginali', in A. Labriola, *Finanza ed economia*, Napoli: Società Editrice Partenopea, 1925.

Leone, E. (1909), *La revisione del marxismo*, Roma: Biblioteca del Divenire Sociale.

Marshall, A. (1879), *The Pure Theory of Foreign Trade. The Pure Theory of Domestic Values*, originally printed for private circulation, Cambridge: H. Sidgwick and reprinted Clifton, N. J.: Augustus M. Kelley, 1974.

Marshall, A. (1961), *Principles of Economics*, C. W. Guillebaud, ed., London: Macmillan for the Royal Economic Society, ninth (variorum) edition in two volumes: vol. 1–text; vol. 2–notes.

Martello, T. (1912), *L'economia politica e l'odierna crisi del darwinismo*, Bologna: Laterza.

Montemartini, G. (1899a), *Introduzione allo studio della distribuzione delle ricchezze*, Milano: Fusi.

Montemartini, G. (1899b), *La teoria delle produttività marginali*, Pavia: Società Editrice Libraria.

Pantaleoni, M. (1889), *Principii di economia pura*, Firenze: Barbera.

Pantaleoni, M. (1897), 'A proposito del *Cours d'économie politique* di V. Pareto', *Rivista popolare di politica, lettere e scienze sociali*, vol. 2, March.

Pantaleoni, M. (1904), *Lezioni di economia pura*, Roma: Sandron.

Pareto, V. (1960), *Lettere a Matteo Pantaleoni*, G. De Rosa, ed., Banca Nazionale del Lavoro, 3 volumes.

Roncaglia, A. (1972), *Sraffa e la teoria dei prezzi*, Bari: Laterza.

Schumpeter, J. A. (1954), *History of Economic Analysis*, E. Schumpeter, ed., New York: Oxford University Press.

Sraffa, P. (1925), 'Sulle relazione tra costo e quantità prodotta', *Annali di Economia*, no. 2.

Sraffa, P. (1926), 'The laws of return under competitive conditions', *Economic Journal*, vol. 36, December.

Walras, L. (1965), *Correspondence of Leon Walras and Related Papers*, W. Jaffé, ed., Amsterdam: North Holland, 3 volumes.

Whitaker, J. K., ed. (1975), *The Early Economic Writings of Alfred Marshall 1867–1890*, London: Macmillan for the Royal Economic Society, two volumes.

# 8.  Marshall and ethics

## A. W. Coats

## I. Preamble

> In all economic questions, considerations of the higher ethics will always assert themselves, however much we try to limit our inquiry for an immediate practical purpose (Alfred Marshall, 1887, p. xxvi).

> The key note . . . of the whole of Marshall's life as an economist, was that double nature—scientist and pastor, thinker and moralizer—that Keynes perceived as the clue to Marshall's mingled strength and weakness; to his conflicting purposes and wasted strength (Whitaker, 1972, pp. 37–38).

The interrelationship between economics and ethics is a fundamental and pervasive theme in Marshall's career and writings. An adequate treatment of this theme is obviously impossible within the space available here since it would call for a detailed analysis of the condition and development of the two disciplines during Marshall's lifetime against the broader background of mid- and late-Victorian British intellectual, social and economic history, with special reference to the growing specialisation and professionalisation of the social (or moral) sciences. Consequently, what follows is highly selective.

## II. Economics among the moral sciences

Given my special interests, and John Maloney's recent perceptive account of Marshall's role in the development—perhaps one should say the emergence—of the economics profession in Britain (Maloney, 1985), it is convenient to begin with the last of the above-mentioned subjects. As is well known, Marshall did not practise what Beatrice Webb termed 'a Self-Contained, Separate, Abstract Political Economy' (Webb, 1926, p. 422); and Maynard Keynes was seriously misleading in describing him as

*K methodig*

the first great economist . . . who devoted his life to building up the subject as a *separate* science, standing on its own foundations with as high standards of scientific activity as the physical or biological sciences (Keynes, 1925, pp. 56–57; emphasis added).

To discuss 'standards of scientific activity' or 'the professional scientific attitude' (another phrase in the same passage) would take us too far into methodology and sociology. The more immediately relevant issue here is the concept of a 'separate' science, a term Marshall himself occasionally applied to his economics, which pointed towards the growing division of labour in an expanding academic universe. No doubt Keynes was right in claiming that after Marshall 'Economics could never again be [merely?] one of a number of subjects which a Moral Philosopher would take in his stride, one Moral Science out of several, as Mill, Jevons and Sidgwick took it' (ibid., p. 57).

Developments in economics during Marshall's lifetime were part of a much broader process—though, admittedly, the eventual success of Marshall's protracted campaign to establish an independent Economics Tripos (Groenewegen, 1988) had significant repercussions, both within Cambridge and beyond. He would surely have deplored the narrowing, fragmentation, excessive abstraction and mathematisation that has occurred in economics since his death, although he would have welcomed the growth of quantification, within limits.

Nevertheless, given the pedagogical and professional circumstances of his time, he favoured greater specialisation, since the ambitious Comtean plan for a unified social science 'showed no signs of coming into existence'. The progress of knowledge, Marshall argued, required a 'common sense' breakdown of social problems into their component parts, and a corresponding division of academic labour, with each discipline utilising its 'specialised scientific organon, if there be one ready'.[1] Needless to say, economics was fully prepared for the new dispensation, even if the other social sciences were not.

Five years later, when the *Principles* first appeared, Marshall professed indifference to academic demarcation disputes, declaring that 'the less we trouble ourselves with the scholastic inquiries as to whether a certain consideration comes within the scope of economics, the better' (Marshall, 1961, vol. 1, p. 9). In his hands this constituted a licence for a comprehensive approach that some critics have dubbed 'imperialistic' (Boulding, 1969, p. 8; Collini *et al.* 1984, p. 312). Marshall's own procedure was characteristically ambivalent. As recently noted, he sought

> to retain a hold on all possibilities simultaneously—to claim that there was a well-delimited area for economic science, one that could be expanded indefinitely by the cumulative efforts of dedicated students, while at the same time maintaining immediate contact with all ethical questions of the present and future, without claiming to solve them by its own methods, or losing its qualities as a science in the process (Collini *et al.*, 1984, p. 318).

This was, indeed, a curious species of separateness. Like many of his generation, Marshall initially studied and taught what would nowadays be regarded as several distinct disciplines before deciding to dedicate his life to economics. But unlike his close colleague and contemporary, Henry Sidgwick, who wrote major treatises on *Ethics* (1874), *Political Economy* (1883) and *Politics* (1891), he subsequently more or less stuck to his last, thereby directly contributing to the irresistible march of scholarly compartmentalisation that has subsequently dominated 20th-century academic knowledge.

Ethics was one of the subjects, together with mathematics, philosophy, politics and psychology, that absorbed Marshall's energies during his early years, and his characterisations of its relationship to economics provide a rare opportunity to derive some amusement from this solemn occasion. Ethics was both the 'sister' of economics (Marshall, 1874, p. 430) and 'the good Abigail', the 'mistress' of economics (Marshall, 1893, pp. 390, 389); and as has been wittily observed of the latter designation: 'Although . . . separate establishments were, as usual with such relationships, the wisest arrangement, Marshall continued to speak as though economics enjoyed privileged access to that establishment' (Collini *et al.*, 1984, p. 318). For those familiar with Margaret Attwood's chilling novel, *The Handmaid's Tale* (parts of which were filmed at Duke University), the scope for Freudian interpretations is further enhanced by A. C. Pigou's guileless suggestion that Marshall saw ethics as 'a handmaid of economics and a servant of practice' rather than 'an intellectual gymnastic [or] even as a means of winning truth for its own sake' (Pigou, 1925, p. 84).

Although the ethics–economics connection was being actively discussed throughout much of his career (Maloney, 1985, ch. 9), Marshall did not actively participate in the debate.[2] He steadfastly refrained from engaging in philosophical controversy or committing himself to any formal ethical doctrine, preferring instead to rely on 'our ethical instincts and common sense, when they as *ultimate* arbiters come to apply to practical issues the knowledge obtained by economics and other sciences' (Marshall, 1961, vol. 1, p. 28; emphasis in original).

Marshall's reservations about utilitarianism—or, for that matter, any other formal philosophical system—are well known,[3] hence his insistence that while

> some of the greatest economists have been utilitarians . . . that was an accident. Their analysis was wholly independent of utilitarian doctrine; it was, when rightly understood, *common property to all ethical creeds* (Marshall, 1893, p. 388; emphasis in original).

Given his reluctance to explicate his ethical beliefs, it is hardly surprising that so many commentators have concluded that Marshall simply took for granted the conventional moral ideas and standards of his social and intellectual group. There is substantial warrant for this general interpretation; but it is possible to be more specific. For example, in *Industry and Trade*, as earlier in his sermon to the younger generation of economists, he acknowledged the difficulty of defining the true nature of the 'social good', but added that there was a fundamental 'substratum' of agreement that consisted 'mainly in that healthful exercise and development of faculties which yields happiness without pall, because it sustains self-respect and is sustained by hope' (Marshall, 1923, p. 664; cf. Marshall, 1897, p. 310). The key term here is not 'happiness', but 'self-respect'. As Marshall informed the evolution sociologist, Benjamin Kidd, his 'religion of self-respect' required no 'supernatural sanctions' of the kind needed 'in an earlier stage of development'; for

> the sanctions of religion are moral, and that morality may be a product of instinct, but in the ultimate appeal must rely mainly on reason. My reason . . . tells me that an unmoral life is not likely to be a happy one at all, and cannot be a very happy one; because—according to my personal experience, and according to that of all those whom I know, who have tried both methods of living—the times I have least respect for myself have been my unhappiest, physical conditions count for little in comparison.[4]

In a rare concession to contemporary ethical debate, in two revealing footnotes, Marshall endeavoured to dispel the misconception that the desire to do one's duty is no different from any other 'pleasure', by proposing the broad, neutral term 'satisfaction' to refer to 'the aims of all desires, whether appertaining to man's higher or lower nature'. For the Benthamites, however, an additional 'independent major premise was required' to 'serve as a bridge by which to pass from individualistic Hedonism to a complete ethical creed'. For some, the Kantian 'Categorical Imperative' would serve the purpose; but for others, obviously including Marshall himself, whatever 'the origin of our moral instincts', it would be sufficient to rely on 'self-respect', which 'is to be had only on the condition of endeavouring so to live as to promote the progress of the human race'.[5]

The ethical significance of Marshall's concern with 'the progress of the human race' appears more clearly in his 1875 unpublished talk on 'Some Features of American Industry', which ends with the statement that he was working his way 'towards that ethical creed which is according to the Doctrine of Evolution'. There were two key factors in the human evolutionary process: firstly, 'the peaceful moulding of character into harmony with the conditions by which it is surrounded, so that a man . . . will without conscious moral effort be impelled in that course which is in union with the actions, the sympathies, and the interests of the society amid which he spends his life', and secondly, 'the education of a firm will through the overcoming of difficulties . . . [a will that] submits every particular action to the judgement of reason' (reproduced in Whitaker, 1975a, vol. 2, pp. 375, 377). As John Whitaker has observed, Marshall's approach combined a powerful internalised individual commitment to duty with the external pressure to conform to community ethical standards. But

> only if there are agreed ethical axioms can the internal and external pressures be regarded as always working together . . . This kind of ethical absolutism—the belief that there exist universal values which merely need to be discovered—was a quite common unconscious presumption of nineteenth century thinkers.[6]

## III. 'Pure' economic science and applied economic ethics?

There are at least four reasons why Marshall could not contemplate a complete severance of economics from ethics.

1. On a personal level he was, as Keynes said, 'too anxious' to do good, and this led him to undervalue the more theoretical as against the practical aspects of economics. In his later years he seemed to lose interest in pure theory, apart from continuing efforts to reinterpret and defend his own work in response to criticism; and he became

increasingly preoccupied with ethical ideals, historical development, and problems of economic and social policy.

2. To Marshall, the economist's mission was itself an ethical undertaking. Its purpose was not merely to relieve poverty and suffering, but to help raise the 'quality of human life'; and the scientific economist's work could, at least sometimes, 'suggest a moral or practical precept' which, through human effort, could 'modify the action of laws of nature' (Marshall, 1961, vol. 1, p. 36). And, as the economist (ideally?) has 'no class or personal interests to make him afraid of any conclusions which the figures [or the analysis?] when carefully interpreted may indicate', he was 'fortified by the consciousness of his own rectitude' (ibid., vol. 2, p. 757; Marshall, 1897, p. 305). Like others of his intellectual circle, Marshall had abandoned his youthful religion and could salve his conscience by viewing his career as a species of secular priesthood. Indeed, on his deathbed he told Keynes 'how he first came to study economics and how such a study was a sort of religious work for the sake of the human race'.[7]

3. In 'positive' scientific terms, the economist was obliged to take ethical forces 'into account' (Marshall, 1961, vol. 1, p. vi), because they directly and significantly influenced individual and social behaviour and, therefore, the operation of economic laws and tendencies. For example, in the *Economics of Industry* (1879, ch. 2), 'moral character' was listed as one of the principal 'agents of production', and this agent played a central role in Marshall's conception of evolutionary socio-economic change. (See *infra*, Section IV).

4. Together with his rejection of the concept of 'economic man', Marshall incorporated ethical factors into his economics also because he wished to align himself, in general terms, with the 'new economic movement' (Foxwell, 1887) associated with the reformist ideas of Thomas Carlyle, John Ruskin, Arnold Toynbee (Marshall's predecessor at Balliol College, Oxford), and the more moderate Christian Socialists. Like Marshall, these writers held that political economy should be a study of human welfare rather than merely material wealth.[8]

In Marshall's sociological system the relationship between economics, ethics and psychology was crucial. It explains both his rejection of the concept of an economic man 'who is under no ethical influences and who pursues pecuniary gain warily and energetically, but mechanically and selfishly' (Marshall, 1961, vol. 1, p. vi), and his claim that one of the 'chief features' of his *Principles* was the inclusion of all motives relevant to human action. More important still, it underlies the claim of economics to be a 'separate' science, because economic motives are measurable, albeit indirectly. Admittedly, not all motives are measurable; and the available indirect monetary measure is imperfect and inexact, so that economics cannot hope to achieve the precision and generality of physics. Nevertheless, 'it is this definite and exact measurement of the steadiest motives in business life, which has enabled economics to far outrun every other branch of the study of man' (ibid., vol. 1, p. 14). Ethics, of course, lacks this advantage:

> The pure science of Ethics halts for lack of a system of measurement of efforts, sacrifices, desires, etc., fit for her wide purpose. But the pure science of Political Economy has found a system that will serve her narrower aims. This discovery, rather than any particular proposition, is the great fact of the pure science (Marshall, 1876, p. 126).

However, as noted above, Marshall was unwilling to confine himself within the boundaries of 'the pure science of Political Economy'. He was eager to embrace all motives, both higher and lower, whether measurable or non-measurable; and as one of his more penetrating critics, Walter Weisskopf, has argued, he provided no solution to the problem of handling the qualitative ethical differences entailed in taking account of the higher motives of life:

> Although the restriction of economics to the money motive seems to be completely vindicated on purely intellectual grounds, . . . [because] conduct motivated by money gains is supposedly measurable, verifiable, predictable, and subject to laws, regularities and uniformities . . . its combination with deliberate rationality contains an ethical element, because deliberateness is considered by Marshall to be a moral virtue. At the end of his discussion Marshall acknowledges the importance of the ethical: the money measurement is used for the sake of greater exactness; but for practical issues we must 'take some sort of account of our ethical instincts and common sense'.[9]

Marshall's determination to take account of ethical factors explains his rejection of Sidgwick's conventional distinction between the 'science' and the 'art' of political economy (Sidgwick, 1883, pp. xix, 12, 21ff, 403) and John Neville Keynes' tripartite division between: (a) the 'positive' scientific study of economic laws, (b) 'applied' political economy, focusing on the practical precepts for attaining given ends;

and (c) the ethical norms and criteria required for policy recommendations (Keynes, 1890, pp. 31–36). Unlike Sidgwick, who devoted nine chapters of his *Principles* to the art of political economy, including such topics as 'The Principles of Distributive Justice' and 'Political Economy and Private Morality', Marshall had no patience with elaborate classifications. He simply drew the line between the relatively 'pure' and the relatively 'applied' parts of the science, arguing that

> it seems better to regard the science as pursuing its inquiries with more or less direct reference to certain practical issues, and as pointing the way towards solutions of them, than to make pretension to the authority of an Art, complete and self-contained, and responsible for the entire direction of conduct in certain matters (Marshall, 1961, vol. 2, p. 154).

However, in his quest for realism and his impatience with mere abstraction, he severely limited the sphere of the 'pure' science, even claiming that 'in a sense the whole of economics is an applied science' (ibid., vol. 2, p. 153). In this respect his approach resembled that of his predecessor, Henry Fawcett (cf. Deane, 1989, pp. 97–98).

Marshall clearly believed it was both possible and desirable to avoid the confusions between the imperative and the indicative mood which had bedevilled the writings of earlier economists, including Adam Smith (Marshall, 1961, vol. 1, pp. 756–58; p. vi), and he periodically issued strong injunctions against this malpractice. An unusually specific example occurs in his *Bee-Hive* article, where he distinguished between the consequences of a certain course of action and the question whether actions having such consequences were justifiable. In many cases, he said, the issues 'are so clear that our moral judgement is given without hesitation, almost instinctively, and we are scarcely aware that any other judgement than that of political economy can be given'. However other cases 'which political economy presents to our judgement' are not so clear, and here:

> It is absolutely necessary to keep entirely distinct two questions, that which must be decided according to the laws of political economy, viz. what consequences will follow from a postponed (sic)[10] course of action, and that which will be decided by our moral judgement, viz. whether an action which produces these consequences is right (Marshall, 1874, p. 425).

The economist's 'special science' gives him no special competence to answer the second question, for political economy:

lacks the power of giving direct and complete answers on points involving questions of right and wrong . . . and if the rigidly scientific character of political economy be forgotten, those questions even, which belong strictly to her domain, will not be discussed with scientific calm and thoroughness (ibid., pp. 425–26).

In later years Marshall seems to have been somewhat more flexible towards 'the rigidly scientific character of political economy'; and in differentiating between conclusions based securely on scientific method and judgements on matters lying outside the economist's professional competence and authority he employed what later became the familiar (and notorious) Robbinsian distinction between the economist *qua* scientist and *qua* citizen—one that has provoked perennial controversy and mixed responses from 20th-century economic writers, many of them angry, sceptical, or merely cynical. Marshall's own practice was, to say the least, permissive;[11] and he overlooked, or perhaps simply chose to ignore the problem of individual judgement involved in deciding where the boundary should be drawn between scientific and non-scientific matters.[12] In the absence of an explicit definition of the discipline's scope—which he was certainly unwilling to provide—the decision must necessarily be based either on personal, extra-scientific value premises or, alternatively, on an inter-subjective professional consensus which necessarily has normative and/or ideological implications. As Maloney has persuasively argued, the establishment of such a consensus under Marshall's leadership, and on his terms, became one of his long-term career objectives (Maloney, 1985, especially chs 2, 10 and 11).

## IV. Ethics, psychology and the evolutionary process

Although Marshall said he had 'come to economics out of ethics, intending to stay there only a short while' (Marshall, 1961, vol. 2, p. 36), his study of psychology left a lasting imprint on his mind for, late in life he remarked: 'If I had to live my life over again I should have devoted it to psychology. Economics has too little to do with ideals. If I said much about them I should not be read by businessmen' (Keynes, 1925, p. 37); and the business community was a major segment of the audience he wished to address.

Psychological—or, more strictly speaking, characteriological—factors were central in Marshall's account of economic, social and moral development, and in this he was probably influenced by John Stuart Mill's conception of a science of 'ethology'—i.e., the study of character formation, which Mill thought might possibly constitute the foundation of a general science of society. In his *System of Logic* (1843), Mill referred to 'progressive changes both in the character of the human race' and in 'their outward circumstances as far as moulded by themselves' (cited in Hollander, vol. 1, p. 194), whereas Marshall spoke in similar terms of 'the ever changing and subtle forces of human nature' and the social scientist's need to recognise that there would be 'no sudden improvement in man's conditions of life, because he forms them as much as they form him, and he himself cannot change fast' (Marshall, 1897, p. 311). At first sight Marshall's statements about the speed of change of human nature seem inconsistent. He frequently referred to 'human nature being what it is', as though it were a fixed datum, whereas at other times he gave a quite different impression of human pliability and adaptability (for example, Marshall, 1885, pp. 173–74; cited in Reisman, 1987, p. 370). The differences could, however, be reconciled by distinguishing between the 'tactics' and the 'strategy' of man's conflict with nature; for

> . . . though there is a kernel of man's nature that has scarcely changed, yet many elements of his character, that are most effective for economic uses, are of modern growth. . . . To carry over from one age to another both strategical and tactical lessons, is to incline somewhat towards a mechanical view of economics; to carry over strategical lessons is characteristic of a biological view.[13]

Unlike his price theory, where the analytical distinction between the immediate, short, and long periods was clearly specified, in discussing changes in character, morals, and social conditions he suggested no time periods, although he was probably thinking in terms of secular, or very long-term developments.[14] The 'progress of industry', for example, was attributable to a combination of influences including: 'the religious, the moral, the intellectual and the artistic faculties . . . [and the] organization of a well-ordered state . . . [It is] the product of an infinite variety of motives, many of which have no direct connection with the pursuit of wealth.'[15] This was no simple deterministic scheme, although

> man's character has been moulded by his everyday work, and the material resources which he thereby procures; more than by any other influence unless it be that of his religious ideals; and the two great forming agencies of the world's

history have been the religious and the economic (Marshall, 1961, vol. 1, p. 1; see also 'Some features of American industry' in Whitaker, 1975, vol. 2, p. 359).

Religious motives were more intense than economic motives; but the latter were more pervasive, and Marshall attached extraordinary weight to the influence of occupation on character and behaviour. 'Work, in its best sense, the healthy and energetic exercise of faculties, is the aim of life, is life itself' (Marshall, 1873, p. 115) and ideally no man (or woman?) 'should have any occupation which tends to make him less than a gentleman' (ibid., p. 110). In his youthful enthusiasm, Marshall believed that the progress of society would eventually obliterate the distinction between the working man and the gentleman; and once this was achieved 'everyone who is not a gentleman will have only himself to blame for it' (ibid., p. 111). Under such circumstances, 'no one is to do in the day so much manual work as will leave him little time or little aptitude for intelligent and artistic enjoyment in the evening' (ibid., p. 110).

These passages may seem naive to modern readers, but they illustrate the importance Marshall attached to activities as against mere wants. Human beings were not simply Benthamite pleasure machines, consuming for the sake of consumption—although that might unfortunately be the case with some of the lowest income groups; and, contrary to William Stanley Jevons' idea that 'the Theory of Consumption is the scientific basis of economics', Marshall believed that

> much that is of chief interest in the science of wants is borrowed from the science of efforts and activities. These two supplement each other; each is incomplete without the other. But if either, more than the other, may claim to be the interpreter of the history of man, whether on the economic side or any other, it is the science of activities and not that of wants (Marshall, 1961, vol. 1, p. 90).

Thus, although the causal relationship between them was sometimes expressed in neutral terms, and a cumulative process of deterioration presumably could not be entirely ruled out, the general thrust of Marshall's account was undeniably optimistic, with activities as the more powerful element; for 'Although it is man's wants in the early stages of development that give rise to activities, yet afterwards each new step *upwards* is to be regarded as the development of new activities giving rise to new wants' (ibid., p. 38; emphasis in original).

The ethical significance of the distinction between wants and activities underlies Marshall's concept of the standard of life, which is much broader than the standard of comfort, that is, mere conventional necessities (ibid., vol. 1, p. 504). Thus,

> a rise in the standard of life implies an increase in intelligence and energy and self-respect; leading to more care and judgement in expenditure, and to an avoidance of food and drink that gratify the appetite but afford no strength, and of ways of living that are unwholesome physically and morally (ibid., vol. 1, p. 689; cf. p. 504).

Given Marshall's 'religion of self-respect', the long-run inter-dependence and compatibility of economic, social, characterological and ethical changes seemed assured; and this constituted the basis of Marshall's belief in the superiority of late 19th-century British society by comparison with both its past, and the contemporary state of less developed nations. To some critics this complacent attitude has seemed outrageous. For example, following his pathbreaking analysis of the wants/activities' interrelationship in Marshall's system, Talcott Parsons offered some scathing comments on Marshall's sociology in general, and his concept of character in particular:

> Englishmen have often ridiculed Hegel for supposing that the evolution of the *Weltgeist* had taken place solely for the purpose of producing the Prussian State of the early nineteenth century. And yet Marshall, good Englishman that he was, supposes that the whole process leads to the production of the English businessman and artisan of the latter part of the same century. With all due respect for these worthy gentlemen, does anyone really suppose that they alone will inherit the earth? I am not here concerned with disputing the validity or propriety of Marshall's ethical conviction of the supreme value of one type of character. What is important is whether such subjective ethical convictions should be allowed to colour the whole perspective of the past and present tendencies of social development as it undoubtedly does in the case of Marshall. The complete disregard of most other things which it entails is a narrowness hardly compatible with the ideal of scientific objectivity.[16]

## V. Marshall's ethics and the new movement in English economics

In his important survey published in the second volume of the new *Quarterly Journal of Economics,* Marshall's former pupil and colleague, Herbert Somerton Foxwell, who was by no means an uncritical admirer, characterised the new movement in English economic thought as comprising three main elements: 'theoretic criticism, historical method, and humanistic feeling' (Foxwell, 1887,

p. 87). Marshall's contribution to the last of these is of special interest in the present context for it has been unduly neglected by historians of economics—though not by social and more general intellectual historians.

According to Foxwell, the strengths of the authors who emphasised 'the moral and humanistic criticism of our economic life and institutions' lay in 'their opposition to materialism, and their healthy estimate of the real objects of existence'; whereas their weakness was the tendency to 'sometimes allow reason to be overbalanced by emotion'. However, economists like General Walker in the United States, and Jevons and Marshall in England, were contributing to the current convergence of the three lines of inquiry—those of the theorist, the historian and the moralist—so as to form a 'new school', whose members reject

> the old notion that a positive science of economics can be constructed, which even in the industrial sphere can be independent of morality and justice, purely rigid and mechanical in its principles. . . . It is the mechanical unmoral economics, even more than the policy of laissez faire, which the new school has banished to Saturn . . . It is their decided conviction that, if competition is to remain the basis of economic relations, society must see that it is so held in check that it shall not violate the older and deeper principles of justice and humanity (ibid., pp. 90–91, 100–101).

*[handwritten margin notes: reasonable interpretation of Marshall's overall position; basic justification for intervention]*

Whether Marshall saw and/or approved of this passage is not clear; but, setting aside some of the more recent methodological connotations of the phrase 'positive science of economics', it represents a reasonable interpretation of his overall position. And it provides a suitable entrée to a brief account of the contemporary significance of the humanistic side of his work.

In the oft-quoted peroration that concluded his inaugural lecture Marshall disclosed his

> most cherished ambition . . . to increase the number of those, whom Cambridge, the great mother of strong men, sends out into the world with cool heads but warm hearts, willing to give some at least of their best powers to grappling with the social suffering around them; resolved not to rest content till they have done what in them lies to discover how far it is possible to open up to all the material means of a refined and noble life (Marshall, 1885, p. 174).

In this characteristically evangelical Victorian manifesto, with its combination of moral earnestness, duty, manliness, professional commitment and social responsibility, the juxtaposition of 'cool heads' and 'warm hearts' is especially pertinent given Marshall's 'double nature'.[17] For most of his career he felt obliged to rein in his natural moral enthusiasm; so there was an unmistakable sense of relief in his confidential admission of his intention, in the final part of his forthcoming book 'to give a little freedom to my *sentiment*, as distinguished from my reason, and to speak as a citizen rather than especially as an economist'. And yet immediately he reimposed the restraint, adding that 'sentiment is like a butterfly; no amount of discipline will make him go by a rational bee-line'.[18] As sometimes suggested, Marshall may have absorbed some of the Toynbee aura while at Balliol. But the influence of T. H. Green's concept of citizenship was probably more powerful for Marshall certainly believed that Toynbee had been altogether too emotional.[19] Nevertheless, there is a curiously Toynbeean implication in the above-quoted letter to the effect that the economist as such was entirely lacking in sentiment—a view fully compatible with Toynbee's well known contrast between the economists and the human beings.[20]

During the years when Marshall was writing the first edition of the *Principles*, England was in a ferment of social reform; and it is in this sense that the book was 'a kind of counter-Reformation . . . directed against doubts from within and without the fold' (Shove, 1942, p. 310). As a recent social historian has observed:

> Alfred Marshall was a liberator of the more cautious. Christians worried by the relation of economics to social justice found in him a thinker more systematic than Toynbee (whom he succeeded at Balliol) and more respectable than George (with whom he debated publicly at Oxford). . . . Whether or not they read Marshall in detail, Christians with a desire for social justice but a respect for the body of professional opinion could assure themselves and others that here was an orthodox economist who blessed efforts to remove social misery, whose notion of economic theory was quite friendly to what Scott Holland called the 'unfaltering assertion of moral as supreme over mechanical laws' (Inglis, 1963, pp. 257–58).

The question of the relationship between moral and mechanical (or economic) laws was the subject of a fundamental debate between the economists and certain sections of the clergy in England, as in the United States, during the 1880s and 1890s; and this constitutes an essential part of the context of Marshall's treatment of the economics–ethics issue. The aforementioned Canon Henry Scott Holland was chairman of the Christian Social Union (CSU), an organisation formed in 1889 by a group of scholarly Oxford clergy who had been deeply influenced by the Toynbee–Green reformist movement; and their action in launching a new periodical, the *Economic Review*, in 1890, shortly before the appearance of the inaugural issue of the *Economic Journal*, was deeply disturbing to Marshall, for it was an open public challenge to the hegemony of Cambridge economics, of which he was undeniably the leading exponent and custodian (Kadish, 1982, ch. 6).

By proposing to concentrate on 'the moral and social bearing of economic problems', the *Review*'s editors were evidently trying to divide the territory between the two camps. But the establishment of the CSU and its new organ reveal the continuing sensitivity to the respective spheres of the more narrowly scientific and the broader ethical–social approaches to the subject; and this helps to explain Marshall's desire to encompass both in his *Principles*. The issues were complex, for they included religious, philosophical, methodological, doctrinal, policy and professional elements, which have been carefully explored by Alon Kadish and John Maloney (Kadish, 1982; Maloney, 1985). Theologian–economists like Wilfred Richmond, who lacked professional credentials (whatever they were at the time) nevertheless reached a considerable audience;[21] and by flatly asserting the superiority of moral over economic principles they tended to undermine the economists' intellectual authority and thereby limit their sphere of influence. Marshall did not challenge this claim directly; and he characteristically occupied an ambivalent middling position on the spectrum of economists' views on the ethics–economics issue,[22] although he was clearly unwilling to abandon all claims to the ethical implications of economic and social problems.

It seems doubtful that Marshall made any significant adjustments to the *Principles* in response to the Oxford clerical–reformist movement, although he was already in general sympathy with its broader aims and objectives, which formed part of the general current of Christian socialism.[23] This is clear from his conception of the economist's 'mission', and his statement of the qualities the economist requires for the effective performance of his task. These include the qualities of 'a shrewd mother-wit, of a sound sense of proportion, and of a large experience of life'. Beyond this, the economist must possess not only

the three great intellectual faculties, perception, imagination and reason; and most of all he needs imagination. . . . [but also] the faculty of sympathy, and especially that rare sympathy which enables people to put themselves in the place, not only of their comrades, but also of other classes (Marshall, 1961, vol. 1, pp. 43 and 45).

One may only speculate how far modern professional training helps to develop these capacities.

## VI. Conclusion

Marshall invariably emphasised—many historians of economics nowadays would say overemphasised—the essential unities and continuities in the long-run development of economic ideas; and it is therefore fitting, in this centenary year, that he should appear to us as a great transitional and synthesising figure spanning the classical and modern ages of our discipline. Moreover, notwithstanding his characteristic British complacency and insularity, we now more fully appreciate that he incorporated a considerable variety of non-British components into his capacious architectonic edifice.

Of course, late 20th-century economics is very different from anything Marshall himself could have foreseen or would have wished to see, and not merely in respect of its sheer scale, fragmentation and technical complexity. Surely he would disapprove of the massive investment of intellectual and material resources into the 'pure' science, and especially into highly abstract mathematisation. On the other hand, he would no doubt welcome the immense expansion of the 'applied' side—data collection and analysis and economic/historical research; and he might feel gratified, albeit with some reservations, by the manifest success of his professionalisation campaign, which paved the way for the employment of thousands of economists in a remarkable variety of useful and important non-academic positions. Whether the profession still has the requisite commitment to the relief of poverty and other good causes so dear to Marshall's heart is quite another matter.

But while much of the core of Marshall's theoretical analysis still survives, and has been absorbed so effectively into 20th century mainstream economics that it takes a conscious effort of historical reconstruction to identify it, what can be said of the ethical components of his writings? Is it the case, as even some of the more sympathetic commentators have asserted, that his 'pious asides and prim moralisings have "dated" badly; that the line of attack against which they were in part a defence has faded out' (Shove, 1942, p. 316); and that consequently the reader of the *Principles* should 'pass over, without too much feeling of annoyance, those passages which are a reflection, in Schumpeter's phrase, of Marshall's "mid-

Victorian morality seasoned by Benthamism", much of which the present generation finds almost intolerably tiresome' (Guillebaud, 1952, pp. 113, 114). A more recent, somewhat less sympathetic, commentator has questioned the wisdom of this advice, not only because 'Marshall's constant sermonizing page after page was integral and substantive to his work, that indeed in a strange and fundamental way this *was* his work' (Levitt, 1976, p. 44; emphasis in original), but because (as Keynes remarked), its 'concealed crevices' contain 'buried treasure' of value to our own and subsequent generations (quoted by Levitt, ibid.).

Of course, most of professional economics in the 1990s is far more formal, precise and rigorous than its Marshallian counterpart, and correspondingly narrower in vision, scope and content, notwithstanding determined efforts in some quarters to extend its domain by applying a simplified utility-maximising model to every conceivable subject under the sun. Ironically, Marshall, who was so wary of the dangers of utilitarianism and simple theories, would undoubtedly have deplored this species of social science imperialism.

While much Marshallian ground has undoubtedly been lost (admittedly with some compensatory gains) in the process of whoring after false positivist scientific gods, there has recently been increasing evidence of a counteracting tendency that promises to bear fruit in the foreseeable future. This involves, in particular, a considerable number of varied and thoughtful efforts to incorporate into the main body of economic analysis elements that Marshall deemed integral to his broad concept of economic science (pure and applied). A central theme here is the revival of serious interest in economics as a 'moral' science that takes ethics more fully 'into account'.

This revival goes much deeper than the vague, amorphous, and too often untheoretical expanding field of 'social' or 'humanistic' economics (e.g., Lutz and Lux, 1979; cf., *supra*, fn. 1). It includes such varied works as: Boulding, 1969, 1973; Etzioni, 1988; Hardin, 1988; Hirschman, 1981; McPherson, 1984; Matthews, 1981; and Sen, 1987. Titles such as *Economics for a Civilized Society* (Davidson and Davidson, 1988) suggest that Marshall's concept of economic 'chivalry', which seems so quaint to some modern readers, still has purchase. Studies of 'non-selfish' economics such as: Baumol, 1986; Collard, 1978; and Phelps, 1975; co-operation: Axelbrod, 1984; status and the passions: Frank, 1985; 1988 (*pace* David Hume, of blessed memory), indicate that some current economists wish, as did Marshall, to go beyond the confines of a disembodied 'agent' or 'economic man' to a human being of flesh and blood. And the fruitful revival of interdisciplinary work, both in economics and psychology (cf. Earl, 1988; Hogarth and Reder, 1987) and more generally, might also earn Marshall's approval—though he became suspicious of academic psychology.

Needless to say, this brief catalogue gives no adequate impression of the richness and variety of the recent range of literature on what might be termed 'some neglected Marshallian themes'. No attempt has been made to include, for example, the huge body of writing on the subjects of evolutionary institutional change, or on the traditional value-laden topic of efficiency versus equity (or the ethics of the market), which appears so often in the public policy literature.

Of course, in most instances where comparisons can be found between recent contributions and Marshall's broader interests, the similarities are superficial, given the great differences in method and approach. And although there has been a marked recovery of interest in ethical or normative economics, the positivist, 'objective' natural-science conception of economics is still dominant. The promise of Marshall's organismic–biological approach has yet to be realised.

## Notes and references

[1] Marshall (1885, p. 164); from his inaugural address. Most historians of economics do not realise that, for a time, 'that noble science of politics' was conceived in Cambridge as the umbrella under which economics and other moral sciences should be classified. This helps to explain why Marshall was eager to drop the term 'Political' from the title of his discipline, although in 1889, probably for tactical reasons, he proposed that Political Economy should be included in a new Political Sciences Tripos. (Note the plural.) For a revealing account of this situation see Collini *et al.* (1984, ch. 11). In the third and fourth editions of the *Principles*, Marshall implied that Social Economics would be as acceptable a title for his subject as Economics *simpliciter* (Marshall, 1961, vol. 1, p. 159).

[2] There are, of course, occasional brief comments on the economics–ethics relationship in Marshall's writings. The most explicit and/or detailed are in the *Bee-Hive* articles (which few of his fellow economists probably read), and in his response to Lord Goschen's *Presidential Address* to the British Economic Association (Marshall, 1874; 1893).

[3] R. D. Collison Black has recently questioned the conventional view that 'Jevons was a thoroughgoing Benthamite, whereas Marshall was hardly a Utilitarian at all', arguing that both men 'blended the new evolutionism with the old Utilitarianism' in their efforts to reconstruct economic studies, but in different

proportions (Black, 1990, pp. 7, 14). The implications for Marshall's work are considered below on pp. 154–55.

⁴ Marshall to Benjamin Kidd, 6 June 1894, Cambridge University Library, Add 8069 M251. Rita McWilliams Tullberg kindly provided a copy of this letter. Marshall was often evasive on matters of ethical principle, as indeed on other matters too. In the course of a public discussion on Henry George's views, for example, he said he did not know what was meant by a 'just distribution of proceeds between capital and labour' (Marshall, 1883, p. 198). However, this did not prevent him from making frequent observations on the desirability of redistribution on both economic and ethical grounds. For an unusually outspoken example, in a letter to Bishop Wescott, with respect to schemes 'to take from the rich and give to those who are less rich', he said: 'I would promote all such by every means in my power that were legitimate; and I would not be especially scrupulous in interpreting that word' (24 January 1900; cited in Pigou, 1925, p. 386). Presumably this was Marshall the citizen speaking!

⁵ See Marshall (1961, vol. 1, p. 17; vol. 2, p. 137). For a valuable discussion of these matters, see Henderson (1989 and 1990); also Whitaker (1977). I greatly appreciate the opportunity to examine Professor Henderson's paper of 1990 in advance of publication.

⁶ Whitaker (1977, p. 172). Marshall may have derived his 'common sense' view of ethical principles from Kant, via Sidgwick, whose work he presumably read, although there is no reference to Sidgwick's *Ethics* in Marshall's writings. According to the Kant–Sidgwick approach, the object of ethics (moral philosophy) is not to discover new truths but to systematise available knowledge so as to demonstrate the ultimate rationale of the moral knowledge and practices man already has. 'There should be no wholesale rejection of practical moral claims, but an attempt should be made to unify and show the objective justification of most of those claims' (Nielsen, 1967, p. 117). Sidgwick tried to provide a logical bridge between inclination and obligation, 'is' and 'ought', by 'combining the Kantian theory of rational duty with the utilitarian theory of value, maintaining that we are intuitively aware of the duty to obey moral principles at the expense of self interest but that moral principles, in turn, are justified by their utility in promoting the common good' (Abelson and Nielsen, 1967, p. 97). This seems to capture the essence of Marshall's approach. See also Schneewind (1977).

⁷ Hill and Keynes (1989, p. 195); I owe this reference to Rita McWilliams Tullberg. Religious language and imagery occurs so frequently in Marshall's writings it would repay separate study, It was by no means uncommon at the time. For a thoughtful discussion of the context see Skidelsky (1983, ch. 2 'Cambridge Civilization: Sidgwick and Marshall').

⁸ See below, Section V, p. 164 for further discussion.

⁹ Weisskopf (1955, p. 70); citing vol. 1, p. 28. Weisskopf complains of Marshall's 'moral–economic casuistry' because so often in his account ethical problems are implied in the logical ones. Marshall's strong emphasis on the value of rational, deliberative conduct involves 'a moral–economic calculus of a compulsively obsessional and neurotic character' (ibid., pp. 184, 183).

¹⁰ [A number of corrections have been made, probably in Marshall's hand, to the press-cuttings from the *Bee-Hive* of Marshall's two articles, kept in the Marshall

Archive. The word 'postponed' is crossed through and 'proposed' written above—Ed.]

[11] Recent scholars have derived some harmless amusement from this permissiveness which, in the past, has often been the focus of severe criticism. For example, John Maloney refers to the 'unhealthy give-and-take between Marshall the economist and Marshall the private citizen'. To Marshall, the economist as private citizen had much to do. And Marshall the private citizen was everywhere. He attended Professor Marshall's lectures doggedly; his constant interruptions must have been very frustrating to the latter, who had not come along to tell students that one of the best ways to use their wealth was to buy pictures, exhibit them and leave them to the nation, or to tell them that keeping up with fashion was a "crime". . . . In the end, Marshall the moralist dressed up as Marshall the economic biologist, egged on Marshall the ordinary citizen to speak out in public by telling him he was speaking more or less professionally after all' (Maloney, 1985, pp. 198, 200; cf. Levitt, 1976, p. 435: 'Even when speaking strictly *qua* economist, Marshall unhesitatingly intruded normative and moral prescripts into his discussion, and these his readers learned to ignore almost totally; and if not ignore, treat as either solecistic quaintness or irrelevant mush. Yet they show that Marshall each time he faced an impasse in the use of economics to solve problems of general social well-being, was forced, and had no hesitation in returning, to strictly personal judgments of moral rightness and social oughtness'). Levitt provides a comprehensive catalogue of these pronouncements. See also Reisman (1987, chs. 1 and 2).

[12] In this respect the parallel with Mill is striking. Mill informed a correspondent that his *Principles* was 'essentially, a book of applications exhibiting the principles of the science in the concrete . . . I was the more prompted to do this inasmuch as it would enable me to bring in, or rather to bring out, a great number of opinions on incidental matters, moral and social, for which one has not often so good an opportunity, and I have used this privilege as freely as Adam Smith did, and I fully expect to offend and scandalise ten times as many people as I shall please' (quoted by Whitaker, 1975b, p. 1047). On the issue of principle involved, see Hutchison (1964, p. 142). He considers that Marshall violated sound methodological practice much less frequently than Pigou and some of his Cambridge colleagues (cf. Hutchison, 1981, especially pp. 65, 99, 110).

[13] Marshall (1898, p. 44). Elsewhere Marshall stated that 'partly through the suggestions of biological study, the influence of circumstances in fashioning character is generally recognized as the dominant fact in social science' (Marshall, 1961, vol. 1, p. 48).

[14] As Weisskopf has noted, changes of character completely undermine the concept of diminishing marginal utility, which presupposes fixed preferences and tastes. Marshall ignored this problem. 'By making constancy of character a prerequisite for the stationary state and, with this, for the establishment of an equilibrium price, Marshall has unified his system and assured its ethical justification with one stroke' (Weisskopf, 1955, p. 217; cf. p. 177. For a more sophisticated analysis of this problem, see Whitaker, 1977, pp. 183–85).

[15] Chasse (1984, p. 392). Cf. Whitaker (1977, especially pp. 182–83).

[16] Parsons (1932, p. 335). For a somewhat less negative interpretation, see Chasse (1984).

[17] See the second epigraph to this paper, *supra*, p. 1. Also Keynes' beautifully expressed reference to Marshall's 'evangelical moraliser of an imp somewhere inside him, that was so ill advised as to disapprove' of any preoccupation with the purely abstract (in Pigou, 1925, p. 37).

[18] To A. W. Flux, 19 March 1904; in Pigou (1925, p. 408); emphasis in original. Oddly enough, when *Industry and Trade* appeared, a reviewer in the *Athanaeum* complained that its moral tone was out of place in a scientific work (cf. Flubacher, 1950, p. 390).

[19] For valuable comments on this relationship, see Kadish (1986, pp. 234–36). Foxwell seems to have been somewhat more sympathetic to Toynbee. On the Toynbee–Green relationship, Richter (1964), is indispensable.

[20] 'At last it is apparent to all the world, that the long and bitter controversy between the economists and human beings has ended in the conversion of the economists. The economist now dares to say that the end of his practical science is not wealth but man; and further, he owns that his intellectual theories have undergone a vast change. He has learnt to recognise that the laws which he supposed were universal are only partial and provisional' (quoted from p. 1 of his posthumously published Lectures on the Industrial Revolution, 1884, with valuable supplementary comments in Kitson Clark, 1973, pp. 289–90).

[21] Richmond (1888 and 1890). The latter work contains a remarkably revealing preface by Scott Holland. Richmond is one of the ethicists discussed in Henderson (1990).

[22] Maloney (1985, ch. 9), reviews a representative, but incomplete, selection of contemporary economists' views on this subject.

[23] For a comprehensive review, see Jones (1968); also Norman (1976).

## Bibliography

Abelson, R. and Nielsen, K. (1967), 'Ethics, History of', P. Edwards, ed., *The Encyclopedia of Philosophy*, New York: Macmillan and Free Press, vol. 3, pp. 81–116.

Axelrod, R. (1984), *The Evolution of Cooperation*, New York: Basic Books.

Baumol, W. (1986), *Superfairness: Applications and Theory*, Cambridge, Mass.: MIT Press.

Black, R. D. C. (1990), 'Jevons, Marshall and the utilitarian tradition', *Scottish Journal of Political Economy*, vol. 37, pp. 5–17.

Boulding, K. (1969), 'Economics as a moral science', *American Economic Review*, vol. 59, pp. 1–12.

Boulding, K. (1973), *The Economy of Love and Fear: A Preface to Grant Economics*, Belmont, Ca.: Wadsworth.

Chasse, J. D. (1984), 'Marshall, the human agent and economic growth: wants and activities revisited', *History of Political Economy*, vol. 16, pp. 381–404.

Collard, D. (1978), *Altruism and Economy: A Study in Non-Selfish Economics*, Oxford: Martin Robertson.

Collini, S., Burrow, J. and Winch, D. (1984), *That Noble Science of Politics*, Cambridge: Cambridge University Press.

Davidson, G. and Davidson, P. (1988), *Economics for a Civilized Society*, New York: Norton.

Deane, P. (1989), 'Henry Fawcett: the plain man's economist', in L. Goldman, ed., *The Blind Victorian: Henry Fawcett and British Liberalism*, Cambridge: Cambridge University Press, ch. 4.

Earl, P. (1988), *Psychological Economics: Development, Tensions, Prospects*, Boston, Dordrecht: Kluwer.

Etzioni, A. (1988), *The Moral Dimension: Toward a New Economics*, New York: Free Press.

Flubacher, J. (1950), *The Concept of Ethics in the History of Economics*, New York: Vantage Press.

Foxwell, H. S. (1887), 'The economic movement in England', *Quarterly Journal of Economics*, vol. 2, pp. 84–103.

Frank, R. H. (1985), *Choosing the Right Pond: Human Behavior and the Quest for Status*, Oxford: Oxford University Press.

Frank, R. H. (1988), *Passions Within Reason: The Strategic Role of the Emotions*, New York: Norton.

Groenewegen, P. D. (1988), 'Alfred Marshall and the establishment of the Cambridge Economic Tripos', *History of Political Economy*, vol. 20, pp. 627–67.

Groenewegen, P. D. (1990), 'Teaching economics at Cambridge at the turn of the century: Alfred Marshall as Lecturer in Political Economy', *Scottish Journal of Political Economy*, vol. 37, pp. 40–60.

Haan, N., Bellah, R., Rabinow, P. and Sullivan, W. N. (1983), *Social Science as Moral Inquiry*, New York: Columbia University Press.

Hardin, R. (1988), *Morality within the Limits of Reason*, Chicago: University of Chicago Press.

Henderson, J. P. (1989), 'The relation of ethics to economics: J. S. Mackenzie's challenge to neoclassical economics', *Review of Social Economy*, vol. 47, pp. 240–65.

Henderson, J. P. (1990), 'The ethicists' view of Marshall's *Principles*', unpublished paper, 41 pp.

Hill, P. and Keynes, R. (1989), *Lydia and Maynard*, London: Andre Deutsch.

Hirschman, A. O. (1981), 'Morality and the social sciences: a durable tension', in his *Essays in Trespassing: Economics to Politics and Beyond*, Cambridge: Cambridge University Press, pp. 294–306; also in Haan, N. et al., 1983, pp. 21–32.

Hogarth, R. M. and Reder, M. W. (1987), *Rational Choice: The Contrast Between Economics and Psychology*, Chicago: Chicago University Press.

Hollander, S. (1985), *The Economics of John Stuart Mill*, vol. 1, *Theory and Method*, Oxford: Basil Blackwell.

Hutchison, T. W. (1964), *'Positive' Economics and Policy Objectives*, London: George Allen and Unwin.

Hutchison, T. W. (1981), *The Politics and Philosophy of Economics: Marxists, Keynesians and Austrians*, New York: New York University Press.

Inglis, K. S. (1963), *Churches and the Working Classes in Victorian England*, London: Routledge.

Jones, P. D'A. (1968), *The Christian Socialist Revival: Religion, Class and Social Conscience in Victorian England*, Princeton: Princeton University Press.

Kadish, A. (1982), *The Oxford Economists in the Late Nineteenth Century*, Clarendon Press: Oxford.

Kadish, A. (1986), *Apostle Arnold: The Life and Death of Arnold Toynbee 1852–1883*, Durham, N.C.: Duke University Press.

Keynes, J. M. (1925), 'Alfred Marshall, 1842–1924', in Pigou, 1925, pp. 1–65.

Keynes, J. N. (1904) [1890], *The Scope and Method of Political Economy*, London: Macmillan, third edition.

Kitson Clark, G. (1973), *Churchmen and the Condition of England, 1832–1885: A Study in the Development of Social Ideas and Practice from the Old Regime to the Modern State*, London: Methuen.

Levitt, T. (1976), 'Alfred Marshall: Victorian relevance for modern economics', *Quarterly Journal of Economics*, vol. 90, pp. 425–43. Reprinted in Wood, 1982, vol. 1, no. 23.

Lutz, M. A. and Lux, K. (1979), *The Challenge of Humanistic Economics*, Menlo Park California: Benjamin/Cummings.

Maloney, J. (1985), *Marshall, Orthodoxy and the Professionalisation of Economics*, Cambridge: Cambridge University Press.

Marshall, A. (1873), 'The future of the working classes', in Pigou, 1925, pp. 101–18.

Marshall, A. (1874), 'The laws of political economy' and 'The province of political economy', in R. Harrison, 1963, 'Two early articles by Alfred Marshall', *Economic Journal*, vol. 73, pp. 422–30, originally published in *The Bee-Hive*. Reprinted in Wood, 1982, vol. 4, no. 106.

Marshall, A. (1876), 'Mr. Mill's theory of value', in Pigou, 1925, pp. 119–33.

Marshall, A. (1883), 'Three lectures on progress and poverty', in G. J. Stigler, 'Alfred Marshall's lectures on progress and poverty', *Journal of Law and Economics*, 1969, vol. 12, April, pp. 184–226. Reprinted in Wood, 1982, vol. 4, no. 106.

Marshall, A. (1885a), 'The present position of economics', in Pigou, 1925, pp. 152–74.

Marshall, A. (1885b), 'How far do remediable causes influence prejudicially (a) the continuity of employment, (b) the rate of wages? with four appendices', in C. W. Dilke, ed., *Report of Proceedings and Papers on the Industrial Remuneration Conference*, London: Cassel.

Marshall, A. (1887), Preface to L. L. F. R. Price, *Industrial Peace: Its Advantages, Methods and Difficulties. A Report on an Inquiry Made for the Toynbee Trustees*, London: Macmillan.

Marshall, A. (1889), 'Cooperation', in Pigou, 1925, pp. 227–55.

Marshall, A. (1893), Response to the President's Address, *Economic Journal*, vol. 3, pp. 387–90.

Marshall, A. (1897), 'The old generation of economists and the new', in Pigou, 1925, pp. 295–311.

Marshall, A. (1898), 'Mechanical and biological analogies in economics', in Pigou, 1925, pp. 312–18.

Marshall, A. (1900) [1892], *Elements of Economics of Industry: Being the First Volume of Elements of Economics*, London: Macmillan, third edition.

Marshall, A. (1907), 'Social possibilities of economic chivalry', *Economic Journal*, vol. 17, pp. 7–29. Reprinted in Pigou, 1925, pp. 323–46.

Marshall, A. (1923) [1919], *Industry and Trade: A Study of Industrial Technique and Business Organization; and of Their Influences on the Conditions of Various Classes and Nations*, London: Macmillan, fifth edition.

Marshall, A. (1961) [1890], *Principles of Economics*, C. W. Guillebaud, ed., London: Macmillan for the Royal Economic Society, ninth (variorum) edition in two volumes, vol. 1– text; vol. 2–notes.

Marshall, A. and Marshall, M. P. (1879), *Economics of Industry*, London: Macmillan, first edition.

Matthews, R. C. O. (1981), 'Morality, competition and efficiency', *The Manchester School*, vol. 49, pp. 289–309.

McPherson, M. S. (1983), 'Want formation, morality, and some interpretative aspects of economic inquiry', in Haan *et al.*, 1983, pp. 96–124.

Nielsen, K. (1967), 'Ethics, problems of', in P. Edwards, ed., *The Encyclopedia of Philosophy*, New York: Macmillan and Free Press, vol. 3, pp. 117–34.

Norman, E. R. (1976), *Church and Society in England 1770–1970: A Historical Study*, Oxford, Clarendon Press.

Parsons, T. (1931/32), 'Economics and sociology; Marshall in relation to the thought of his time', *Quarterly Journal of Economics*, vol. 46, pp. 310–45.

Parsons, T. (1931/32), 'Wants and activities in Marshall', *Quarterly Journal of Economics*, vol. 46, pp. 101–40.

Paul, E. F., Miller, F. D. and Paul, J., eds (1985), *Ethics and Economics*, Oxford: Basil Blackwell.

Phelps, E. S., ed. (1975), *Altruism, Morality and Economic Theory*, New York: Russell Sage Foundation.

Pigou, A. C., ed. (1925), *Memorials of Alfred Marshall*, London: Macmillan.

Reisman, D. (1987), *Alfred Marshall: Progress and Politics*, London: Macmillan.

Richmond, W. (1888), *Christian Economics*, London: Rivingon's.

Richmond, W. (1890), *Four Lectures on Economic Morals*, London: W. H. Allen.

Richter, M. (1964), *The Politics of Conscience: T. H. Green and His Age*, London, Weidenfeld and Nicholson.

Schneewind, J. B. (1977), *Sidgwick's Ethics and Victorian Moral Philosophy*, Oxford: Clarendon Press.

Sen, A. (1987), *On Ethics and Economics*, Oxford: Basil Blackwell.

Shove, G. F. (1942), 'The place of Marshall's *Principles* in the development of economic theory', *Economic Journal*, vol. 52, pp. 294–329. Reprinted in Wood, 1982, vol. 2, no. 38.

Sidgwick, H. (1901) [1883], *The Principles of Political Economy*, London: Macmillan, third edition.

Skidelsky, R. (1983), *John Maynard Keynes, Vol. 1: Hopes Betrayed, 1883–1920*, London: Macmillan, and New York: Viking Penguin Inc., 1986.

Webb, B. (1926), *My Apprenticeship*, London and New York: Longman Green.

Weisskopf, W. A. (1955), *The Psychology of Economics*, London: Routledge and Kegan Paul.

Whitaker, J. K. (1972), 'Alfred Marshall: the years 1877–1885', *History of Political Economy*, vol. 4, pp. 1–61. Reprinted in Wood, 1982, vol. 1, no. 8.

Whitaker, J. K., ed. (1975a), *The Early Economics Writings of Alfred Marshall 1867–1890*, London: Macmillan for the Royal Economic Society, and New York: Free Press, 2 volumes.

The Econ Journal HB1 E3
Camb Jo Econ HB1 A2C34
Jo Post K Econ HB1 J72

Whitaker, J. K. (1975b), 'John Stuart Mill's methodology', *Journal of Political Economy*, vol. 83, pp. 1033–49.

Whitaker, J. K. (1977), 'Some neglected aspects of Alfred Marshall's economic and social thought', *History of Political Economy*, vol. 9, pp. 161–97. Reprinted in Wood, 1982, vol. 1, no. 25.

Wood, J. C., ed. (1982), *Alfred Marshall: Critical Assessments*, London: Croom-Helm, four volumes.

# 9. Marshall and business

*John Maloney*

Marshall liked and admired businessmen. This sounds a very bare statement. Has anyone ever liked and admired *all* businessmen? Yet Marshall's entrepreneur is hardly ever more than a stereotype. This is odd in the work of one who was ever qualifying his economic analysis, banishing diagrams to the footnotes in case they made the world a simple place for his readers, attacking the short statement and even eschewing the short sentence on the grounds that brevity and truth did not mix. And it must be said that the Marshallian businessman, too, is complex and subtle even in his uniformity. But not everyone thought so in Marshall's lifetime. 'G. S.', reviewing *Industry and Trade* in the *Athenaeum*, was critical of a book which had

> substituted for the proverbial human calculating machine a new 'economic man'—'bold', 'far-sighted', 'alert', 'resourceful', bearing in fact a striking resemblance to the captains of industry with whom war-saving advertisements and American moving pictures have made us familiar, and almost as far removed from real life as they are.[1]

The innuendo that Marshall was misspending his old age watching silent precursors of *Citizen Kane* can, perhaps, be discounted. Yet other reviewers of *Industry and Trade* said much the same thing,[2] the book being particularly unpopular with the socialists. Did Marshall idealise the businessman? What reasons did he have for doing so? And what, if anything, did the business community think of Marshall?

## I

One could write a book about 'man in his business life' (Marshall's delineation of the territory of the *Principles*), without making the professional businessman its epitome. But, in the *Principles*, an epitome is what he is. Economists, Marshall tells us at the outset, deal with a man who is largely influenced by egoistic motives in his business life, to a great extent with reference to them; but who is neither above vanity and recklessness, nor below delight in doing his work well for its own sake, or in sacrificing himself for the good of his family, his neighbours and his country; a man who is not below the love of a virtuous life for its own sake (Marshall, 1920, p. 27).

These qualities are raised to their strongest pitch in the portrait of the entrepreneur begun in the *Principles*, matured on the smaller canvas of 'Social possibilities of economic chivalry' (1907) and etched with fervour and anxiety—as trusts and cartels extended their deadening grip—into the otherwise rather pedestrian second half of *Industry and Trade*. The portrait is least flattering in the *Principles*, though even here Marshall asserts that 'a just appreciation of the nobility of business work rightly done' waits not upon more noble businessmen but upon a more constructive and less critical spirit in the universities and colleges (Marshall, 1920, p. 300fn.). Nonetheless when Marshall himself defends the businessman against the charge of excessive love of money, the motives he substitutes are not obviously any more laudable:

> . . . even business work, that seems at first sight unattractive, often yields a pleasure by offering scope for the exercise of men's faculties, and for their instincts of emulation and power . . . a manufacturer or trader is often stimulated much more by the hope of victory over his rivals than by the desire to add something to his fortune (ibid., p. 23).

Yet even when the motive is below the highest, abilities entirely admirable in themselves can be developed, such as the ability

> to go straight to the kernel of the practical problems with which he was to deal, to see almost instinctively the relative proportions of things, to conceive wise and far-reaching policies, and to carry them out calmly and resolutely (ibid., p. 606).

In the same year as the *Principles* was first published, Marshall addressed Section F of the British Association for the Advancement of Science as its president, and here his defence of businessmen was less restrained. Their motives in competing for wealth, he said, were less sordid than the world in general 'and, I am forced to admit, economists in particular', had been wont to assume. A chemist's motives, he said, were, first, to earn enough money to provide a cultured life for himself and his family, and then 'that once provided, he spends himself in seeking knowledge, partly for its own sake, partly for the good it may do to others, and last, but often least, for the honour it may do himself'. How, if at all, did businessmen's motives differ? Very little, was Marshall's answer. They were as likely as scientists to desire a cultured life. In the search of knowledge, they had the same 'instincts of the chase', and many of them had 'the same power of being stimulated to great and feverish exertions by emulations that are not sordid or ignoble'. The main difference was that the businessman found it hard to do honour to himself by any means other than becoming rich. As a mark of excellence, money was regarded by those 'for whose opinion he cares' as more trustworthy than 'highly coloured stories about new innovations . . . And so all the best businessmen want to get money . . . (Marshall, 1890, p. 281).

The point is reiterated in 'Social possibilities of economic chivalry', (Marshall, 1907), but only after the businessman has been allowed to cut a far more romantic figure than before. His 'constantly shifting' visions of goals, routes to those goals, obstacles on the route, and contrivances to overcome the obstacles are compared to those of a master chess-player 'constantly rejecting brilliant solutions because he has pictured himself the counter-strokes to them'. The business imagination, Marshall, says,

> gains little credit with the people because it is not allowed to run riot; its strength is disciplined by a stronger will; and its highest glory is to have attained great ends by means so simple that no one will know, and none but experts will even guess, how a dozen other expedients, each suggesting as much brilliance to the hasty observer, were set aside in favour of it (ibid., p. 332).

However, Marshall continues, the fact that many large incomes owe their existence to the success of these noble designs in no way alters the waste and deprivation which accompanies maldistribution of wealth:

> Now there is a general agreement among thoughtful people, and especially among economists, that if society could award . . . honour, position and influence by means less blind and less wasteful; and if it could at the same time maintain all that stimulus which the free enterprise of the strongest businessmen derives from present conditions, then the resources thus set free would open out to the mass of people new possibilities of a higher life, and of larger and more varied intellectual activities (ibid., p. 325).

This is what 'economic chivalry' means. It includes not only public spirit, but also 'a delight in doing noble and difficult things because they are noble and difficult . . . It includes a scorn for cheap victories and a delight in succouring those who need a helping hand' (ibid., p. 330).

But the picture of *Industry and Trade* is more sombre. For while Marshall provides a demanding list of the qualities needed by the head of a business (Marshall, 1919, p. 355), very little attempt is made to judge how widely these qualities are realised in practice. It is surprising that this of all Marshall's works should stand accused of sycophancy towards business.

## II

For most of his life at least, Marshall presumed that those qualities required, and elicited, by modern business were present, if latent, in all sections of society. The emphasis varied with the audience. Opening a Co-operative Productions Exhibition in 1896, he enjoined the co-operative movement to 'bring out the faculties that were born in man', rescue working-class abilities going to waste and compete away the scarcity rents of the entrepreneurial minority:

> He did not suppose they would abolish the capitalist employer, but they were moving in the way of making him unnecessary and they would make him a much rarer person than he was now, and make him do his work for a much less share of the common produce that he now got.[3]

By 1907 such ambitions seem to have been sharply reined in. It is, in fact, rather surprising that Marshall should extend his discussion of economic chivalry to its possibilities within the working man, given that the whole purpose of the article is to reduce the supply price of entrepreneurship. But, since he does so, we can infer much from the brevity and dismissiveness of his remarks. Utopian communities around the world, Marshall assures us, are dragged down by rancour over who does the least and receives the most, amply demonstrating that ' . . . in the breast of the common man—that is, of the man who is not endowed with the qualities of leadership . . . jealousy is a more potent force than chivalry' (Marshall, 1907, p. 341).

Marshall's growing hostility in later life to socialism has often been noted. But is is only a part, albeit an important one, of his growing pessimism about the possibilities of change in general. The passages about the higher life that would one day be attained by the worker remained in the *Principles* as it went through successive editions. But elsewhere there is little on this theme after 1890. The emphasis shifts from civilising the worker to civilising the businessman, and even the businessman is cast in an increasingly passive role. The day for speaking directly to the employer, lecturing him as to what was fair and unfair industrial practice (Marshall 1887) was apparently over. By 1907 economic chivalry was a Pavlovian response to be elicited from businessmen by largely unspecified means.

Yet as Marshall muted his visions of betterment for the working-class and the capitalist class alike, he also came to repent of his rather querulous attitude to individual mobility *between* social classes. His dislike of the upwardly mobile—at any rate if their speed exceeded a crawl—was repeatedly expressed, sounds deeply felt, and lasted well into his middle years. He assured his students that 'the *nouveau riche* is a trial to himself and his friends'.[4] Individual mobility, both upwards and downwards, hurt the working class, yearly forced to exchange their own best and brightest for the stupidest and most idle offshoots of the bourgeoisie. Where members of a working-class family did rise to managerial positions, it was best that this should be accomplished over two generations—workmen who rose too quickly to posts of command were usually harsh and tyrannical, while their children had 'the worst faults of the older aristocracy without their virtues' (Marshall, 1920, p. 309).

*Industry and Trade* marks a notable advance on all this. Marshall's concern is that now, with the dominance of the large corporation, business will be an *ineffective* supplier of ladders for the working class to climb. For while 'there is a rapid increase in the number of those who have the strength and the elasticity of mind and character needed for the larger responsibilities of industry' (Marshall, 1919, p. 661), the modern manager, provided only with written records of a worker's achievement in one grade of industry, is unlikely to be able to pick such candidates out. By contrast:

> The small employer, who knew all his men, could draw a broad distinction between the value to the business of a particular operative, and the value of his work: and would go out of his way to retrain anyone who, though not specially expert and quick with his hands, would be likely to develop such faculties of judgement and resource that considerable responsibilities might be thrown upon him later on . . . (ibid., p. 662).

The simplicity and continuity, then, was in Marshall's approval of the habits and abilities instilled by the management of a modern business. The complexity was in his view as to whether such virtues potentially resided in everyone and, insofar as they did, whether collective betterment or individual mobility was the best way to realise them.

But which *country* was best at realising them? *Industry and Trade* is far from hesitant when it comes to grading nations for entrepreneurial spirit. The Spanish, we hear, had it crushed out of them by the Inquisition (ibid., p. 107). German discipline is a foe of the spontaneity which must be encouraged in the potential innovator (ibid., p. 129). England became the first industrial nation 'mainly because her people had never been either inclined or compelled to look to authority for instructions' (ibid., p. 580). But, almost from the day of his arrival in the United States in 1875, Marshall never doubted who was the most inspired nurse of business ability and, in particular, of those habits of forethought and deliberation which he prized so highly. These were instilled in the American youth from the moment that he thoughtfully and deliberately chose his own career, exempt from the interference of 'parents and masters, policemen and church ministers'. 'Fathers do not in general contend that they have a *right* to control the actions of their sons after they are able to think for themselves' (Whitaker, vol. 2, p. 359). Marshall makes no attempt to explain *why* this happy state should particularly prevail in the United States, any more than he explains *why* American youth in particular makes a hero of the 'money king' and is thus uniquely restless in humdrum and monotonous work. But, whatever the reasons, the money king displaces parents and policemen, his energising influence supplemented by the intemperate American climate and its effects on steadiness of employment: 'Every time a man is thrown out of work he is as it were directly prompted to ask himself the question "Is it worth my while to stay in this place or in this employment?"' (ibid., p. 363). Even the American co-operative societies aroused in Marshall stronger affection than he could feel for their English counterparts:

> I did not know the full power of the Cooperative spirit until at an annual national congress of delegates I heard terse, pointed, business-like arguments mingled with utterance of high aspiration, and saw in the rough, shrewd face of the speaker the bright eye sparkle with enthusiasm as he spoke of "the grand Cooperative Faith" (ibid., p. 369).

And, as economy and culture shifted in Europe and America alike, Marshall found few problems in shifting his grounds for believing in American superiority. By 1890 he was contrasting England's damaging split into rich rentiers and risk-averse managers with

> the restless energy and the versatile enterprise of a comparatively few very rich and able men who rejoice in that power of doing great things by great means that

their wealth gives them, and who have but partial respect for those who always keep their violins under glass cases (Marshall, 1890, p. 266–67).

By 1919, this particular contrast was much diminished, and Marshall was reverting to the reverence of American youth for money:

A powerful process of natural selection has thus called out the leaders of American industry from the many millions of lads who were born to the last generation from alert parents of many races; and who entered on life with the resolve that they would prove themselves to be abler and greater than their fellows by becoming rich. . . (Marshall, 1919, p. 156).

The uncharacteristic indulgence with which Marshall treats this attitude, together with his repeated failure to explain *why* it should especially prevail in America, suggest perhaps that happy memories of 1875 were strong enough to break down Marshall's critical guard on some topics for the rest of his life.

## III

So far we have been talking, in an undifferentiated way, about Marshall and 'the businessman'. Yet no economist of his time was more aware than Marshall of the opportunities and dangers that arose as the salaried manager supplanted the capitalist-entrepreneur. Speaking to the Cambridge Economic Club in 1897, Marshall revealed mixed feelings. The fact that more businessmen were now managers raised fears of ossification as the manager, with less incentive than the capitalist to succeed but just as strong a fear of failure, put risks aside and turned in a dull, if satisfactory, performance. But there were compensations. The changing nature of the manager, if not necessarily the rise of the manager in itself, gave grounds for hope that scientific expertise and sympathy would be the key traits of the businessman of tomorrow. The increase in the size of industries (does Marshall mean industries or firms?) was ensuring that 'scientific' methods were being substituted for 'empirical' ones. The company research department, the professional journal, the business congress were all helping to reap for expertise the reward of approbation. The chemist-turned-manager was entering the world of economic chivalry even if the capitalist-entrepreneur stayed largely outside it. And approbation, Marshall concluded, equalled sympathy

and sympathy is the one solid and strong force acting steadfastly throughout the whole of human nature, which has in it nothing sordid. The coming generation of economists will have no more urgent, and perhaps no more pleasant task, than to inquire . . . how far this class of forces may take the place of the cruder force of the pursuit of private material gain . . . (Marshall, 1897, p. 309).

But the sympathy of expert with expert was sympathy in a very partial form. Marshall aimed higher than this, and the promotion of managerial sympathy for the working man was high on his list of arguments for an economics degree at Cambridge. The tale of the founding of the Tripos has often been told: it will not be repeated here except insofar as Marshall invoked the Tripos as useful for businessmen and fell back on the businessman as useful for securing the Tripos.

A business education that strengthened the intellect—as opposed to pouring inert information into inert brains—had been a preoccupation of Marshall's since his early days as Principal and Professor of Political Economy at University College, Bristol. There he had used his inaugural lecture to excoriate business 'education' which consisted of 'barren facts which the boy threw off when he went into business as a bird shakes the raindrops from its feathers when the rain is over'. Business education—any education—should verse the student in human nature, or at any rate those sides of human nature not to be plumbed by playground and factory experience alone. This meant history, literature—also required to develop 'the power of appreciating what is beautiful'—and the moral sciences, among which might be reckoned 'Political Economy, the science of business . . .'.

But secondly, said Marshall, education should give the mind strength, give 'the power of reasoning correctly and knowing when a thing is proved'. No other study would do this half as well as mathematics 'which is to the mind what bread is to the body, the staff of life'—though applying mathematics in mechanics and physics should not be forgotten, training the businessman as they did in the ways of systematic experiment.

All this—the power of appreciating the beautiful aside—sounds thoroughly utilitarian. However keen the reasoning, however refined the observation developed, their ultimate purpose was to make and sell a better water pump. But the lecture's peroration strikes a more uplifting note. The quality of the businessman's motives, not the material wants of his consumers, comes on to the centre of the stage

because he has pursued those studies which will be called into play in his business, therefore his business will every day give him scientific problems which he will glory in solving because they are problems: therefore he will be helped by his business, he will almost be forced by his business to lead an intellectual life. Though a business man, nay because a business man he will play an important part in making this age an intellectual age.[5]

If Marshall could say this kind of thing at University College Bristol—where the audience, in his wife's words were 'businessmen, trade unionists and a few women; they were less academic than those at Cambridge' (Marshall, M. P., 1947, pp. 23–24)—it should cause no surprise that his eventual recommendation for Cambridge was that future businessmen should get the same undergraduate education as future economics dons. There were, of course, good political reasons for arguing this—any other plans would have involved still more demands on the resources of a grudging university administration— but cynical manoeuvring alone could hardly have conjured up the eloquence and enthusiasm with which Marshall fought his case. A fight it was, and the most contentious issue of all was the usefulness of the proposed Tripos to business. The philosopher J. McT. E. McTaggart even managed to find a businessman to assure him that there was no better training for business than Latin verses. Comments such as this were more likely to help Marshall than worry him. All the same, they may have underlined for him the difficulty of the balancing act that he was performing. For if he relied too heavily on the direct relevance of an economics degree to a career in business, supplemented with detailed examples of the kind of occasion when it would be useful, he was losing ground in an even more important mission, that of rescuing 'analytical and scientific' economics from the clutches of the kind of 'empiricist' who ruled the London School of Economics.[6] But unless some fairly specific link between economic education and business practice could be forged, he would be defenceless against the argument that economics simply provided a training of the mind which, however valuable to the businessman, could just as well be acquired by studying, say, physics or law.

Marshall resolved the dilemma by appealing to the market. He wrote to a selection of businessmen and public officials, inviting them to write back and say why they supported the proposed Tripos. In summarising their views he did not explicitly deny—though naturally he did not assert—that other subjects might train the mind for business as well as economics did. But this consideration became irrelevant if no one planning a business career was prepared to study them. Thus the report of the Economics and Political Science Syndicate, penned by Marshall and published in March 1903, found a particularly warm welcome for the Tripos among

> businessmen who, while anxious to secure for their sons the advantages of residence at one of the older Universities, yet often hesitate because there is not among the existing Honours examinations one which already during their student days will concentrate their main intellectual activity upon the field of their future labours.[7]

This point settled, Marshall was free to take the high road to the Tripos. This suited his own inclinations; and again support from his business correspondents was forthcoming. Thus Albert Fry, master engineer, Master of Merchant Venturers (Bristol) and chairman of the council of University College, Bristol, complained that

> a man now arriving from a university and entering a business office has no key to the wider interests of what is going on and is only wearied with unnecessary detail; after a while if he is the right sort he sees what it is all about and is interested, but he has had a bad time first. A proper education would save him most of this I think.[8]

And many of Marshall's correspondents stressed the difference between the middle manager, who needed a good technical education so as to see to the details, and the 'captains of industry' that Cambridge was, or should be, producing, for whom 'the highest and most complete education—in its broadest sense—is required'.[9] Marshall, of course, had no incentive to argue publicly that an economics degree at Cambridge was particularly *unsuitable* for the lower ranks of management. He did, however, consistently take the view that the number of undergraduates who could benefit from an economics degree was fairly limited, telling Foxwell in 1906 that he was

> compelled to turn out of my lecture room nearly half—this year it was more than half—of the students whom ill-advised College tutors send to me. I do it by saying at once that I shall assume the text books, and going almost at once to some intricate reasoning which no one can possibly understand unless he knows his books fairly well.[10]

And with the Tripos under way there were unsuitable subjects as well as unsuitable students to be frozen out. When *The Times* (11 December 1905) pointed out that the Cambridge curriculum made no direct mention of such subjects as 'balance-sheets, sinking funds, depreciation, goodwill and the finance of machinery', Marshall's reply was that honours students might be trusted to read about such things for themselves and confirmed, with what sounds more like satisfaction than grief, that 'no place has been found in our staff for an accountant'. He can hardly have expected what happened next—a prompt offer of funds for such a post from a Cambridge businessman, Mr J. Odell Vinter. If the University showed it 'meant business' as regards commercial education, said Vinter, then he and his associates could doubtless endow a chair in accountancy. We would like one, Marshall assured Mr Vinter with glacial enthusiasm, before flattening him with the information that 'the ablest business men tell us that it is faculty rather than knowledge which the business man of today needs'.[11]

Yet Marshall was not entirely reticent about specific lessons which a businessman might learn from having taken the Economics Tripos. In his final flysheet (5 June 1903) before the Senate voted on the matter, he invoked the profit-sharing movement that was catching on abroad, arguing that British industrialists with economics degrees could have both studied it and anticipated it. And there was one very specific purpose indeed, he confided to John Neville Keynes on 30 January 1902, which he hoped the Tripos would serve, and that was to reduce 'the hostility which business men and men of affairs show to economics'. It may be that the notably friendly letters he received from such men in support of the Tripos put these fears to rest.

## IV

To reiterate: for Marshall the businessman epitomised 'the fundamental characteristics of industrial life': ||

> a certain independence and habit of choosing one's own course for oneself, a self-reliance; a deliberation and yet a promptness of choice and judgement, and a habit of forecasting the future, and of sharing one's course with reference to distant aims (Marshall, 1920, p. 5).

|| *business man's virtues*

To some extent (and *Industry and Trade* reiterated this point, Marshall, 1919, p. 163) these virtues encroached on life as a whole. But their presence when man is away from 'the business part of his life' is not insisted on with any urgency, and indeed matters little to the success or failure of the *Principles* as a piece of persuasion. Whereas the achievement—and much of the charm—of Wicksteed's *Common Sense* (1910) lies in the way it persuades the reader that marginal equivalence pervades the atmosphere like oxygen, the

*Principles* allows its readers to keep their economic affairs, if they so desire, strictly behind the office door and before the grocer's counter.

Indeed they are encouraged to do so. 'Business' says Marshall 'is more clearly marked off from other concerns than previously' (Marshall, 1920, p. 5): and the claim turns out to be an essential buttress to the validity of neoclassical analysis. From the beginning to the end of his career, there was nothing Marshall wanted to do more than cut economics loose from classical, wealth-maximising, egoistical 'economic man'. In fact, he would never concede that any classical economist had ever set up so crude a figure, but that was beside the point. He knew very well that in the public mind economists would be stuck with this caricature as long as they did no more than disown it. An alternative had to be put in its place, and Marshall found, or thought he had found, an acceptable substitute when he used his inaugural lecture at Cambridge in 1885 to christen economics 'the science of measurable motives'.

The very definition emphasised that any motive, however exalted, was within the economist's remit as long as its intensity could be gauged with 'the measuring-rod of money'. The trouble was, however, that by 1885 orthodox economics was under attack from the relativist notions of the English historical school. To decouple the subject from an exclusive concern with money-grubbing man was indeed to dent one prong of the historical attack. But if historicists were to challenge that the power to measure motives could be applied only to a few, exceptional, periods and places, then the main thrust of relativism would merely have been diverted from economic man to a different, and by no means less obviously vulnerable, target.

No such attack was made upon Marshall's inaugural—though the economic historian William Cunningham criticised almost everything else about it. Nonetheless in the first edition of the *Principles*, Marshall abstained from any suggestion that the measurability of motives might easily be extended outside modern commercial life. In doing so he became the last English economist—disciples of Austria aside—to acquiesce in the methodological treaty proposed by Bagehot in 1876:

> We need—not that the authority of our Political Economy should be impugned, but that it should be *minimised*; that we should realise distinctly where it is established, and where not; that its sovereignty should be upheld, but its frontiers marked (Bagehot, 1876, p. 22)

To Marshall there was little point in mitigating the claims of economics to universality unless this *did* shore up its rule in a more limited domain, and this was the exact purpose of 'marking business off from other concerns'. But if business were to be so marked off, and the boundary was to be represented as 'more clear . . . than previously', then further historical explanations were required.

The simplest explanation would have been an evolutionary one—behave in a businesslike way or your firm will die. Perhaps even: maximise profits or your firm will die. With such a dictum Marshall could have thrown a bridge across from the static to the dynamic half of the *Principles* and cured the bifurcated state in which it reaches us. Instead he left it for Alchian to think of the point 60 years later (Alchian, 1950).

Why? It may be that Marshall did think of this very proposition but could not convince himself of its truth. Even so, unless his belief was that it was wholly untrue, one might expect to find it pressed into service somewhere. A second possibility is that the point genuinely did not occur to him. The third, and perhaps the most likely, explanation for this particular dog's silence in the night is that its bark would have undermined all Marshall's attempts to get round the problem of increasing returns. The biological metaphor he needed to stop the most efficient firms from running away with all the customers was the biological metaphor he actually used—the inevitable old age and decay of each tree, without any change in the state of the forest. It is hard to think of anything having less to do with the idea of evolution.

Darwinian analogies do enter the *Principles* from time to time, but none plays a significant role. Indeed the principal 'Darwinian' chapter (Book 4, ch. 8) is the most curious in the whole book. Most of the evolutionary analogies are precisely that—no more than figures of speech. Marshall stresses the range of occasions on which natural selection will *fail* to operate in the economic sphere (and omits to put forward a single case where it does). Thus:

> A mere desire on the part of employees for a share in the management and the profits of the factory in which they work, or the need on the part of clever youths for a good technical education, is not a demand in the sense in which the term is used when it is said that supply naturally and surely follows demand (Marshall, 1920, p. 242).

Later in the chapter he slaps down Smith's invisible hand as an instrument of natural selection, exempting Smith himself from criticism but complaining of the exaggeration with which Smith's followers had 'argued . . . that, if a man had a talent for managing business, he would surely be led to use that talent for the benefit of mankind' (ibid., p. 246). Finally he eschews the Lamarckian doctrine that acquired characteristics can be inherited, to fall back on the conclusion that social progress depends on how rapidly the poor are able to climb off the 'cycle of deprivation'—a point already made, without any biological trimmings whatever, in the opening pages of the book.

*Industry and Trade* goes a little further down the evolutionary path, discussing 'the origins of business trust and confidence' in terms of natural selection (Marshall, 1919, p. 164). But the case is scarcely made out: no good reason is given why honest businessmen are more likely to survive than dishonest: indeed Marshall's point that 'as small communities increase in size, an offender could more easily move from the scene of his transgression' if anything implies the opposite (ibid., p. 164).

In short, Marshall failed to harness evolutionary arguments either to his account of the rise of the 'business point of view' or to anything else. Biological metaphors abound in the *Principles*. Static equilibrium analysis is downgraded to 'a necessary introduction to a more philosophic treatment of society as an organism' (Marshall, 1920, p. 461). And yet, at the end of it all, the biological analogies themselves remain resolutely static. The firms which make up an industry grow and decay like the trees in the forest, the men and women of England, the leaves on the branch.

No coherent place in the great evolutionary chain, then, is offered either to firms or to the entrepreneurs who run them. And, with his failure to explain *how* modern commercial life comes to possess attitudes which mark it off from other concerns and other ages, he lays his work open to the charge that the demarcation is illusory. Throughout the *Principles* the predominance in business of  businesslike virtues (and especially the virtue of optimising under constraint) is asserted as a *datum*. The mystery, if any, is not why Marshall acquiesced in Bagehot's methodological treaty but why the historicists did. The Marshallian citadel was never more than lackadaisically defended. The problem of reconciling competition with increasing returns prevented him from equating survival of the fittest with survival of the maximiser. And once this option was ruled out Marshall was left with little with which to buttress his picture of business rationality, a picture which in 1890 was not axiomatic or self-evident or even routine.

## V

Marshall said more than once that he hoped businessmen would read the *Principles*. It is hard to find evidence that they did. No industrialist appears among those who wrote congratulating him on the book, and assurances that it would be useful to business invariably came from academic critics. Jowett located its value to employers and workers alike in its ability 'to mediate between the old state of industrial society and the new. Neither employers nor employed have any reason to regard you as otherwise than a friend'.[12] The *Manchester Guardian* recommended the book to businessmen for advice as to 'the aims of technical education, of the practical advantages and difficulties of getting more value out of machinery by working a factory on a system of shifts and of the economic aspects of limited liability and of restrictions on the output of industry'.[13] The *Observer* praised the guidance given to the working man who wished to start his own business.[14]

But notice of the book from the trade press was negligible. The present writer has been able to find only two such reviews. And of these, the notice in the *Railway Times* was more concerned with Marshall's deficiencies as an historian of the 17th century than with anything that might relate to railways:

> The statement that 'our Stuart Kings sold their country for French gold; and it was not till 1688 that England awoke from the slumber of Circean degradation barely in time to save Holland from destruction' would be irrelevant if it were true, which it is not.[15]

In extreme contrast, the *Journal of Gas Lighting and Water Supply* (14 October 1890) spent more time upon Marshall's recent presidential address to Section F of the British Association than on the *Principles*, praising him for describing 'Leeds gas affairs' very accurately. This, said the *Journal*'s correspondent, set him off from the average 'college professor' with whom 'worldly people' were justifiably impatient.

But whether from academia, Fleet Street or commerce, the vast majority of reviews of the *Principles* were not only laudatory, but contained no queries as to the value, or disputation as to the purpose, of studying economics. Twenty-nine years later *Industry and Trade* was to meet a more mixed reception. Here the reviews divided, as those of the *Principles* had not, very much along ideological lines. Socialists criticised the book and most other people praised it. The *New Statesman* (13 September 1919) objected that there was nothing about the wage-earner and next to nothing about co-operation. R. H. Tawney, writing in the *Daily News* (13 October 1919), accused Marshall of simply asserting that private enterprise was more efficient than nationalisation, without even expressing an opinion about, let alone demonstrating empirically, how far industry, as currently organised, 'performs its function with reasonable efficiency'.

But not all the criticism was from the socialist camp. Marshall's not especially complimentary remarks about business education in Germany drew the patriotic wrath of the *Times Educational Supplement*, according to whom he had 'exalted the German system of education', whose most salient characteristic was 'duelling of the grossest type', at the expense of Britain's own.[16] On his personal copy of this review Marshall inscribed the comment 'He does not know that the duellers are not in the main "students" proper' and 'I was afraid of being condemned as over-rating German deficiencies, so this is some comfort'. The subject could hardly be unprovocative in 1919.

But other reviewers went all the way up the evaluatory scale to extravagant praise. The *Irish Times* could 'imagine no book more likely to impress the thoughtful leader of a trade union or a manufacturer'.[17] The *Outlook* assured its readers that 'the book is *not* academic; it is indeed one of the most readable books on business questions we have ever met'.[18] To the *Liverpool Post* 'Dr Alfred Marshall is a modern Johnson, as learned and as venerable, though more tolerant and urbane . . . the book affords topics and materials to absorb a vigorous business club for the whole winter'.[19] The *Economist*'s reviewer closed the book

with the feeling that there has come to an end a long and delightful series of after dinner conversations, during which a mellowed mind has been pouring out to an impetuous and youthful guest its stores of ripe reflection and experience.[20]

Only Gerald Shove, with his comparison of Marshall with Joseph Conrad, was able to provide a simile as intriguing as this.

Once again, however, the comments overwhelmingly took the form of academics and journalists telling industrialists that they ought to read the book. The sole exception was the *Yorkshire Observer*, whose reviewer clearly was, or had been, active in the woollen industry. It can hardly have been the sort of industrial response Marshall was hoping for:

> In a description of the topmaking process on page 231 . . . 'short yarns' should, of course, be short fibres, and 'bundle' is scarcely an appropriate name for the continuous riband of wool delivered from the cob and afterwards rolled into a ball . . . Moreover, Professor Marshall seems to misconceive the functions of the Bradford Conditioning House when he states that tops are to some extent standardised under its direction.[21]

## VI

Business, then, kept its distance from Marshall. But have we also perhaps been too prone to take at face value Marshall's protestations of his closeness to business? The letters in support of the Tripos aside, not one letter to or from a businessman survives in his correspondence. Of the 56 complimentary copies of *Elements of the Economics of Industry*—of all Marshall's books the one most likely to appeal to the general reader—only one was presented to a business-man, Thomas Scott Cree of Glasgow, and even he was also a writer on economic subjects destined to become president of Section F of the British Association for the Advancement of Science and to receive an obituary in the *Economic Journal*. Mrs Marshall refers to the indus-trialists who stayed at Balliol Croft—no one has discovered who they might have been. Even Marshall's trip to America in 1875, the supposed foundation of an immense practical knowledge of business in after-life, does not yield a record of extensive connections with businessmen. Only two are mentioned in his letters home to his family, and one of these was an Englishman who 'looks forward to coming home'. We have descriptions of staying with the President of Harvard, and there meeting General Sherman and the editors of the *Atlantic Monthly* and the *Nation*. But industry merely receives 'I have seen eight factories since Tuesday' before Marshall continues with minute descriptions of two church services he has attended.[22] It could be that he thought his parents would be uninterested in his industrial experiences—yet he thought it worth sketching a piece of modern glass-blowing equipment and a plan of a Manhattan docks for their benefit. The 'American Notes' to be found in the Marshall Papers tell the story with much the same emphasis, albeit on a more cryptic scale.

With such facts (or rather lack of facts) in mind, it is possible for a reader of the *Principles* to doubt some of the genuineness of Marshall's enthusiasm and solicitude for the businessman. He had, after all, every incentive to exaggerate such feelings. Marshall *needed* the businessman as a paragon of what marked off modern industrial society from other times and places; and he needed this demarcation in order to justify the neoclassical view of the world without getting bogged down in endless and irresolvable argument. But he also needed the businessman to resolve his own warring predilections. The urge to soar into high theory, and the fear that such soaring would not turn the world into a better place, could be reconciled by establishing the necessity for advanced thinking in education for business. Economics, furthermore, could assist its own survival as a moral science by assuming responsibility for the professional ethics of the businessmen whom it educated. These were not mean goals. Even if we ultimately conclude that Marshall used business more profitably than business used Marshall, the smooth operator should not be allowed to climb, in our minds, above his true status as the (reasonably) humble servant of the missionary.

## Notes and references

[1] *Athenaeum*, 31 October 1919.

[2] See *Observer*, 14 December 1919.

[3] Speech reported in *Labour Co-Partnership*, May 1896.

[4] Cannan notes on Marshall's lectures, 18 November 1891. Cannan Papers, British Library of Economic and Political Science, London School of Economics.

[5] The text of the lecture is in the Marshall Papers, Marshall Library of Economics, Cambridge.

[6] See Marshall to J. N. Keynes, 30 January 1902, Marshall Library of Economics, Cambridge, Keynes 1(125).

[7] *Cambridge University Reporter*, 10 March 1903.

[8] A. Fry to Marshall, 3 May 1902, Marshall Papers, Marshall Library of Economics, Cambridge, Marshall, 1/121.

[9] *Banker's Magazine*, July 1903.

[10] Marshall to Foxwell, 12 February 1906, Marshall Library of Economics, Cambridge, currently Marshall 3(49).

[11] *The Times*, 11, 18, 26, 29 December 1905.

[12] Jowett to Marshall, 24 July 1890, Marshall Papers, Marshall Library of Economics, Cambridge, Marshall, 1/53.

[13] *Manchester Guardian*, 29 August 1890.

14 *Observer,* 24 August 1890.
15 *Railway Times,* October 1890.
16 *Times Educational Supplement,* 8 January 1920.
17 *Irish Times,* 12 September 1919.
18 *Outlook,* 1 November 1919.
19 *Liverpool Post,* 26 November 1919.
20 *The Economist,* 13 December 1919.
21 *Yorkshire Observer,* 6 September 1919.
22 Marshall to Rebecca Marshall (mother), 25 June 1875, Marshall Papers, Marshall Library of Economics, Cambridge, Marshall, 1/292.

## Bibliography

Alchian, A. (1950), 'Uncertainty, evolution and economic theory', *Journal of Political Economy,* vol. 58, no. 3, June.

Bagehot, W. (1876), 'The postulates of English political economy', in R. Holt Hutton, ed., *Economic Studies,* London: Longmans (1895) [1879].

Marshall, A. (1875), 'Some features of American industry', paper read at a meeting of the Cambridge Moral Science Club, 17 November 1875. Reprinted in Whitaker, 1975, vol. 2, pp. 352–77.

Marshall, A. (1887), Preface to L. L. F. R. Price, *Industrial Peace: Its Advantages, Methods and Difficulties. A Report on an Inquiry Made for the Toynbee Trustees,* London: Macmillan.

Marshall, A. (1890), 'Some aspects of competition', the Section F Presidential address to the Leeds meeting of the British Association for the Advancement of Science, reprinted in Pigou, 1925, pp. 256–91.

Marshall, A. (1897), 'The old generation of economists and the new', in Pigou, 1925, pp. 295–311.

Marshall, A. (1907), 'Social possibilities of economic chivalry', in *Economic Journal,* vol. 17, pp. 17–29. Reprinted in Pigou, 1925, pp. 323–46; page references here are to Pigou.

Marshall, A. (1919), *Industry and Trade: A Study of Industrial Technique and Business Organization; and of Their Influences on the Conditions of Various Classes and Nations,* London: Macmillan, first edition.

Marshall, A. (1920), *Principles of Economics,* London: Macmillan, eighth edition.

Marshall, M. P. (1947), *What I Remember,* Cambridge: at the University Press.

Pigou, A. C., ed. (1925), *Memorials of Alfred Marshall,* London: Macmillan.

Price, L. L. F. R. (1887), *Industrial Peace; Its Advantages, Methods and Difficulties,* London: Macmillan.

Whitaker, J. K. (ed.) (1975), *The Early Economic Writings of Alfred Marshall 1867–1890,* London: Macmillan for the Royal Economic Society and New York: Free Press, two volumes.

Wicksteed, P. H. (1910), *Common Sense of Political Economy, including a study of the human basis of economic law,* London: Macmillan & Co.

# Appendix A.
# A list of the Marshall correspondence in the Marshall Library of Economics, Cambridge

*Frances Willmoth*

This list is intended as a brief guide only. By the time it appears in print a full descriptive catalogue of all these items, a list by date and a conspectus of old and new reference numbers should be available to assist visitors to the Marshall Library and enquirers by post. The cataloguing of the rest of the collection is in progress.

A complete rearrangement of the correspondence has been necessary because of the confusion created by additions to the collection at various dates, by the inadequacy of the former numbering system and by significant omissions from it. A list surviving from the 1940s indicates that letters to Alfred, drafts or copies of his replies, and letters to Mary were once kept as a single sequence, and the main series is now arranged on this principle; the contents of bundles dated 1902 (concerning the Economics Tripos), 1907, and 1923 (concerning publications) have been kept together, as has Marshall's correspondence with his publisher (Macmillan). Finally there are the letters he received respecting his 1908 *Memorandum on the Fiscal Policy of International Trade*, letters from John Maynard Keynes found misplaced in the John Neville Keynes collection, and letters written and sent by Marshall but eventually returned to him or to the Marshall Library. All this forms Section 1 of the Marshall collection, with a single sequence of subnumbers (Marshall 1/1—Marshall 1/306). The 32 letters forming the Mary Paley Marshall correspondence can be identified in the catalogue under her name.

Letters to Herbert Somerton Foxwell, formerly numbered Marshall 3(6)—3(56), and to Charles Ryle Fay by various writers, formerly numbered Misc.1(23)—1(68) and Misc. 1(93)—1(94), are now being treated as separate collections and are not listed here. This is also true of the group of letters by Henry Fawcett bought by the Marshall Library in 1936 and of a few other items formerly numbered as 'Misc.' with no direct connection with Marshall.

In using the present list readers should note the following points. Because of constraints of space, numbers are given without a preceding collection name. The appropriate collection name must nevertheless be used in citing references. That is, 'Marshall' must be prefixed to all numbers excepting only those 'former numbers' for which a different prefix ('Misc' or 'Keynes') is given. In the column 'Former number', * indicates an item was previously unnumbered. Full names are given where possible but space has not allowed this in the case of titled personages. To enable our computer to manipulate the data it has been necessary to give dates in the form 'year.month.day'. Inferred dates are indicated by '(?)'; in the few cases where the name of a recipient has been inferred this is not indicated, as there is rarely much room for doubt. The abbreviation 'LBB' stands for the 'Large Brown Box', which contained comparatively late additions to the collection listed under this heading in the brief catalogue of the papers given in *History of Economic Thought Newsletter*, no. 3, November 1969 and reprint in Wood, 1982, vol. 4, no. 110.[1]

The preservation and detailed cataloguing of Alfred Marshall's papers has been made possible by financial support from the Marshall Library Fund II, with the approval of the Faculty of Economics and Politics, University of Cambridge, and by the generosity of St John's College, Cambridge, and of the Royal Economic Society. The project is led by Frances Willmoth, as Archivist to the Marshall Library, with the assistance of Philomena Guillebaud and Rita Tullberg. Alison Wilson has acted as a computerisation consultant.

---

[1] Wood, J. C., ed. (1982), *Alfred Marshall: Critical Assessments*, London: Croom Helm, four volumes.

| Writer (W) or recipient (R) | Date | Current number | Former number |
|---|---|---|---|

*All catalogue numbers given here are preceded by the word 'Marshall' unless otherwise specified.*
*\* in the column 'Former number' indicates that the item was previously unnumbered.*

| | | | |
|---|---|---|---|
| Acton, Lord (W) | 1895.11.16 | 1/1 | 1(1) |
| Acworth, William Mitchell (W) | 1902.4.20 | 1/113 | 1(49) |
| Alston, Leonard (W) | 1923.1.27 | 1/150 | 1(85) |
| Armitage-Smith, Sydney (W) | 1908.6.20 | 1/258 | in LBB(24) |
| (R) | 1908.6.27 | 1/260 | in LBB(24) |
| (W) | 1908.7.4 | 1/261 | in LBB(24) |
| Avebury, Lord (W) | 1902.4.16 | 1/114 | 1(50) |
| | | | |
| Balfour, Arthur James (W) | 1891.3.23 | 1/2 | 1(2) |
| (W) | 1902.4.16 | 1/3 | 1(3) |
| (W) | 1919.9.30 | 1/4 | 1(4) |
| Bateson, William (R) | 1908.10.24 | 1/272 | 3(1) |
| (R) | 1908.10.26 | 1/273 | 3(2) |
| Bauer, Stephan (W) | 1923.1.29 | 1/151 | 1(86) |
| Bechaux, A. (W) | 1907.3.6 | 1/132 | 1(69) |
| Benians, Ernest Alfred (W) | 1923.6.29 | 1/152 | 1(87) |
| Berry, Arthur (W) | 1891.4.1 | 1/282 | Misc. 1(99) |
| Booth, Charles (W) | 1902.4.17 | 1/115 | 1(51) |
| Bowes, Robert (W) | 1885.2.16 | 1/185 | 2(54) |
| Browne, George Forrest (W) | 1902.3.7 | 1/116 | 1(64) |
| Bryce, James (W) | 1890s(?) 8.23 | 1/5 | 1(5) |
| Bullock, Charles Jesse (W) | 1907.10.21 | 1/133 | 1(70) |
| Burt, Thomas (W) | 1887.2.16 | 1/6 | 1(120) |
| (W) | 1890.10.24 | 1/7 | 1(6) |
| (W | 1892.5.10 | 1/8 | 1(7) |
| (R) | 1892.5.11 | 1/9 | 1(8) |
| (W) | 1892.5.14 | 1/10 | 1(8) |
| (W) | 1899.4.28 | 1/11 | 1(121) |
| | | | |
| Calwer, Richard (W) | 1906.2.12 | 1/12 | 3(100) |
| Cannan, Edwin (W) | 1923.1.25 | 1/153 | 1(88) |
| Carver, T.N. (W) | 1923.2.17 | 1/154 | 1(89) |
| Cassel, Karl Gustav (W) | 1923.1.31 | 1/155 | 1(90) |
| Chapman, Sydney John (W) | 1923.3.6 | 1/156 | 1(91) |
| Clapham, John Harold (R) | 1912.5.17 | 1/13 | 3(90) |
| (R) | 1912.11.4 | 1/14 | 3(90) |
| Clark, William Henry (R) | 1908.11.22 | 1/262 | in LBB(24) |
| (W) | 1910.3.23 | 1/263 | in LBB(24) |
| (W) | 1910.3.26 | 1/266 | in LBB(24) |
| Cohen, N.L. [Nathaniel Louis] (R) | 1902.6.14 | 1/131 | Misc. 2(31) |

| Writer (W) or recipient (R) | Date | Current number | Former number |
|---|---|---|---|
| Cunynghame, Henry Hardinge (W) | 1888.10.4 | 1/15 | 1(10) |
| Cust, Nina (W) | 1914.10.16 | 1/16 | 1(164) |
| (R) | 1914.10.17 | 1/17 | 1(165) |
| | | | |
| Dale, Sir David (W) | 1902.4.28 | 1/117 | 1(52) |
| Dalla Volta, Riccardo (W) | 1923.2.8 | 1/18 | 1(65) |
| Davies, T. Llewellyn (W) | 1903.7.2 | 1/252 | in LBB(24) |
| (R) | 1903.7.14 | 1/253 | in LBB(24) |
| (W) | 1903.8.13 | 1/254 | in LBB(24) |
| (W) | 1903.8.25 | 1/255 | in LBB(24) |
| Dawkins, Clinton Edward (W) | 1902.4.18 | 1/118 | 1(53) |
| Dawson, William Harbutt (R) | 1916.2.2 | 1/274 | 3(3) |
| (R) | 1916.6.5 | 1/275 | 3(4) |
| (R) | 1916.11.18 | 1/276 | 3(5) |
| Dibblee, George Binney (W) | 1902.4.25 | 1/119 | 1(54) |
| Dicey, Albert Venn (W) | 1893.11.7 | 1/19 | 1(11) |
| (W) | 1903.11.25 | 1/20 | 1(12) |
| (W) | 1903.12.11 | 1/21 | 1(122) |
| Dixon, Frank Haigh (W) | 1907.10.10 | 1/134 | 1(71) |
| | | | |
| Edgeworth, Francis Ysidro (R) | 1891 | 1/277 | 3(58) |
| (R) | 1891.2.16 | 1/278/1,2 | 3(57) |
| (R) | 1891.4.1 | 1/282 | Misc. 1(99) |
| (R) | 1891.4.4 | 1/279 | 3(59) |
| (R) | 1892.4.26 | 1/280 | 3(60) |
| (R) | 1892.4.28 | 1/281 | 3(61) |
| (R) | 1907.2.11 | 1/23 | 1(163) |
| (W) | 1907.2.9 | 1/22 | 1(163) |
| (W) | 1923.2.7 | 1/157 | 1(106) |
| Elliott, Thomas Henry (W) | 1902.4.1 | 1/120 | 1(111) |
| (W) | 1906.5.24 | 1/24 | 1(13) |
| (R) | 1906.5.25 | 1/25 | 1(13) |
| (W) | 1906.5.26 | 1/26 | 1(14) |
| | | | |
| Florence, Philip Sargant (W) | 1927.2.13 | 1/27 | 1(140) |
| Flux, Alfred William (R) | 1901.6.4 | 1/283/1,2 | 3(83) |
| (W) | 1923.1.28 | 1/158 | 1(92) |
| Foxwell, Herbert Somerton (W) | 1907.10.2 | 1/136 | 1(73) |
| (W) | 1923.1.27 | 1/159 | 1(93) |
| Fry, Albert (W) | 1902.5.3 | 1/121 | 1(55) |
| Fry, Rt. Hon. Lewis (W) | 1902.4.18 | 1/122 | 1(56) |
| | | | |
| Galton, Francis (W) | 1891.8.3 | 1/28 | 1(23) |
| Garnett, William (W) | 1902.6.4 | 1/123 | 1(57) |

| Writer (W) or recipient (R) | Date | Current number | Former number |
|---|---|---|---|
| Gibb, George S. (W) | 1902.4.19 | 1/124 | 1(58) |
| Gide, Charles (W) | 1923.2.1 | 1/160 | * |
| Giffen, (Sir) Robert (R) | 1886.6.25 | 1/284 | 3(86) |
| (W) | 1886.6.28 | 1/285 | 3(86) |
| (W) | 1902.2.10 | 1/125 | 1(59) |
| Girdlers, Worshipful Co. of (R) | 1909.6.2 | 1/29 | 3(91) |
| Gladstone, William Ewart (W) | 1866.7.4 | 1/251 | * |
| Glover, Sir John (W) | 1902.6.14 | 1/131 | Misc. 2(31) |
| | | | |
| Hadley, Arthur Twining (W) | 1923.2.15 | 1/161 | 1(94) |
| Henry, Professor (W) | 1885.1.2 | 1/184 | 2(48) |
| Hilton, John (R) | 1919.4.14 | 1/30 | 3(62) |
| Hobson, Charles Kenneth | 1909.10.16 | 1/286 | Library file* |
| (R) | 1944.12.31 | 1/287 | Library file* |
| (W) | 1961.2.21 | 1/288 | Library file* |
| Hollander, Jacob Henry (W) | 1907.10.1 | 1/137 | 1(74) |
| | | | |
| Jack, William (W) | 1877.6.9 | 1/177 | 2(38) |
| (W) | 1877.7.19 | 1/180 | 2(41) |
| (W) | 1877.7.26 | 1/181 | 2(42) |
| Jackson, Henry (W) | no date | 1/32 | 1(166) |
| James, Montague Rhodes (W) | 1913.12.19 | 1/33 | 1(66) |
| Jenks, Jeremiah Whipple (W) | 1907.10.29 | 1/138 | 1(75) |
| Jenkyn Jones, William (W) | 1923.2.1 | 1/163 | 1(96) |
| Jevons, Herbert Stanley (W) | 1923.2.15 | 1/162 | 1(95) |
| Jevons, William Stanley (W) | 1875.1.7 | 1/34 | 3(101) |
| (W) | 1879.5.12 | 1/35 | 3(103) |
| Jowett, Benjamin (W) | 1879 (before) 10.6 | 1/37 | 1(14A) |
| (W) | 1879.10.6 | 1/38 | 1(15) |
| (W) | 1881.7.16 | 1/39 | 1(123) |
| (W) | 1881.8.9 | 1/40 | 1(16) |
| (W) | 1881.8.21 | 1/41 | 1(17) |
| (W) | 1883.3.28 | 1/42 | 1(18) |
| (W) | 1884.12.14 | 1/43 | 1(124) |
| (W) | 1884.12.25 | 1/44 | 1(19) |
| (W) | 1885.2.22 | 1/45 | 1(125) |
| (W) | 1886(?).1.5 | 1/46 | 1(20) |
| (W) | 1886.12.30 | 1/47 | 1(126) |
| (W) | 1887.4.11 | 1/48 | 1(127) |
| (W) | 1887.7.3 | 1/49 | 1(128) |
| (W) | 1888.12.19 | 1/50 | 1(129) |
| (W) | 1889.1.6 | 1/51 | 1(130) |
| (W) | 1890.5.22 | 1/52 | 1(131) |
| (W) | 1890.7.24 | 1/53 | 1(21) |

| Writer (W) or recipient (R) | Date | Current number | Former number |
|---|---|---|---|
| (W) | 1890.9.18 | 1/54 | 1(132) |
| (W) | 1890.10.20 | 1/55 | 1(22) |
| (W) | 1890.12.30 | 1/56 | 1(135) |
| (W) | 1891.7.23 | 1/57 | 1(134) |
| (W) | 1891.9.30 | 1/58 | 1(135) |
| (W) | 1892.6.10 | 1/59 | 1(136) |
| (W) | 1892.10.16 | 1/60 | 1(137) |
| (W) | 1893.1.2 | 1/61 | 1(138) |
| (W) | 1893.8.7 | 1/62 | 1(139) |
| Kawabe, Kumakichi (R) | 1910.5.2 | 1/63 | 3(85) |
| Keynes, John Maynard (W) | 1910.7.11 | 1/269 | Keynes 5(28) |
| (W) | 1910.7.12 | 1/270 | Keynes 5(29) |
| (W) | 1910.9.13 | 1/271 | Keynes 5(30) |
| (W) | 1914.10.10 | 1/64 | 1(67) |
| (W) | 1919.9.29 | 1/65 | 1(68) |
| (W) | 1922.6.7 | 1/66 | 1(150) |
| (W) | 1922.7.25 | 1/67 | 1(149) |
| (W) | 1944.12.31 | 1/287 | Library file* |
| Keynes, John Neville (W) | 1891.5.3 | 1/69 | 1(108) |
| (W) | 1898.10.18 | 1/70 | 1(109) |
| (W) | 1902.1.29 | 1/71 | 1(110) |
| (W) | 1884.12.29 | 1/68 | 1(107) |
| Kidd, Benjamin (R) | 1894.6.6 | 1/72 | 3(63) |
| Koebner, W. for J. G. Cotta' sche Buchhandlung Nachfolger (W) | 1903.9.3 and 5 | 1/214 | * |
| Laughlin, James Laurence (W) | 1908.11.12 | 1/74 | 1(24) |
| Lavington, F. (W) | 1923 (inferred) | 1/164 | 1(97) |
| Leaf, Walter (W) | 1902.4.17 | 1/126 | 1(60) |
| LeMarchant, F.C. (W) | 1902.4.17 | 1/127 | 1(62) |
| Leslie, Thomas Edward Cliffe (W) | 1878(?).6.3 | 1/75 | 1(9) |
| Levasseur, Emile (W) | 1908(?) before 3 June | 1/76 | 1(25) |
| (W) | 1908.6.3 | 1/77 | 1(26) |
| Lieben, Richard (W) | 1906.6.17 | 1/78 | 1(27) |
| (R) | 1906.6.19 | 1/79 | 1(27) |
| (W) | 1906.6.29 | 1/80 | 1(28) |
| Lloyd George, David (R) | 1908.6.27 | 1/259 | in LBB(24) |
| Ludlow, John Malcolm Forbes(W) | 1887.11.27 | 1/81 | 1(141) |
| (W) | 1901.6.2 | 1/82 | 1(29) |
| (W) | 1901.6.6 | 1/83 | 1(30) |

| Writer (W) or recipient (R) | Date | Current number | Former number |
|---|---|---|---|
| Macdonald, J.A. Murray (W) | 1910.4.22 | 1/264 | in LBB(24) |
| (R) | 1910.4.23 | 1/265 | in LBB(24) |
| (W) | 1910.4.25 | 1/267 | in LBB(24) |
| Macdonell, John (W) | 1902.4.1 (copy) | 1/129 | 1(61) |
| (W) | 1902.4.1 | 1/128 | 1(61) |
| Macmillan & Co. (R) | 1878.7(?) | 1/182 | 2(49) |
| (W) | 1886.11.15 | 1/191 | 2(45) |
| (W) | 1886.6.2 | 1/187 | 2(55) |
| (W) | 1886.11.10 | 1/190 | 2(44) |
| (R) | 1887(?) | 1/192 | 2(1) |
| (W) | 1887.4.14 | 1/193 | 2(7) |
| (W) | 1890.3.27 | 1/195 | 2(9) |
| (W) | 1890.7.7 | 1/196 | 2(8) |
| (W) | 1891.1.9 | 1/198 | 2(2) |
| (W) | 1893.1.23 | 1/207 | 2(53) |
| (R) | 1919.8.26 | 1/238 | 2(29) |
| (W) | 1920.4.1 | 1/241 | 2(32) |
| (W) | 1920.4.9 | 1/242 | 2(33) |
| Macmillan, Alexander (W) | 1877.4.17 | 1/175 | 2(36) |
| (W) | 1877.5.14 | 1/176 | 2(37) |
| (W) | 1877.7.3 | 1/178 | 2(39) |
| (W) | 1877.7.16 | 1/179 | 2(40) |
| (W) | 1880.6.22 | 1/183 | 2(43) |
| Macmillan, (Sir) Frederick (W) | 1892.1.5 | 1/200 | 2(50) |
| (W) | 1892.2.24 | 1/202 | 2(52) |
| (W) | 1892.2.26 | 1/203 | 2(51) |
| (R) | 1892.2.27 | 1/204 | 2(51) |
| (W) | 1892.2.29 | 1/205 | 2(3) |
| (W) | 1895.9.16 | 1/208 | 2(4) |
| (W) | 1895.10.3 | 1/209 | 2(5) |
| (W) | 1896.1.31 | 1/210 | 2(10) |
| (R) | 1896.10.5 | 1/211 | 2(6) |
| (W) | 1896.10.6 | 1/212 | 2(6) |
| (W) | 1903.6.22 | 1/213 | 2(56) |
| (W) | 1907.10.5 | 1/215 | 2(11) |
| (W) | 1908.11.23 | 1/216 | 2(12) |
| (W) | 1910.4.6 | 1/217 | 2(13) |
| (W) | 1910.4.25 | 1/268 | in LBB(24) |
| (W) | 1913.5.14 | 1/218 | 2(14) |
| (W) | 1916.4.4 | 1/219 | 2(15) |
| (W) | 1916.4.7 | 1/220 | 2(16) |
| (W) | 1917.8.22 | 1/221 | 2(17) |
| (R) | 1917.8.25 | 1/222 | 2(17) |
| (W) | 1917.8.29 | 1/223 | 2(18) |
| (R) | 1918.6.8 | 1/224 | 2(19) |

| Writer (W) or recipient (R) | Date | Current number | Former number |
|---|---|---|---|
| (W) | 1918.6.10 | 1/225 | 2(19) |
| (R) | 1918.6.11 | 1/226 | 2(20) |
| (W) | 1918.6.12 | 1/227 | 2(20) |
| (R) | 1918.10.12 | 1/228 | 2(21) |
| (W) | 1918.10.14 | 1/229 | 2(21) |
| (W) | 1918.10.24 | 1/230 | 2(22) |
| (W) | 1919.6.2 | 1/231 | 2(23) |
| (W) | 1919.7.1 | 1/232/1,2 | 2(24) |
| (R) | 1919.7.2 | 1/233 | 2(25) |
| (W) | 1919.7.3 | 1/234 | 2(25) |
| (W) | 1919.8.19 | 1/235 | 2(26) |
| (W) | 1919.8.21 | 1/236 | 2(27) |
| (W) | 1919.8.26 | 1/237 | 2(28) |
| (W) | 1919.9.11 | 1/239 | 2(30) |
| (W) | 1919.9.18 | 1/240 | 2(31) |
| (W) | 1920.11.29 | 1/243 | 2(34) |
| (W) | 1920.12.1 | 1/244 | 2(35) |
| Mann, Thomas (W) | 1890 (approx.) | 1/84 | 1(32) |
| (W) | 1891.3.14 | 1/85 | 1(33) |
| (W) | 1892.5.12 | 1/86 | 1(34) |
| Marshall, Mary Paley (R) | 1881.7.16 | 1/39 | 1(123) |
| (R) | 1881.9.29 | 1/109 | 1(146) |
| (R) | 1884.12.14 | 1/43 | 1(124) |
| (R) | 1885.2.22 | 1/45 | 1(125) |
| (R) | 1886(?).1.5 | 1/46 | 1(20) |
| (R) | 1886.12.30 | 1/47 | 1(126) |
| (R) | 1887.2.16 | 1/6 | 1(120) |
| (R) | 1887.4.11 | 1/48 | 1(127) |
| (R) | 1887.7.3 | 1/49 | 1(128) |
| (R) | 1887.11.27 | 1/81 | 1(141) |
| (R) | 1888.12.19 | 1/50 | 1(129) |
| (R | 1889.1.6 | 1/51 | 1(130) |
| (R) | 1890.5.22 | 1/52 | 1(131) |
| (R) | 1890.9.18 | 1/54 | 1(132) |
| (R) | 1890.12.30 | 1/56 | 1(135) |
| (R) | 1891.7.23 | 1/57 | 1(134) |
| (R) | 1891.9.30 | 1/58 | 1(135) |
| (R) | 1892.2.27 | 1/93 | 1(143) |
| (R) | 1892.6.10 | 1/59 | 1(136) |
| (R) | 1892.10.16 | 1/60 | 1(137) |
| (R) | 1893.1.2 | 1/61 | 1(138) |
| (R) | 1893.8.7 | 1/62 | 1(139) |
| (R) | 1903.12.11 | 1/21 | 1(122) |
| (R) | 1909.5.14 | 1/99 | 1(40) |

| Writer (W) or recipient (R) | Date | Current number | Former number |
|---|---|---|---|
| (R) | 1909.12.11 | 1/102 | 1(145) |
| (W) | 1910.5.2 | 1/63 | 3(85) |
| (R) | 1922.6.7 | 1/66 | 1(150) |
| (R) | 1922.7.25 | 1/67 | 1(149) |
| (R) | 1925.12.2 | 1/92 | 1(142) |
| (R) | 1927.2.13 | 1/27 | 1(140) |
| (R) | 1927.10.13 | 1/112 | 1(198) |
| (R) | 1929.12.30 | 1/110 | 1(147) |
| Marshall, Rebeccah (R) | 1875.6.5 | 1/289 | 3(66) |
| (R) | 1875.6.12 | 1/290 | 3(67) |
| (R) | 1875.6.20 | 1/291 | 3(68) |
| (R) | 1875.6.25 | 1/292 | 3(69) |
| (R) | 1875.7.5 | 1/293 | 3(70) |
| (R) | 1875.7.10 | 1/294 | 3(71) |
| (R) | 1875.7.18 | 1/295 | 3(72) |
| (R) | 1875.8.22 | 1/296 | 3(73) |
| (R) | 1875.9.5 | 1/297 | 3(74) |
| (R) | 1875.9.23 | 1/298 | 3(75) |
| (R) | 1875.9.25 | 1/299 | 3(76) |
| Mavor, James (W) | 1923.2.21 | 1/165 | 1(98) |
| McEwen, Alexander (R) | 1866.7.4 [from Gladstone, q.v.] | | |
| Menger, Carl (W) | 1890.6.8 | 1/87 | 1(35) |
| (W) | 1891.1.10 | 1/88 | 1(36) |
| Mozley, J.R. (W) | 1916.9.29 | 1/89 | 1(31) |
| Nicholson, Joseph Shields (W) | 1907.9.21 | 1/139 | 1(78) |
| North, S. (W) | 1907.6.4 | 1/140 | 1(79) |
| Ogden, Charles Kay (R) | 1917.3.15 | 1/90 | 3(99) |
| Oshima, H. (W) | 1923.2.7 | 1/166 | 1(99) |
| Papi, Giuseppe Ugo (W) | 1923.(?).26 | 1/167 | 1(100) |
| Pate, Miss M. (R) | 1908.4.25 | 1/302 | 3(78) |
| (R) | 1908.5(?) | 1/303 | 3(80) |
| (R) | 1908.7.27 | 1/304 | 3(79) |
| Phelps, Lancelot Ridley (W) | 1907.9.25 | 1/141 | 1(80) |
| Pigou, A. C. (W) | 1923(?).1.25 | 1/168 | 1(101) |
| Plastounoff, Roman R. (W) | 1886.10.16 | 1/188 | 2(46) |
| (W) | 1886.10.29 | 1/189 | 2(47) |
| Pollock, (Sir) Frederick (W) | 1891.1.17 | 1/91 | 1(37) |
| (W) | 1925.12.2 | 1/92 | 1(142) |
| Potter, Beatrice (R) | 1891.7.11 | 1/305 | 3(81) |
| (W) | 1892.2.27 | 1/93 | 1(143) |
| Ramsay, (Sir) William (R) | 1902.4.21 | 1/94/1,2 | 3(82) |

| Writer (W) or recipient (R) | Date | Current number | Former number |
|---|---|---|---|
| Rayleigh, Baron (W) | 1908.5.20 | 1/95 | 1(38) |
| Ritchie, Charles Thomson (W) | 1903(?).9.19 | 1/256 | in LBB(24) |
| (R) | 1903.9.21 | 1/257 | in LBB(24) |
| Roberts, Ernest Stewart (R) | 1910.8.22 | 1/96 | 3(92) |
| Rogers, James Edwin Thorold (W) | 1888(?).3.19 | 1/97 | 1(39) |
| Rothenstein, William (W) | 1908.4.21 | 1/98 | 1(40) |
| (W) | 1909.5.14 | 1/99 | 1(40) |
| Schmoller, Gustav (W) | 1890.8.6 | 1/100 | 1(41) |
| (W) | 1893.11.10 | 1/101 | 1(42) |
| Scott, Robert Forsyth (W) | 1909.12.11 | 1/102 | 1(145) |
| Seager, Henry Rogers (W) | 1907.10.10 | 1/142 | 1(81) |
| Shove, Gerald Frank (W) | 1923.1.25 | 1/169 | 1(102) |
| Smith, George Armitage (W) | 1907.9.19 | 1/143 | 1(82) |
| Smith, Hastings Bertrand Lees (W) | 1907.9.17 | 1/144 | 1(77) |
| Smith, (Sir) Hubert Llewellyn (R) | 1919 (or 1920) | 1/103 | 3(84) |
| (W) | 1923.1.30 | 1/170 | 1(103) |
| Stephen, Leslie (W) | 1891.3.2 | 1/104 | 1(43) |
| Sutherland, (Sir) Thomas (W) | 1902.4.18 | 1/130 | 1(63) |
| Taussig, Frank William (W) | 1907.8.2 | 1/145 | 1(83) |
| (W) | 1907.10.14 | 1/146 | 1(84) |
| (W) | 1923.2.20 | 1/171 | 1(104) |
| Taylor, W.G. Langworthy (W) | 1907.10.20 | 1/147 | 1(76) |
| Unidentified (R) | 1889.10.20 | 1/306 | 3(77) |
| Wagner, Adolph Heinrich G. (W) | 1891.3.22 | 1/105 | 1(44) |
| (W) | 1901.5.3 | 1/106 | 1(45) |
| Ward, Adolphus William (W) | 1908.5.30 | 1/107 | 1(46) |
| Webb, B. see Potter | | | |
| Wieser, Friedrich von (W) | 1895.11.24 | 1/108 | 1(47) |
| Wilson, James Maurice (W) | 1881.9.29 | 1/109 | 1(146) |
| (W) | 1929.12.30 | 1/110 | 1(147) |
| Young, Allyn Abbot (W) | 1927.10.13 | 1/112 | 1(198) |
| (W) | 1909.2.3 | 1/111 | 1(48) |
| Yule, George Udny (W) | 1923.1.25 | 1/172 | 1(105) |

# Appendix B.
# General bibliography

*The date in square brackets is that of the first edition of the cited work.*

Marshall, A. (1890), *Principles of Economics*, vol. 1, London: Macmillan, first edition.

Marshall, A. (1891), *Principles of Economics*, vol. 1, London: Macmillan, second edition.

Marshall, A. (1895), *Principles of Economics*, vol. 1, London: Macmillan, third edition.

Marshall, A. (1898), *Principles of Economics*, vol. 1, London: Macmillan, fourth edition.

Marshall, A. (1907), *Principles of Economics*, vol. 1, London: Macmillan, fifth edition.

Marshall, A. (1910), *Principles of Economics, An Introductory Volume*, London: Macmillan, sixth edition.

Marshall, A. (1916), *Principles of Economics, An Introductory Volume*, London: Macmillan, seventh edition.

Marshall, A. (1920), *Principles of Economics, An Introductory Volume*, London: Macmillan, eighth edition.

Marshall, A. (1949), *Principles of Economics*, London: Macmillan, eighth edition, reset and with a comparative index of new and old page settings.

Marshall, A. (1961), *Principles of Economics*, C. W. Guillebaud, ed., London: Macmillan for the Royal Economic Society, ninth (variorum) edition in two volumes, vol. 1– text; vol. 2–notes.

Abelson, R. and Nielsen, K. (1967), 'Ethics, History of', P. Edwards, ed., *The Encyclopedia of Philosophy*, New York: Macmillan and Free Press, vol. 3, pp. 81–116.

Alchian, A. (1950), 'Uncertainty, evolution and economic theory', *Journal of Political Economy*, vol. 58, no. 3, June.

American Economic Association (1953), *Readings in Price Theory*, Homewood, Ill: Irwin.

Amery, J. (1951), 'Joseph Chamberlain and the tariff reform campaign', in vol. 4 of J. L. Garvin and J. Amery, *Life of Joseph Chamberlain*, London: Macmillan, in six volumes, 1932–69.

Andrews, P. W. S. (1951), 'Industrial analysis in economics', in T. Wilson and P. W. S. Andrews, eds, *Oxford Studies in the Price Mechanism*, Oxford: Oxford University Press.

Auerbach, A. J. (1987), 'The theory of excess burden and optimal taxation', in A. J. Auerbach and M. Feldstein, eds, *Handbook of Public Economics*, Amsterdam & New York: North Holland, vol. 1, chap. 2.

Axelrod, R. (1984), *The Evolution of Cooperation*, New York: Basic Books.

Bagehot, W. (1876), 'The postulates of political economy'. Reprinted in R. Holt Hutton, ed., *Economic Studies*, London: Longmans, 1895 [1879].

Bagehot, W. (1953) [1880], *Economic Studies*, Stanford: Academic Reprints.

Balfour, A. J. (1903), *Economic Notes on Insular Free Trade*, London: Longman Green.

Barnard, A. (1958), *The Australian Wool Market, 1840–1900*, Melbourne: Melbourne University Press.

Barone, E. (1894), 'Sul trattamento di quistioni dinamiche', *Giornale degli Economisti*, vol. 9, no. 5, November.

Bartley, N. (1892), *Opals and Agates: or Scenes under the Southern Cross and the Magelhans*, Brisbane: Gardina Gotch.

Barucci, P. (1972), 'The spread of marginalism in Italy, 1871–1890', *History of Political Economy*, vol. 4, pp. 512–32.

Bastable, C. F. (1895) [1892], *Public Finance*, London: Macmillan, second edition.

Baumol, W. (1986), *Superfairness: Applications and Theory*, Cambridge, Mass.: MIT Press.

Becher, H. (1971), *William Whewell and Cambridge Mathematics*, unpublished Ph.D. thesis, University of Missouri.

Berkeley Jones, Rev. H. (1853), *Adventures in Australia in 1852 and 1853*, London: Richard Bentley.

Bharadwaj, K. (1978), *Classical Political Economy and the Rise to Dominance of Supply and Demand Theories*, New Delhi: Orient Longmans.

Bharadwaj, K. (1978), 'The subversion of classical analysis', *Cambridge Journal of Economics*, vol. 2, pp. 253–72. Reprinted in Wood, 1982, vol. 3, no. 94.

Bickerdicke, G. F. (1902), 'Taxation of site value', *Economic Journal*, vol. 12, no. 4, December, pp. 472–84.

Black, R. D. C., ed. (1977), *Papers and Correspondence of W. S. Jevons*, vol. 3, London: Macmillan for the Royal Economic Society.

Black, R. D. C., ed. (1981), *Papers and Correspondence of W. S. Jevons*, vol. 7, London: Macmillan for the Royal Economic Society.

Black, R. D. C. (1987), 'Fleeming Jenkin', in J. Eatwell, M. Milgate and P. Newman, eds, *The New Palgrave: A Dictionary of Economics*, London: Macmillan, New York: Stockton Press and Tokyo: Maruzen Co.

Black, R. D. C. (1990), 'Jevons, Marshall and the utilitarian tradition', *Scottish Journal of Political Economy*, vol. 37, pp. 5–17.

Blaug, M. (1985), *Economic Theory in Retrospect*, Cambridge: Cambridge University Press, fourth edition.

Boulding, K. (1969), 'Economics as a moral science', *American Economic Review*, vol. 59, pp. 1–12.

Boulding, K. (1973), *The Economy of Love and Fear: A Preface to Grant Economics*, Belmont, Ca.: Wadsworth.

Brems, H. (1975), 'Marshall on mathematics', *Journal of Law and Economics*, vol. 18, no. 2, pp. 583–85. Reprinted Wood, 1982, vol. 1, no. 22.

Brentano, L. (1903), 'The proposed reversal of English commercial policy', *The Fortnightly Review*, vol. 74.

Brownlie, A. and Lloyd Prichard, M. (1963), 'Professor Fleeming Jenkin 1833–1885: pioneer in engineering and political economy', *Oxford Economic Papers*, 15, pp. 204–16.

Cairnes, J. E. (1874), *Some Leading Principles of Political Economy Newly Expounded*, New York: Harper.

Cassel, G. (1901), 'The theory of progressive taxation', *Economic Journal*, vol. 11, no. 4, December, pp. 481–91.

Cassel, G. (1932), 'The mechanism of pricing', in his *The Theory of Social Economy*, translated to English by S. L. Barron, London: Ernest Benn, as reprinted in H. Townsend, ed., *Price Theory*, Harmondsworth: Penguin, 1971.

Chamberlin, E. (1938) [1933], *The Theory of Monopolistic Competition*, Cambridge, Mass: Harvard University Press.

Chapman, S. J. (1912), 'The incidence of some land taxes and the dispersion of differential advantage', *Economic Journal*, vol. 22, no. 3, September, pp. 489–92.

Chapman, S. J. (1913), 'The utility of income and progressive taxation', *Economic Journal*, vol. 23, no. 1, March, pp. 25–35.

Chasse, J. D. (1984), 'Marshall, the human agent and economic growth: wants and activities revisited', *History of Political Economy*, vol. 16, pp. 381–404.

Clapham, J. H. (1922), 'Of empty economic boxes', *Economic Journal*, vol. 32, no. 3, September, pp. 305–14.

Clapp, B. W. (1962), 'A Manchester merchant and his schedules of supply and demand', Economica, vol. 29, pp. 185–87.

Coase, R. H. (1975), 'Marshall on method', *Journal of Law and Economics*, vol. 18, no. 1, pp. 25–31. Reprinted Wood, 1982, vol. 1, no. 21.

Coase, R. H. (1984), 'Alfred Marshall's mother and father', *History of Political Economy*, vol. 16, no. 4.

Coats, A. W. (1964), 'The role of authority in the development of British economics', *Journal of Law and Economics*, vol. 7.

Coats, A. W. (1968), 'Political economy and the tariff reform campaign of 1903', *Journal of Law and Economics*, vol. 11.

Collard, D. (1978), *Altruism and Economy: A Study in Non-Selfish Economics*, Oxford: Martin Robertson.

Collini, S., Burrow, J. and Winch, D. (1984), *That Noble Science of Politics*, Cambridge: Cambridge University Press.

Colwyn Committee (1927), *Report of the Committee on the National Debt and Taxation*, Cmnd 2800, London: HMSO.

Corry, B. (1968), 'Marshall, Alfred', in D. L. Sills, ed., *International Encyclopedia of the Social Sciences*, vol. 10, p. 25.

Cournot, A.-A. (1897) [1838], *Researches into the Mathematical Principles of the Theory of Wealth*, translated to English by N. T. Bacon, New York: Macmillan.

Dalla Volta, R. (1885), 'A. Marshall, "The present position of economics"', *L'Economista*, 25 October.

Dalla Volta R. (1890), 'A. Marshall, *Principles of Economics*', *L'Economista*, 28 September.

Davidson, G. and Davidson, P. (1988), *Economics for a Civilized Society*, New York: Norton.

Deane, P. (1989), 'Henry Fawcett: the plain man's economist', in L. Goldman, ed., *The Blind Victorian: Henry Fawcett and British Liberalism*, Cambridge: Cambridge University Press, ch. 4.

Dickens, C. (1971) [1854], *Hard Times*, New York: Signet.

Dorfman, J. (1941), 'The Seligman correspondence', *Political Science Quarterly*, 56, pp. 407–409.

Dupuit, J. (1952), 'On the measurement of the utility of public works', *International Economic Papers*, 2, pp. 83–110.

Earl, P. (1988), *Psychological Economics: Development, Tensions, Prospects*, Boston, Dordrecht: Kluwer.

Einaudi, L. (1980), 'La scienza economica in Italia. Reminescenze', in M. Finoia ed., *La scienza economica in Italia, 1850–1950*, Bologna: Cappelli.

Ekelund, R. and Shieh, Y. (1989), 'Jevons on utility, exchange, and demand theory', *Manchester School*, 57, pp. 17–33.

Ekelund, R. B., Jr, and Hebert, R. F. (1990), *A History of Economic Theory and Method*, New York: McGraw-Hill, third edition.

Ellis, H. S. and Fellner, W. J. (1943), 'External economies and diseconomies', *American Economic Review*, vol. 33, September, pp. 493–511. Reprinted in American Economic Association (1953).

Etzioni, A. (1988), *The Moral Dimension: Toward a New Economics*, New York: Free Press.

Fanno, M. (1914), *Contributo alla teoria dell' offerta a costi congiunti*, supplement to *Giornale degli Economisti*, vol. 19.

Fanno, M. (1926), 'Contributo alla teoria economica dei beni succedanei', *Annali di Economia*, no. 3.

Fawcett, H. (1878), *Free Trade and Protection: An Inquiry into the Causes which have Retarded the General Adoption of Free Trade since its Introduction into England*, London: Macmillan.

Feiwel, G., ed. (1989), *Joan Robinson and Modern Economic Theory*, New York: New York University Press.

Flubacher, J. (1950), *The Concept of Ethics in the History of Economics*, New York: Vantage Press.

Foa, B. (1928), *Di alcune influenze del tempo sul valore*, Milano: Edizioni del Lavoro.

Forsyth, A. R. (1935), 'Old Tripos days at Cambridge', *Mathematical Gazette*, vol. 19, p. 167.

Foxwell, H. S. (1887), 'The economic movement in England', *Quarterly Journal of Economics*, vol. 2, pp. 84–103.

Frank, R. H. (1985), *Choosing the Right Pond: Human Behavior and the Quest for Status*, Oxford: Oxford University Press.

Frank, R. H. (1988), *Passions Within Reason: The Strategic Role of the Emotions*, New York: Norton.

Frisch, R. (1950), 'Alfred Marshall's theory of value', *Quarterly Journal of Economics*, vol. 64, November, pp. 495–524. Reprinted in Wood, 1982, vol. 3, no. 61.

Gollin, A. (1965), *Balfour's Burden: Arthur Balfour and Imperial Preference*, London: Anthony Blond.

Gonce, R. A. (1982), 'Alfred Marshall on industrial organization: from *Principles of Economics* to *Industry and Trade*. Reprinted in Wood, 1982, vol. 4, no. 123.

Graziadei, A. (1899), *La produzione capitalistica*, Torino: Bocca.

Graziadei, A. (1909), *Saggio di un' indagine sui prezzi in regime di concorrenza e di sindacato tra gli imprenditori*, Imola: Galeati.

Groenewegen, P. D. (1988), 'Alfred Marshall and the establishment of the Cambridge Economic Tripos', *History of Political Economy*, vol. 20, pp. 627–67.

Groenewegen, P. D. (1990), 'Teaching economics at Cambridge at the turn of the century: Alfred Marshall as Lecturer in Political Economy', *Scottish Journal of Political Economy*, vol. 37, pp. 40–60.

Haan, N., Bellah, R., Rabinow, P. and Sullivan, W. N. (1983), *Social Science as Moral Inquiry*, New York: Columbia University Press.

Hague, D. C. (1958), 'Alfred Marshall and the competitive firm', *Economic Journal*, vol. 68, December, pp. 673–90. Reprinted in Wood, 1982, vol. 3, no. 71.

Hall, Thomas (no date), *The Early History of Warwick District and Pioneers of the Darling Downs*, Warwick.

Hardin, R. (1988), *Morality within the Limits of Reason*, Chicago: University of Chicago Press.

Harrod, R. F. (1951), *The Life of John Maynard Keynes*, New York: Harcourt and Brace, and London: Macmillan.

Hawtrey, F. M. (1903), *The History of the Hawtrey Family*, London: G. Allen, two volumes.

Henderson, J. (1973), 'William Whewell's mathematical statements of price flexibility, demand elasticity and the Giffen paradox', *Manchester School*, vol. 41, pp. 329–42.

Henderson, J. P. (1989), 'The relation of ethics to economics: J. S. Mackenzie's challenge to neoclassical economics', *Review of Social Economy*, vol. 47, pp. 240–65.

Henderson, J. P. (1990), 'The ethicists' view of Marshall's *Principles*', unpublished paper, 41 pp.

Herbert, C. (1936), *A Merchant Adventurer: Being a Biography of Leonard Hugh Bentall, Kingston on-Thames*, London: Waterflow.

Hewins, W. A. S. (1903), 'The present state of the case for Mr Chamberlain's policy', *The Fortnightly Review*, vol. 74.

Hewins, W. A. S. (1929), *The Apologia of an Imperialist*, London: Constable.

Hicks, J. R. (1983), *Classics and Moderns*, Oxford: Basil Blackwell.

Hill, P. and Keynes, R. (1989), *Lydia and Maynard*, London: Andre Deutsch.

Hirschman, A. O. (1981), 'Morality and the social sciences: a durable tension', in his *Essays in Trespassing: Economics to Politics and Beyond*, Cambridge: Cambridge University Press, pp. 294–306; also in Haan, N. et al. (1983), pp. 21–32.

Hogarth, R. M. and Reder, M. W. (1987), *Rational Choice: The Contrast Between Economics and Psychology*, Chicago: Chicago University Press.

Hollander, S. (1961), 'The representative firm and imperfect competition', *Canadian Journal of Economics and Political Science*, vol. 27, May, pp. 236-41.

Hollander, S. (1985), *The Economics of John Stuart Mill*, vol. 1, *Theory and Method*, Oxford: Basil Blackwell.

Hollander, S. (1987), *Classical Economics*, Oxford: Blackwell.

Hook, A. (1905), 'The present position of the land tax', *Economic Journal*, vol. 15, no. 3, September, pp. 374–80.

Houghton, W. E. (1957), *The Victorian Frame of Mind, 1830–1870*, New Haven: Yale University Press.

Hutchison, T. W. (1964), *'Positive' Economics and Policy Objectives*, London: George Allen and Unwin.

Hutchison, T. W. (1981), *The Politics and Philosophy of Economics: Marxists, Keynesians and Austrians*, New York: New York University Press.

Inglis, K. S. (1963), *Churches and the Working Classes in Victorian England*, London: Routledge.

Jannaccone, P. (1905), *Introduzione* to the Italian translation of Marshall's *Principles of Economics*, fourth edition, Torino: Unione Tipografica Torinese.

Jannaccone, P. (1914), 'Teoria e pratica del dumping', in P. Jannaccone, *Prezzi e mercati*, Torino: Einaudi, 1934.

Jenkin, H. C. F. (1887), *Papers Literary, Scientific, etc.*, S. Colvin and J. Ewing, eds, London: Longmans, Green.

Jenner, R. A. (1964–65), 'The dynamic factor in Marshall's economic system', *Western Economic Journal*, vol. 3, no.1, pp. 21–38. Reprinted in Wood, 1982, vol. 1, no. 18.

Jensen, H. E. (1987), 'Alfred Marshall as a social economist', *Review of Social Economy*, vol. 45, pp. 14–36.

Jevons, W. S. (1905), *The Principles of Economics*, H. Higgs, ed., London: Macmillan.

Jevons, W. S. (1970] [1871], *The Theory of Political Economy*, Baltimore: Penguin.

Jha, N. (1963), *The Age of Marshall*, London: Frank Cass.

Jones, P. D'A. (1968), *The Christian Socialist Revival: Religion, Class and Social Conscience in Victorian England*, Princeton: Princeton University Press.

Kadish, A. (1982), *The Oxford Economists in the Late Nineteenth Century*, Clarendon Press: Oxford.

Kadish, A. (1986), *Apostle Arnold: The Life and Death of Arnold Toynbee 1852–1883*, Durham, N.C.: Duke University Press.

Kaldor, N. and Neild, R. R. (1962), 'A proposal for a levy on the advertising revenue of newspapers', in N. Kaldor, ed., *Reports on Taxation*, London: Duckworth, 1980, pp. 115–23.

Kemp, P. K. (1955), *The Bentall Story, Commemorating 150 Years Service to Agriculture, 1805–1955*, Maldon.

Keynes, J. M. (1925), 'Alfred Marshall, 1842–1924', in Pigou, 1925, pp. 1–65. Given in revised form in Keynes, 1972 [1933].

Keynes, J. M. (1972) [1933], 'Alfred Marshall, 1842–1924', *Essays in Biography*. Reprinted in D. Moggridge, ed., *Collected Writings of John Maynard Keynes*, London, Macmillan for the Royal Economic Society, vol. 10.

Keynes, J. M. (1983) [1922–23], Introduction to *Cambridge Economic Handbooks* for 1922 and 1923. Reprinted in D. Moggridge, ed., *Collected Writings of John Maynard Keynes*, London, Macmillan for the Royal Economic Society, vol. 12.

Keynes, J. N. (1904) [1890], *The Scope and Method of Political Economy*, London: Macmillan, third edition.

Kitson Clark, G. (1973), *Churchmen and the Condition of England, 1832–1885: A Study in the Development of Social Ideas and Practice from the Old Regime to the Modern State*, London: Methuen.

Kreps, D. (1990), *A Course in Microeconomic Theory*, Princeton: Princeton University Press.

Labriola, A. (1900), 'Distribuzione del dividendo e produttività marginali', in A. Labriola, *Finanza ed economia*, Napoli: Società Editrice Partenopea, 1925.

Leone, E. (1909), *La revisione del marxismo*, Roma: Biblioteca del Divenire Sociale.

Levine, A. L. (1980), 'Increasing returns, the competitive model, and the enigma that was Alfred Marshall', *Scottish Journal of Political Economy*, vol. 27, November, pp. 260–75.

Levitt, T. (1976), 'Alfred Marshall: Victorian relevance for modern economics', *Quarterly Journal of Economics*, vol. 90, pp. 425–43. Reprinted in Wood, 1982, vol. 1, no. 23.

Liebhafsky, H. H. (1955), 'A curious case of neglect: Marshall's *Industry and Trade*', *Canadian Journal of Economics and Political Science*, vol. 21, August, pp. 339–53. Reprinted in Wood, 1982, vol. 4, no. 101.

Loasby, B. J. (1978) 'Whatever happened to Marshall's theory of value?', *Scottish Journal of Political Economy*, vol. 25, February, pp. 1–12. Reprinted in Wood, 1982, vol. 3, no. 93.

Lutz, M. A. and Lux, K. (1979), *The Challenge of Humanistic Economics*, Menlo Park, California: Benjamin/Cummings.

Macleod, H. (1884), *An Address to the Board of Electors to the Professorship of Political Economy in the University of Cambridge*, London: Blundell.

Maloney, J. (1985), *Marshall, Orthodoxy and the Professionalisation of Economics*, Cambridge: Cambridge University Press.

Marcet, J. (1827) [1816], *Conversations on Political Economy*, London: Longman, Rees, Orme, Brown & Green, sixth edition.

Marshall, A. (1873), 'The future of the working classes', in Pigou, 1925, pp. 101–18.

Marshall, A. (1874), 'The laws of political economy' and 'The province of political economy', in R. Harrison, 1963, 'Two early articles by Alfred Marshall', *Economic Journal*, vol. 73, pp. 422–30. Originally published in *The Bee-Hive*. Reprinted in Wood, 1982, vol. 4, no. 106.

Marshall, A. (1875), 'Some features of American industry', paper read at a meeting of the Cambridge Moral Science Club, 17 November 1875. Reprinted in Whitaker, 1975, vol. 2, pp. 352–77.

Marshall, A. (1876), 'Mr. Mill's theory of value', in Pigou, 1925, pp. 119–33.

Marshall, A. (1879), *The Pure Theory of Foreign Trade; The Pure Theory of Domestic Values*, originally printed for private circulation, Cambridge: H. Sidgwick. Reprinted as No. 1 in a series of Reprints of Scarce Tracts in Economic and Political Science, Aldwych: London School of Economics, 1930 and Clifton, N. J.: Augustus M. Kelley, 1974. Reprinted, with two additional chapters, in Whitaker, 1975, vol. 2, pp. 111–236.

Marshall, A. (1883), 'Three lectures on progress and poverty', in G. J. Stigler, 'Alfred Marshall's lectures on progress and poverty', *Journal of Law and Economics*, 1969, vol. 12, April, pp. 181–226. Reprinted in Wood, 1982, vol. 4, no. 109.

Marshall, A. (1885), 'The present position of economics', in Pigou, 1925, pp. 152–74.

Marshall, A. (1885), 'How far do remediable causes influence prejudicially (a) the continuity of employment, (b) the rate of wages? with four appendices', in

C. W. Dilke, ed., *Report of Proceedings and Papers on the Industrial Remuneration Conference*, London: Cassel.

Marshall, A. (1887), Preface to L. L. F. R. Price, *Industrial Peace: Its Advantages, Methods and Difficulties. A Report on an Inquiry Made for the Toynbee Trustees*, London: Macmillan. Reprinted in substance in Pigou, 1925 as 'A fair rate of wages', pp. 212–26.

Marshall, A. (1889), 'Cooperation', in Pigou, 1925, pp. 227–55.

Marshall, A. (1890), *Principles of Economics:* see box at beginning of this bibliography for all editions.

Marshall, A. (1890), 'Some aspects of competition', the Section F presidential address for the Leeds meeting of the British Association for the Advancement of Science, reprinted in Pigou, 1925, pp. 256–91.

Marshall, A. (1893), Response to the President's Address, *Economic Journal*, vol. 3, pp. 387–90.

Marshall, A. (1897), 'The old generation of economists and the new', in Pigou, 1925, pp. 295–311.

Marshall, A. (1897), *Memorandum to the Royal Commission on Local Taxation on the classification and incidence of imperial and local taxes.* Published in the Commission's *Report* Cmnd 9528 of 1899 and reprinted in Marshall, 1926, pp. 327–64.

Marshall, A. (1898), 'Mechanical and biological analogies in economics', in Pigou, 1925, pp. 312–18.

Marshall, A. (1900) [1892], *Elements of Economics of Industry: Being the First Volume of Elements of Economics*, London: Macmillan, third edition.

Marshall, A. (1903), *Memorandum on the Fiscal Policy of International Trade*, published 1908 as House of Commons Paper no. 321. Reprinted in Marshall, 1926, pp. 365–420.

Marshall, A. (1907), 'Social possibilities of economic chivalry', in *Economic Journal*, vol. 17, pp. 17–29. Reprinted in Pigou, 1925, pp. 323–46.

Marshall, A. (1917), 'National taxation after the war', in W. H. Dawson, ed., *After-War Problems*, London: George Allen and Unwin.

Marshall, A. (1919), *Industry and Trade: A Study of Industrial Technique and Business Organization; and of Their Influences on the Conditions of Various Classes and Nations*, London: Macmillan, first edition.There were four more editions: 1919, 1920, 1921 and 1923.

Marshall, A. (1923), *Money, Credit and Commerce*, London: Macmillan.

Marshall, A. (1926), *Official Papers by Alfred Marshall*, J. M. Keynes, ed., London: Macmillan for the Royal Economic Society.

Marshall, A. and Marshall, M. P. (1879), *Economics of Industry*, London: Macmillan, first edition.

Marshall, M. P. (1947), *What I Remember*, Cambridge: at the University Press.

Martello, T. (1912), *L'economia politica e l'odierna crisi del darwinismo*, Bologna: Laterza.

Mason, R. (1989), *Robert Giffen and the Giffen Paradox*, Totawa, N.J.: Barnes & Noble.

Matthews, R. C. O. (1981), 'Morality, competition and efficiency', *The Manchester School*, vol. 49, pp. 289–309.

Maxwell, J. A. (1958), 'Some Marshallian concepts, especially the representative firm', *Economic Journal*, vol. 68, December, pp. 691–98. Reprinted in Wood, 1982, vol. 3, no. 72.

McCready, H. W. (1955), 'Alfred Marshall and tariff reform, 1903: some unpublished letters', *Journal of Political Economy*, vol. 63, pp. 259–67. Reprinted in Wood, 1982, vol. 4, no. 100.

McCulloch, J. R. (1825), *Principles of Political Economy*, Edinburgh: Black.

McCulloch, J. R. (1852) [1845], *A Treatise on the Principles and Practical Influence of Taxation and the Funding System*, London: Longman, Brown, Green and Longmans, second edition.

McPherson, M. S. (1983), 'Want formation, morality, and some interpretative aspects of economic inquiry', in Haan *et al.*, 1983, pp. 96–124.

McWilliams, R. (1969), 'The papers of Alfred Marshall deposited in the Marshall Library, Cambridge', *History of Economic Thought Newsletter*, no. 3, November. Reprinted in Wood, 1982, vol. 4, no. 110.

McWilliams Tullberg, R. (1975), 'Marshall's "tendency to socialism"', *History of Political Economy*, vol. 7, pp. 75–111. Reprinted in Wood, 1982, vol. 1, no. 20.

Menger, C. (1871), *Principles of Economics*, English translation by J. Dingwell and B. F. Hoselitz, Glencoe, Ill.: Free Press, 1950.

Mill, J. S. (1899) [1848], *Principles of Political Economy*, New York: Colonial Press, two volumes.

Mill, J. S. (1965) [1848], *Principles of Political Economy, with some of their Applications to Social Philosophy*, in *Collected Works of John Stuart Mill*, Toronto: University of Toronto Press, vol. 3.

Mill, J. S. (1967) [1869], 'Thornton on labour and its claims', in J. M. Robson, ed., *Collected Works of John Stuart Mill*, Toronto: University of Toronto Press, vol. 5.

Mirowski, P. (1986), 'Mathematical formalism and economic explanation', in P. Mirowski, ed., *The Reconstruction of Economic Theory*, Norwell: Kluwer.

Mirowski, P. (1988), *Against Mechanism*, Totawa, N. J.: Rowman & Littlefield.

Mirowski, P. (1989), *More Heat than Light: Economics as Social Physics, Physics as Nature's Economics*, Cambridge and New York: Cambridge University Press.

Mirowski, P. (1990), 'The rise and fall of the equilibrium concept', *Recherches Economiques de Louvain*, vol. 55, pp. 1–22.

Mirowski, P. (1990), 'Problems in the paternity of econometrics: Henry Ludwell Moore', *History of Political Economy*, vol 22.

Mirowski, P. (forthcoming), 'The how, the when and the why of mathematics in neoclassical economics', *Journal of Economic Perspectives*.

Montemartini, G. (1899), *Introduzione allo studio della distribuzione delle ricchezze*, Milano: Fusi.

Montemartini, G. (1899), *La teoria delle produttività marginali*, Pavia: Società Editrice Libraria.

Mummery, A. F. and Hobson, J. A., (1956)[1889], *The Physiology of Industry: Being an Exposure of Certain Fallacies in Existing Theories of Economics*, New York: Kelley & Millman.

Musgrave, R. A. (1959), *The Theory of Public Finance*, New York: McGraw-Hill.

Musgrave, R. A. (1987), 'A brief history of fiscal doctrine', in A. J. Auerbach and M. Feldstein, eds, *Handbook of Public Economics*, Amsterdam & New York: North Holland, vol. 1, chap. 1.

Musgrave, R. A. and P. B. (1984), *Public Finance in Theory and Practice*, New York: McGraw Hill, fourth edition.

National Trust (1976), *Benthall Hall, Shropshire*, Plaistow: Curwen Press for the National Trust, 1976.

Negishi, T. (1985), *Economic Theories in a Non-Walrasian Tradition*, Cambridge: Cambridge University Press.

Negishi, T. (1989), *History of Economic Theory*, Amsterdam, New York, Oxford and Tokyo: North-Holland.

Newman, P. K. (1960), 'The erosion of Marshall's theory of value', *Quarterly Journal of Economics*, vol. 74, November, pp. 587–600. Reprinted in Wood, 1982, vol. 3, no. 75.

Newman, P. (1965), *The Theory of Exchange*, Englewood Cliffs, N. J.: Prentice-Hall.

Nielsen, K. (1967), 'Ethics, problems of', in P. Edwards, ed., *The Encyclopedia of Philosophy*, New York: Macmillan and Free Press, vol. 3, pp. 117–34.

Norman, E. R. (1976), *Church and Society in England 1770–1970: A Historical Study*, Oxford: Clarendon Press.

O'Byrne, W. R. (1861), *A Naval Biographical Dictionary*, London: O'Byrne Bros.

Palgrave, R. H. Inglis (1871), *The Local Taxation of Great Britain and Ireland*, London: The Statistical Society of London.

Pantaleoni, M. (1889), *Principii di economia pura*, Firenze: Barbera.

Pantaleoni, M. (1897), 'A proposito del *Cours d'économie politique* di V. Pareto', *Rivista popolare di politica, lettere e scienze sociali*, vol. 2, March.

Pantaleoni, M. (1904), *Lezioni di economia pura*, Roma: Sandron.

Pareto, V. (1960), *Lettere a Matteo Pantaleoni*, G. De Rosa, ed., Banca Nazionale del Lavoro, 3 volumes.

Parsons, T. (1931/32), 'Economics and sociology; Marshall in relation to the thought of his time', *Quarterly Journal of Economics*, vol. 46, pp. 310–45.

Parsons, T. (1931/32), 'Wants and activities in Marshall', *Quarterly Journal of Economics*, vol. 46, pp. 101–40.

Paul, E. F., Miller, F. D. and Paul, J., eds (1985), *Ethics and Economics*, Oxford: Basil Blackwell.

Peterkin, A. and Johnston, W. (1968), *Commissioned Officers in the Medical Services of the British Army, 1660–1960*, London: Welcome Historical Medical Library, two volumes.

Phelps, E. S., ed. (1975), *Altruism, Morality and Economic Theory*, New York: Russell Sage Foundation.

Philip, P. (1981), *British Residents at the Cape, 1795–1819*, Cape Town: David Philip Ltd.

Pigou, A. C. (1912), *Wealth and Welfare*, London: Macmillan.

Pigou, A. C., ed. (1925), *Memorials of Alfred Marshall*, London: Macmillan.

Pigou, A. C. (1928), *A Study in Public Finance*, London: Macmillan.

Pigou, A. C. (1932) [1920], *The Economics of Welfare*, London: Macmillan, fourth edition.

Plehn, C. C. (1911) [1896], *Introduction to Public Finance*, New York: The Macmillan Company, third edition.

Price, L. L. F. R. (1887), *Industrial Peace: Its Advantages, Methods and Difficulties*, London: Macmillan.

Reisman, D. (1987), *Alfred Marshall: Progress and Politics*, London: Macmillan.

Richards, J. (1988), *Mathematical Visions: the Pursuit of Geometry in Victorian England*, New York: Academic Press.

Richmond, W. (1888), *Christian Economics*, London: Rivington's.

Richmond, W. (1890), *Four Lectures on Economic Morals*, London: W. H. Allen.

Richter, M. (1964), *The Politics of Conscience: T. H. Green and His Age*, London, Weidenfeld and Nicholson.

Robbins, L. C. (1928), 'The representative firm', *Economic Journal*, vol. 38, September, pp. 387–404. Reprinted in Wood, 1982, vol. 3, no. 48.

Robertson, D. H. (1924), 'Those empty boxes', *Economic Journal*, vol. 34, March, pp. 16–21. Reprinted in American Economic Association (1953).

Robertson, D. H. (1930), 'Increasing returns and the representative firm', *Economic Journal*, vol. 40, March, pp. 80–89. Reprinted in Wood, 1982, vol. 3, no. 50.

Robinson, J. V. (1973), *Collected Economic Papers*, Cambridge, Mass.: MIT Press, vol. 4.

Robinson, J. V. (1979), *Collected Economic Papers*, Cambridge, Mass.: MIT Press, vol. 5.

Roncaglia, A. (1972), *Sraffa e la teoria dei prezzi*, Bari: Laterza.

Samuelson, P. A. (1947), *Foundations of Economic Analysis*, Cambridge, Mass: Harvard University Press.

Samuelson, P. A. (1967), 'The monopolistic competition revolution', in R. E. Kuenne, ed., *Monopolistic Competition Theory: Studies in Impact*, New York: Wiley.

Samuelson, P. A. (1972), *Collected Scientific Papers*, Cambridge, Mass.: MIT Press, vol. 3.

Sanger, C. P. (1901), 'The report of the local government commission', *Economic Journal*, vol. 11, no. 3, September, pp. 321–33.

Schabas, M. (1989), 'Alfred Marshall, Stanley Jevons, and the mathematization of economics', *Isis*, vol. 80, pp. 60–73.

Schneewind, J. B. (1977), *Sidgwick's Ethics and Victorian Moral Philosophy*, Oxford: Clarendon Press.

Schumpeter, J. A. (1954), *History of Economic Analysis*, E. Schumpeter, ed., New York: Oxford University Press.

Sen, A. (1987), *On Ethics and Economics*, Oxford: Basil Blackwell.

Shove, G. F. (1930), 'Increasing returns and the representative firm', *Economic Journal*, vol. 40, March, pp. 94–116. Reprinted in Wood, 1982, vol. 3, no. 50.

Shove, G. F. (1942), 'The place of Marshall's *Principles* in the development of economic theory', *Economic Journal*, vol. 52, pp. 294–329. Reprinted in Wood, 1982, vol. 2, no. 38.

Sidgwick, H. [1883], *The Principles of Political Economy*, London: Macmillan, third edition.

Skidelsky, R. (1983), *John Maynard Keynes, Vol. 1: Hopes Betrayed, 1883–1920*, London: Macmillan, and New York: Viking Penguin Inc., 1986.

Smyth, R., ed. (1962), *Essays in Economic Method*, London: Duckworth.

Sraffa, P. (1925), 'Sulle relazione tra costo e quantità prodotta', *Annali di Economia*, no. 2.

Sraffa, P. (1926), 'The laws of return under competitive conditions', *Economic Journal*, vol. 36, December.

Steele, J. G. (1978), *Conrad Martens on Queensland: The Frontier Travels of a Colonial Artist*, Brisbane: University of Queensland Press.

Stigler, G. J. (1941), *Production and Distribution Theories*, New York: Macmillan.

Stigler, G. J. (1951), 'The division of labor is limited by the extent of the market', *Journal of Political Economy*, vol. 59, June, pp. 185–93.

Stigler, G. J. (1982), *The Economist as Preacher and Other Essays*, Chicago: University of Chicago Press; Part 1, 'Economics or ethics?', pp. 3–37.

Stykolt, S. (1956), 'A curious case of neglect: Marshall on the "tangency solution"', *Canadian Journal of Economics and Political Science*, vol. 22, May, p. 251. Reprinted in Wood, 1982, vol. 4, no. 104.

Thornton, H. (1939) [1802], *An Enquiry into the Nature and Effects of the Paper Credit of Great Britain*, F. A. Hayek, ed., London: G. Allen and Unwin.

Thornton, W. (1870), *On Labour*, London: Macmillan, second edition.

Thweatt, W. (1983), 'Origins of the terminology 'supply and demand', *Scottish Journal of Political Economy*, vol. 30, pp. 287–94.

Viner, J. (1931), 'Cost curves and supply curves', *Zeitschrift für National-ökonomie*, vol. 3, September, pp. 23–46. Reprinted in American Economic Association (1953).

Wagner, A. R. (1960), *English Genealogy*, Oxford: Clarendon Press.

Wagner, D. O. (1930), *The Church of England and Social Reform Since 1851*, New York: Columbia University Press.

Walras, L. (1965), *Correspondence of Leon Walras and Related Papers*, W. Jaffé, ed., Amsterdam: North Holland, 3 volumes.

Walras, L. (1954) [1844–77], *Elements of Pure Economics*, translated to English by W. Jaffé from the French definitive edition of 1926, Homewood, Ill.: Irwin; and London: George Allen and Unwin, reprinted Philadelphia: Orion, 1984.

Walsh, V. and Gram, H. (1980), *Classical and Neoclassical Theories of General Equilibrium*, New York and Oxford: Oxford University Press.

Waterson, D. B. (1968), *Squatter, Selector, and Storekeeper: A History of the Darling Downs, 1859–1893*, Sydney: Sydney University Press.

Watts, J. (undated), *Personal Reminiscenses by John Watts*, Brisbane: Oxley Memorial Library, 24.

Webb, B. (1926), *My Apprenticeship*, London and New York: Longman Green.

Wedgewood, J. C. (1912), 'The principle of land value taxation', *Economic Journal*, vol. 22, no. 3, September, pp. 388–97.

Weintraub, E. R. (1985), *General Equilibrium Analysis: Studies in Appraisal*, Cambridge: Cambridge University Press.

Weisskopf, W. A. (1955), *The Psychology of Economics*, London: Routledge and Kegan Paul.

Weisskopf, W. A. (1971), *Alienation and Economics*, New York: Dutton.

Whewell, W. (1829), 'Mathematical exposition of some doctrines of political economy', from the *Transactions* of the Cambridge Philosophical Society. Reprinted in Whewell (1971).

Whewell, W. (1831), 'Mathematical exposition of some of the leading doctrines in Mr. Ricardo's *Principles of Political Economy and Taxation*', from the *Transactions* of the Cambridge Philosophical Society. Reprinted in Whewell (1971).

Whewell, W. (1967) [1862], *Six Lectures on Political Economy*, New York: Kelley.

Whewell, W. (1971), *Mathematical Exposition of Some Doctrines of Political Economy*, from the *Transactions* of the Cambridge Philosophical Society, Cambridge, reprinted New York: Augustus M. Kelley.

Whitaker, J. K. (1972), 'Alfred Marshall: the years 1877–1885', *History of Political Economy*, vol. 4, pp. 1–61. Reprinted in Wood, 1982, vol. 1, no. 8.

Whitaker, J. K. (ed.) (1975), *The Early Economic Writings of Alfred Marshall 1867–1890*, London: Macmillan for the Royal Economic Society and New York: Free Press, two volumes.

Whitaker, J. K. (1975), 'John Stuart Mill's methodology', *Journal of Political Economy*, vol. 83, pp. 1033–49.

Whitaker, J. K. (1977), 'Some neglected aspects of Alfred Marshall's economic and social thought', *History of Political Economy*, vol. 9, pp. 161–97. Reprinted in Wood, 1982, vol. 1, no. 25.

Whitaker, J. K. (1987), 'Marshall, Alfred 1842–1924', in J. Eatwell, M. Milgate and P. Newman, eds, *The New Palgrave: A Dictionary of Economics*, London: Macmillan, New York: Stockton Press and Tokyo: Maruzen Co., vol. 3, pp. 350–63.

Whitaker, J. K. (1987), 'The continuing relevance of Alfred Marshall', in R. D. C. Black, ed., *Ideas in Economics*, London: Macmillan.

Whitaker, J. K. (1989), 'The Cambridge background to imperfect competition', in G. Feiwel, ed., *The Economics of Imperfect Competition and Employment*, London: Macmillan, 1989.

White, M. (1989), 'Why are there no demand and supply curves in Jevons?', *History of Political Economy*, vol. 21, pp. 425–56.

White, M. (1989), 'Invention in the face of necessity: Marshallian rhetoric and the Giffen goods', unpublished paper, Monash University.

White, M. (1989), 'Cuckoo or bowerbird? Jevons, physics and the marginalist revolution', unpublished paper, Monash University.

Wicksell, K. (1896), 'Taxation in the monopoly case', *in Finanztheoretische Untersuchungen*, Jena: Gustav Fisher, ch. 2, Appendix. Reprinted in R. A. Musgrave and C. S. Shoup, eds, *Readings in the Economics of Taxation*, London: Allen and Unwin, 1959, Reading 16, pp. 256–57.

Wicksteed, P. H. (1910), *Common Sense of Political Economy, including a study of the human basis of economic laws*, London: Macmillan & Co.

Williams, P. L. (1978), *The Emergence of the Theory of the Firm*, London: Macmillan.

Wise, M. N. (1989), 'Work and waste: political economy and natural philosophy in 19th century Britain', *History of Science*, vol. 27, pp. 263–301.

Wolfe, J. N. (1954), 'The representative firm', *Economic Journal*, vol. 64, June, pp. 337–49. Reprinted in Wood, 1982, vol. 3, no. 65.

Wood, J. C. (1980), 'Alfred Marshall and the tariff reform campaign of 1903', *Journal of Law and Economics*, vol. 23, pp. 481–9. Reprinted in Wood, 1982, vol. 4, no. 122.

Wood, J. C., ed. (1982), *Alfred Marshall: Critical Assessments*, London: Croom Helm, four volumes.

Young, A. A. (1928), 'Increasing returns and economic progress', *Economic Journal*, vol. 38, December, pp. 527–42.

# Name index

Alchian, A. A.   191
Antonelli, A.   135
Armitage-Smith, G.   ch. 6 fn. 10
Attwood, M.   155
Auerbach, A. J.   ch. 5 fn. 4
Auspitz, R.   54, 138, 139
Axelrod, R.   169

Bagehot, W.   190
Balfour, A. J.   119, 127–28, ch. 6
   fns 4 and 19
Barone, E.   133, 135, 140, 141–43,
   147, 148
Bartley, N.   16
Barucci, P.   134
Bastable, C. F.   68, 95, 102, 121,
   ch. 6 fn. 10
Baumol, W.   169
Becattini, G.   133*
Bentall, E. (née Thornton)   21
Bentall, J. (grandfather of Bentall,
   L.)   21
Bentall, J. (brother of Bentall, L.)
   12, 21
Bentall, L. (Mrs W. Marshall)   11–
   12, 21
Bentall, T.   21
Benthall, Sir P.   21
Bentham, J.   98
Berkeley Jones, H.   15
Bernoulli, D.   97
Bharadwaj, K.   ch. 4 fn. 3
Bickerdicke, G. F.   92
Bishop, S.   17
Black, R. D. C.   ch. 8 fn. 3
Blaug, M.   ch. 2 fn. 11
Boccardo, G.   134
Boulding, K. E.   169
Bowley, A. L.   6, 55–56, ch. 6 fn.
   10
Brems, H.   55, 57

Brentano, L.   120–21, ch. 6 fn. 7
Burnel, R.   21
Böhm Bawerk, E. von   50, 137

Cabiati, A.   141
Campbell, R.   14–15, 19
Cannan, E.   121, ch. 6 fn. 10
Carlyle, T.   158
Carver, T. N.   2
Cassel, G.   52, 92
Chamberlain, J.   93, 118–22, ch. 6
   fn. 16
Chamberlin, E. H.   35
Chapman, S. J.   ch. 5 fn. 15, ch. 6
   fn. 10
Chasse, J. D.   ch. 8 fn. 16
Clapham, J. H.   108, ch. 6 fn. 10
Clark, J. B.   2, 49–50, 56, 143
Coase, R. H.   55, 57
Coats, A. W.   122
Cognetti De Martiis, S.   ch. 7 fn. 5
Collard, D.   169
Collini, D.   ch. 8 fn. 1
Condillac, E.   64
Conrad, J.   194
Corry B.   9
Cossa, L.   134, 136
Cournot, A.-A.   2, 69, 70, 71–72,
   77, 82, ch. 4 fn. 8
Courtney, L.   ch. 6 fn. 10
Cozzi, T.   133*
Cree, T. S.   195
Cunningham, W.   ch. 6 fn. 10, 190

Dalla Volta, R.   133, 134–35, 136–
   37
Davenant, C.   81
Davies, J. Llewellyn   6
De Viti De Marco, A.   135, 136
Dermer, E. C.   23
Descartes, R.   64

Deuchar, J.   15
Dickens, C.   68
Drake, C. A. D. (Mrs C. Marshall)
   15–16
Drake, W. H.   15
Dupuit, J.   72, 98

Earl, P.   170
Edgeworth, F. Y.   6, 14, ch. 1 fn.
   12, 50, 57, 61*, 62, 79, 83, 85, ch.
   4 fns 1 and 9, 121–22, ch. 6 fn. 10,
   136, 139, 140, 142, ch. 4 fn. 4
Einaudi, L.   136, 141–42, ch. 7 fn. 5
Errera, L.   134
Etzioni, A.   169

Fanno, M.   141, 145
Faucci, R.   133*
Fawcett, H.   75, 83, 114–15, 136,
   160, 199
Fay, C. R.   1, 6, 199
Ferrara, F.   134
Ferrara School   134
Fisher, I.   2, 62
Flux, A. W.   ch. 8 fn. 18
Foa, B.   148
Forster, E. M.   22
Foxwell, H. S.   ch. 4 fn. 4, ch. 6 fns
   9 and 10, 164–65, ch. 8 fn. 19, 188,
   199
Frank, R. H.   169
Frisch, R.   62
Fry, A.   188

Galton, F.   83
Gamie, J.   15
George, H.   103, 166, ch. 8 fn. 4
Giffen, R.   70
Giolitti, G.   ch. 7 fn. 7
Gollin, A.   ch. 6 fn. 16
Gonner, E. C. K.   6, ch. 6 fn. 10
Goschen, G. J.   ch. 8 fn. 2
Grant, A.   ch. 4 fn. 7
Graziadei, A.   145, ch. 7 fn. 5
Green, T. H.   166, ch. 8 fn. 19
Guillebaud, C. W.   19, 20
Guillebaud, E. D.   20
Guillebaud, M. (née Marshall)   20
Guillebaud, P.   200

Harcourt, W.   99
Hardin, R.   169
Hawtrey, M.   10, 20
Hawtrey, R.   22
Hegel, G. W. F.   164
Henderson, H.   1
Henderson, J. P.   ch. 8 fns 5 and 21
Herschel, J. F. W.   77
Hewins, W. A. S.   120–22, ch. 6 fns
   9 and 10
Hicks, J. R.   62
Hicks-Beach, M. E.   117–18
Hirschman, A. D.   169
Hobson, J. A.   143
Hogarth, R. M.   170
Hollander, S.   ch. 4 fn. 3
Hume, D.   169
Hutchison, T. W.   ch. 8 fn. 12
Hutton, J.   64

Inglis-Palgrave, R. H.   ch. 6 fn. 10
Ingram, J. K.   83

Jannaccone, P.   141, 147, ch. 7 fn. 5
Jenkin, H. C. Fleeming   64, 74, 77–
   81, 82, 84
Jevons, W. S.   62, 64, 74, 76, 77,
   78–81, 82, 83, 84, 134–35, 136–37,
   154, 163, 165, ch. 8 fn. 3
Jha, N.   144
Jowett, B.   193

Kadish, A.   167, ch. 8 fn. 19
Kahn, R. F.   3–4
Kaldor, N.   110
Kant, E.   ch. 8 fn. 6
Keynes, J. M.   1, 3, 4, 5, 9–10, 14,
   21, 22, 61, ch. 4 fn. 8, 128, 148,
   153, 154, 157, 158, 169, ch. 8 fn.
   17, 199
Keynes, J. N.   159–60, 189, 199
Kidd, B.   ch. 4 fn. 9, 156, ch. 8 fn. 4
King, G.   81
Kitson Clark, G.   ch. 8 fn. 20

Labriola, A.   143, 145
Lampertico, F.   134
Laurier, W.   118
Lavington, F.   1, 4

Lavoisier, A. L.   64
Layton, W. T.   6
Leone, E.   145
Levitt, T.   ch. 8 fn. 10
Lieben, R.   54, 138, 139
List, F.   116
Lloyd George, D.   93, 123
Loria, A.   146
Luzzati, L.   134

MacLeod, H. D.   74
Maloney, J.   167, ch. 6 fn. 15, ch. 8
  fns 10 and 22
Malthus, T. R.   67, 104
Marcet, J.   68, 81, 83
Marshall, Ainslie   10
Marshall, C. (née Drake)   15–16
Marshall, Charles   13–20, 21
Marshall, C. W.   20
Marshall, Edward   13
Marshall, Henry   10, 13, ch. 1 fn.
  19
Marshall, John   9–10, 11, 20
Marshall, L. (Aunt Louisa)   13, 20
Marshall, L. (née Bentall)   11–12,
  21
Marshall, M. (Mrs E. D. Guillebaud)
  20
Marshall, M. P.   6, 9*, 10, 13, 14,
  ch. 1 fn. 2, 199
Marshall, R. (née Oliver)   9, 21,
  195
Marshall, Thornton   13, 22, ch. 1 fn.
  38
Marshall, Walter   20
Marshall, W. (b. 1676)   9–10
Marshall, W. (b. 1780)   10–12, 21
Marshall, W. (b. 1812)   9, 13, 14,
  23
Martello, T.   ch. 7 fn. 1
Martineau, H.   81, 83
Marx, K.   145
Matthews, R. C. O.   169
Mazzola, U.   135
McCready, H. W.   ch. 6 fn. 7
McCulloch, J. R.   68, 96
McPherson, M. S.   169
McTaggart, J. McT. E.   187
Menger, C.   43, 137

Messedaglia, A.   134
Mill, J. S.   2, 56, 62, 73, 74, 81, 82,
  96, 104, 115, 154, 162, ch. 8 fn. 12
Montemartini, G.   136, 143
Moore, H. L.   61*, 84
Munday, G.   17
Musgrave, P. B.   ch. 5 fn. 10
Musgrave, R. A.   92, 107, ch. 5 fns
  4, 10 and 11

Neild, R. R.   110
Newman, P.   53
Newton, I.   85
Nicholson, J. S.   121, ch. 6 fn. 10,
  142
Nitti, F. S.   141

Odell Vinter, J.   189
Oliver, R. (Mrs W. Marshall)   9, 21,
  195

Pantaleoni, M.   133–48
Pareto, V.   85, 133, 135, 136, 137–
  40, 141, 144, 146–49
Parsons, T.   164
Peel, R.   118
Perri, S.   133*
Phelps, E. S.   169
Phelps, L. R.   ch. 6 fn. 10
Physiocrats   113, 116
Pigou, A. C.   vi, 1, 2–3, 4, 6, 43, 92,
  122, ch. 6 fns 10 and 18
Playfair, J.   64
Plunkett, H.   6
Prato, G.   141
Price, L. L. F. R.   61*, ch. 6 fn. 10

Quesnay, F.   104, 108, ch. 5 fn. 12

Ramsay, W.   ch. 4 fn. 1
Reay, Baron (D. J. Mackay)   99
Reder, M. W.   170
Reisman, D.   91
Ricardo, D.   2, 3, 67, 68, 104, 108,
  ch. 5 fn. 12, 139, 140, 147
Ricardian School   116, ch. 7 fn. 4
Ricci, U.   141, 147
Richmond, W.   167
Richter, M.   ch. 8 fn. 19

Ritchie, C.   119–20
Robbins, L.   161
Robertson, D. H.   1
Robinson, J. V.   3–4
Roscher, W. G. F.   2
Ruskin, J.   158

Sanger, C. P.   92, 103, ch. 6 fn. 10
Schmoller, G.   120
Schumpeter, J. A.   49, 62, 133, 168–69
Scialoja, A.   134
Scott Holland, H.   ch. 6 fn. 10, 166, ch. 8 fn. 21
Scott, W. R.   ch. 6 fn. 10
Seligman, E. R. A.   61*, ch. 4 fn. 8, 113, 166
Sella, E.   141
Sen, A.   169
Sherman, H. J.   195
Shove, G. F.   1, 4, 194
Sidgwick, H.   154, 155, 159–60, ch. 8 fns 6 and 7
Skidelsky, R.   23, ch. 8 fn. 7
Slade, W. B.   15, 17–18
Smart, W.   ch. 6 fn. 10
Smith, A.   34, 42, 62, 67, ch. 4 fn. 2, 96, 100, 108, 113, 116, 125, 136, 147, 160, ch. 8 fn. 12, 192
Sorel, G.   ch. 7 fn. 9
Spencer, H.   42, ch. 4 fn. 9
Sraffa, P.   3, 133, 146–49
Steuart, J.   67
Stigler, G. J.   ch. 1 fn. 1, 43

Taussig, F. W.   1, 2
Tawney, R. H.   194
Thornton, E. (Mrs. J. Bentall)   22

Thornton, H.   22
Thornton, R.   22
Thornton, W.   64, 73, 74–78, 81
Thünen, J. H. von   2, 98
Tooke, T.   70
Toynbee, A.   158, 165, ch. 8 fn. 19
Trimmer, S.   81
Turgot, A. R. J.   ch. 5 fn. 12

Venn, J.   ch. 6 fn. 10
Viner, J.   ch. 2 fn. 11

Walker, F. A.   165
Walras, L.   49, 50, 53–55, 62, 83, 133, 134–35, 136, 138–40, 142–43, 144–46
Watts, J.   15
Webb, B.   153
Wedgewood, J. C.   92
Weisskopf, W. A.   159, ch. 8 fns 9 and 14
Wescott, B. F.   6, 97, ch. 8 fn. 4
Whewell, W.   61*, 69, 70–71, 77, 81, 108, ch. 5 fn. 11
Whitaker, J. K.   vi, 7 fn. 1, 62, 91, 98, ch. 5 fns 5 and 11, 133*, 157, ch. 8 fn. 13
White, M.   79
Wicksell, K.   62, ch. 5 fn. 14
Wicksteed, P. H.   83, 189
Wieser, F. von   50
Wilson, A.   200
Wood, J. C.   ch. 6 fn. 13
Wootton, B.   1

Young, A. A.   43
Yule, G. U.   ch. 6 fn. 10

# Subject index

Australia:
  gold rush   14, 16, 20
  sheep farming   14–16, 17–18, 19
  transportation   19–20
  wool and meat trade   18–19

Cambridge:
  Economic Tripos   1–2, 154, 186–89
  Marshallian tradition   ch. 1
Classical theory:   63–64, 65–67, 69–73, 74–75
Consumer's rent   62, 142–43

Demand:
  composite   52
  curves   ch. 4
  elasticity   98, 105, 107
  joint   52

Economies of scale:
  decreasing returns   92, 100, 108, 147–48
  external   31–32, 40–43
  increasing returns   30, 37, 42, 92, 100, 108, 147–48
  internal   29–31, 33, 36–43

Free trade   2, ch. 6

General equilibrium analysis   ch. 3, ch. 7

Imperial preference   118–20, 125
*Industry and Trade*   vi, 4, 6, 7, 37, 91, 129, 146, 156, 179, 182, 183–84, 189, 192, 194–95
Italian school of economics   ch. 7

London School of Economics   4, 120, 187

Manifesto of the Fourteen Economists   121–22
Marginal utility of money   82, 142, 145
Marshall, Alfred:
  ancestry   ch. 1
  as Cambridge student   14, 23
  biological analogies   4, 36, 82–83, ch. 4 fn. 9, 141, 191–92
  Bristol   ch. 4 fn. 1, 186, 187
  business and businessmen   4–5, 161, ch. 9
  childhood   13, 20, 23
  claims to priority   50, 54, 82, ch. 4 fn. 8
  correspondence   App. A
  dynamics   5
  economic chivalry   180–81, 182
  Economic Tripos at Cambridge   1–2, 154, 186–89
  elasticity   98, 105, 107
  ethics   ch. 8
  evolutionary theories   42, 158, 161–64, 191–93
  free trade   2, ch. 6
  influence on Cambridge economics   1–2, 3
  intellectual antecedents   2, 82–85
  literary style   6, 61–63, ch. 4 fn. 1, 179
  monetary questions   2
  needs and wants   136
  on taxation   ch. 5
  professionalisation of economics   161
  'representative firm'   4–5, 36, 37–42
  salaried managers   185
  use of diagrams   53, 54, 55, 74–83
  use of mathematical analysis   49, 50, 51, 54–57, 62, 81–85, 168

227

visit to and views on USA   2, 14,
113–14, 115, 184–85, 195
wants and activities   163–64
Marshall Library, Cambridge:   6, 9*,
126, 128, App. A
Marshallian economics:   1–3
decline of   3–5, 5, 146–49
Mathematics:
use of geometry   71–72, 74–85
use of, in economics   2, ch. 3, 69–
85, 134–35
Marxism   144, 145–46
*Memorandum on the Classification
and Incidence of Imperial and
Local Taxes*   91, 96, 101–103, 104,
105–106
*Memorandum on the Fiscal Policy of
International Trade*   122–27, 128–
29
*Memorials of Alfred Marshall*   vi, 6
*Money, Credit and Commerce*   vi, 2,
4, 129, 146
Moral Science Tripos   2

Natural price   29–30, ch. 4
Neoclassical theory   ch. 4, ch. 7

Partial equilibrium analysis   49, 58,
ch. 7

Price theory   ch. 2, ch. 4
*Principles of Economics*   vi, 1, 6, 20,
30, 33, 36–37, 52, 55, 61, 91, 95,
100, 104, 115–16, 136–37, 138,
140, 141, 154, 159, 167, 168–69,
179–80, 182, 189–94, 196
Protectionism   ch. 6
in USA   113–14, 115

Supply:
composite   52
curves   ch. 4
elasticity   105, 107
joint   18–19, 52, 145

Tariff reform   118–29
Taxation   ch. 5
efficiency   96, 98–100, 101–102
equity   96–98, 101–102
federalism   102
'frontier taxes'   117–18
graduated   97, 99, 101–102
incidence   104–107
local   102–103, 106–107
Taylor's Theorem   83

Walras' Law   53